MAPPING
BRITAIN'S LOST
BRANCH LINES

A DAVID & CHARLES BOOK
F&W Media International, Ltd 2013

David & Charles is an imprint of
F&W Media International, Ltd
Brunel House, Forde Close, Newton Abbot, TQ12 4PU, UK

F&W Media International, Ltd is a subsidiary of
F+W Media Inc.
10151 Carver Road, Cincinnati OH45242, USA

First published in the UK in 2013

Copyright © Paul Atterbury 2013

Paul Atterbury has asserted his right to be identified as
author of this work in accordance with the Copyright,
Designs and Patents Act, 1988.

A catalogue record for this book is available from the British Library.

ISBN-13: 978-1-4463-0283-5
ISBN-10: 1-4463-0283-0

Hardback edition printed in China by RR Donnelley for:
F&W Media International, Ltd
Brunel House, Forde Close, Newton Abbot, TQ12 4PU, UK

10 9 8 7 6 5 4 3 2

Produced for F&W Media International, Ltd by:
OutHouse Publishing
Shalbourne, Marlborough, Wiltshire SN8 3QJ

For OutHouse Publishing:
Project editor: Sue Gordon
Art editor: Dawn Terrey
Image scanning and presentation: Chrissie Atterbury

For David & Charles:
Publisher: Alison Myer
Junior Acquisitions Editor: Verity Graves-Morris
Design Manager: Sarah Clark
Production Manager: Beverley Richardson

F+W Media publishes high-quality books on a wide
range of subjects. For more great book ideas visit:
www.stitchcraftcreate.co.uk

Previous page: This is Moffat station in 1954 – a scene typical of so many branch lines after the ending of passenger services.

Opposite page: The route of Brighton's Dyke branch is clearly visible in the landscape. Here, near the Dyke terminus, it is marked by a line of bushes across the fields.

MAPPING
BRITAIN'S LOST
BRANCH LINES

A NOSTALGIC LOOK AT BRITAIN'S BRANCH
LINES IN OLD MAPS AND PHOTOGRAPHS

PAUL ATTERBURY

D&C
David and Charles

CONTENTS

LLANBERIS, SHOWING FALLS IN DISTANCE.
L. & N W RAILWAY.

Llanberis Falls, Carnarvonshire (Gwynedd) (London & North Western Railway)

Wetton Mill bridge, Manifold valley, Staffordshire (North Staffordshire Railway)

The former Highland Railway Hotel, Dornoch, Sutherland

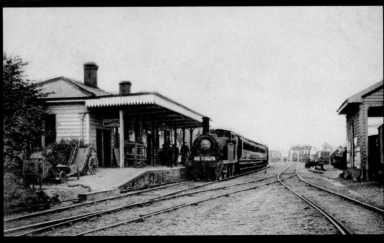

Westerham station, Kent

INTRODUCTION

TODAY THERE IS a nostalgia in Britain for the golden age of the railways, a period usually defined as the first half of the 20th century. Steam was king, and Britain still enjoyed a remarkably comprehensive railway network whose tentacles connected towns, villages and even hamlets across the entire country. At its heart were rural routes and branch lines, the latter often the creation of small companies and driven by local needs and local finance. Firmly at the centre of British life, these lines were, for so many remote areas, a social and economic lifeline.

Branch lines are now part of a lost world, an era when railway maps of Britain showed lines criss-crossing every county — many of them with distinctive, but also lost, names. By bringing together old maps, images of old branch lines and modern photographs of relics that can be discovered today, this book celebrates a Britain of fond memories.

↑In this classic 1950s country railway scene, a Class A1X Terrier tank halts at Langstone, on the Hayling Island branch, Hampshire.

↑Many branch lines lingered on after passenger services ended, kept alive by ever-diminishing freight traffic. Ramsey East, Huntingdonshire, is one example, seen here looking uncared for and overgrown in the late 1950s.

↑Picture postcards became popular in the early 1900s, and many were sent by people who had reached branchline destinations by train. This came from Aldeburgh in 1951.

↓Some branch lines survived. On a wet day in August 1971 a Warship-hauled, London-bound express pauses at St Erth, Cornwall, while the DMU for the St Ives branch waits in the bay platform.

↑ *There were many narrow-gauge branches, often serving remote and underpopulated regions. This is the Rye & Camber Tramway in Kent, probably in the 1920s, with the petrol locomotive then in use. Many of the passengers have chosen to travel in the open freight wagon at the rear.*

↑ *A short branch from the south end of the Tay bridge to Tayport, Fife, opened in 1879. Cut back to Newport-on-Tay after the Tay road bridge opened in 1966, the line closed in 1969. Here, a DMU waits to depart from Tayport in 1961.*

↑ *This entertaining photograph seems to represent branchline freight traffic in a rural goods shed somewhere in Britain, perhaps in the 1930s. The wagon has been stacked to the limit, but clearly could not travel loaded like this.*

↑ *Branchline stations came in all shapes and sizes, but many were just simple shelters on short, wooden platforms. Typical of this basic type was Cassington Halt, on the GWR's long branch to Fairford, Gloucestershire.*

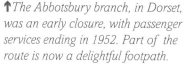

↑The Abbotsbury branch, in Dorset, was an early closure, with passenger services ending in 1952. Part of the route is now a delightful footpath.

←Reminders of lost lines often remain to be discovered. This crossing-gate post was found in the bushes on the Fairford branch, in Gloucestershire.

→Goods traffic continued on the Cheadle branch, in Staffordshire, until 1986 and, surprisingly, some track was still in place in 2012.

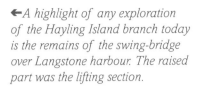

←*A highlight of any exploration of the Hayling Island branch today is the remains of the swing-bridge over Langstone harbour. The raised part was the lifting section.*

↓*This muddy path crossing the landscape under a dramatic sky is the trackbed of the Lossiemouth branch, in Elginshire (now Moray). Some of it is now a footpath.*

↓*Some lines remain as they were left by the demolition teams after closure, overgrown and abandoned in the landscape. This is the Maerdy branch, in the Welsh Valleys, where coal trains ran until the 1980s.*

↓*Disused railways often leave permanent traces, likely to be visible for centuries. Here, near Fontburn, on the Rothbury branch in Northumberland, an embankment carries the curving trackbed across the moorland landscape.*

USING THIS BOOK

BRANCH LINES

For the purposes of this book about Britain's lost branch lines, a branch line is defined as a passenger-carrying railway, generally not more than 25 miles long, running from a mainline junction to a village, town or city terminus. Not included, therefore, are minor lines built to connect two places on main lines, nor routes and branches created by the closure of interconnecting or through routes. Freight-only branches are included only on feature pages. For interest, open and preserved branch lines are also listed.

THE MAPS

The maps in the book are based on a map of the railway network of Britain produced in the 1890s. Some main and branch lines that opened after that date have been added, to give a picture of the British network at its peak, in about 1920. However, the maps do not show every railway line, particularly in the case of towns and cities. The book is not intended to be a comprehensive railway atlas, and the nature of the base map does give rise to occasional inconsistencies.

The aim of the book is to show how the railways of Britain looked in the early 20th century within the context of the counties of Great Britain as they were when the base map was created. The county names and boundaries of that era, along with the national boundaries, have been used. The border between England and Wales was significantly different from today, and some regions now in Wales were then in England. Note also that the 1890s map used English, rather than Welsh, spellings of place names in Wales.

In this book, the counties are grouped to make 25 map sections within five regions: Southern England, Wales, Central & Eastern England, Northern England and Scotland (see right and pages 4–5).

Where the route of a branch line crosses

a county boundary, it is usually featured in the county in which the terminus was situated.

On each map, the railway lines are coloured: blue for closed branch lines; red for closed passenger lines, or freight lines; green for passenger-carrying main lines and branch lines that are still open. Preserved and heritage lines are featured only if they run along complete branch lines. Heritage railways operating on sections of former main or branch lines are not included.

THE DESCRIPTIONS OF THE ROUTES

Following each of the 25 maps are descriptions of the branches in that group of counties. Some lines are covered in depth, with photographs showing the line when it was in use, modern photographs to illustrate the state of the line today, and period postcards. Other branches are covered more briefly, with old photographs and postcards, while others again are presented as a short paragraph of text without illustrations. The distinction between full and partial coverage is not necessarily indicative of the branch's relative importance or length, and may depend on the availability of illustrative material.

Interspersed throughout the book are feature sections focusing on different aspects of branchline history.

A detail from one of the maps, with the key showing the status of passenger railway lines. The numbers refer to a list of branch lines featured in that section.

Closed branch lines

Closed passenger lines

Open passenger lines

THE MAP SECTIONS

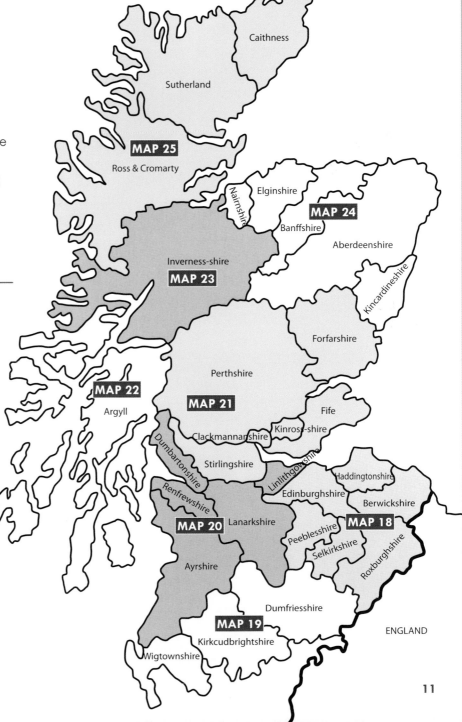

SOUTHERN ENGLAND

TOP LEFT: *In March 1965, the 2.06pm from Seaton Junction sets off for Seaton from Colyton.*

BOTTOM LEFT: *A solitary trainspotter watches the Westerham branchline train arrive at Brasted Halt, in 1959.*

TOP RIGHT: *As the sun sets, a train from Hayling Island slowly makes the crossing to the mainland on the Langstone harbour viaduct.*

BOTTOM RIGHT: *A few passengers have gathered on the platform at Lambourn for the Newbury train.*

MAP 1

CORNWALL & DEVON

BRANCH LINES

❶ **St Ives**
Cornwall (page 25)

❷ **Helston**
Cornwall (page 16)

❸ **Falmouth**
Cornwall (page 25)

❹ **Fowey**
Cornwall (page 17)

❺ **Looe**
Cornwall (page 25)

❻ **Callington**
Cornwall (page 23)

❼ **Gunnislake**
Cornwall (page 25)

❽ **Turnchapel**
Cornwall (page 25)

❾ **Yealmpton**
Devon (page 25)

❿ **Princetown**
Devon (page 18)

⓫ **Kingsbridge**
Devon (page 19)

⓬ **Kingswear**
Devon (page 25)

⓭ **Brixham**
Devon (page 23)

⓮ **Buckfastleigh**
Devon (page 25)

⓯ **Ashburton**
Devon (page 24)

⓰ **Moretonhampstead**
Devon (page 20)

⓱ **Sidmouth**
Devon (page 21)

⓲ **Seaton**
Devon (page 24)

⓳ **Hemyock**
Devon (page 22)

⓴ **Ilfracombe**
Devon (page 25)

Lyme Regis
See Map 2 (pages 28–9)

Closed branch lines

Closed passenger lines

Open passenger lines

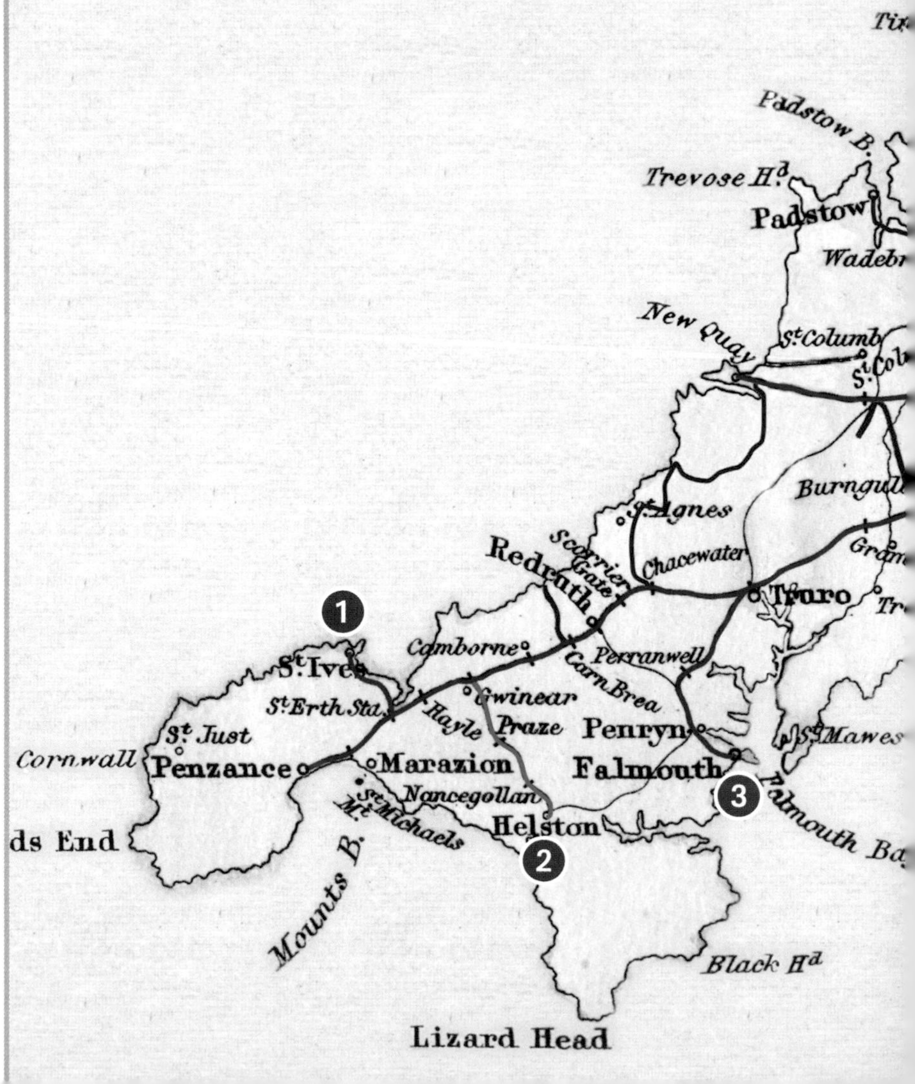

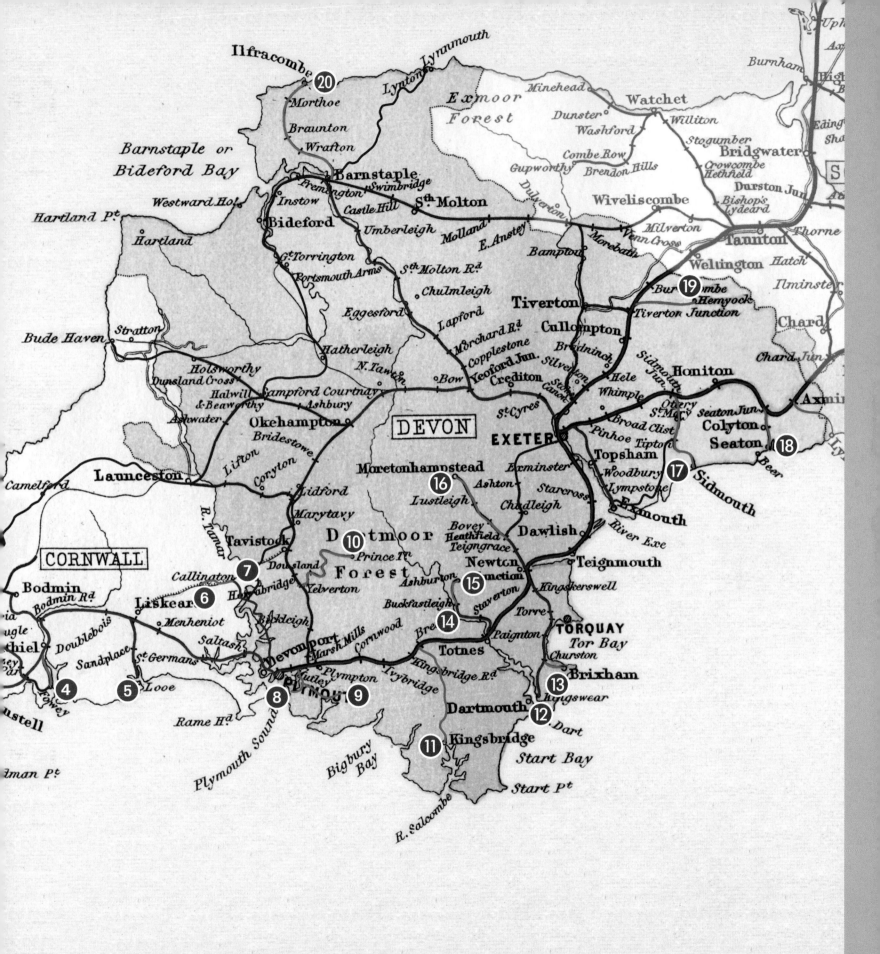

MAP 1

❷ HELSTON

The independent Helston Railway took a long time building its line, which finally opened in 1887. Tourism was by then the main inspiration for building the line, though the transport of local agricultural produce was also important, as in other parts of the region. The branch left the GWR's main line at Gwinear Road, to wind its way through the hills and valleys for 9 miles to Helston. In 1903, by which time the GWR was in charge, a plan to extend the branch to the Lizard was replaced by an early example of a railway-operated bus service. The line remained busy until the 1950s, but a rapid decline in traffic saw the ending of passenger services in 1962. This was the first such closure in Cornwall. Freight continued for another two years. Today, the route can be followed in the landscape, and various structures, including the Cober viaduct, are still standing. Since 2005, the Helston Railway Preservation Company has rebuilt a mile of track and has created a new station near Trevarno. Passenger rides are offered, and there are plans to extend the line.

△The stone arches of the Cober viaduct are an impressive memorial to the Helston branch. Relatively inaccessible today, the viaduct may one day carry trains across the valley again.

◁This artistic postcard view of the Looe Pool near Helston was sent from Camelford in October 1906. The writer was enjoying 'lovely weather'.

▽The branch's terminus at Helston was well equipped for passenger and goods traffic, and the facilities included a small engine shed. In this October 1959 view, a locomotive runs round its train while a railwayman, probably coming off duty, walks towards the station.

❹ FOWEY

The Fowey branch has a complicated history, which started in 1862 with the passing of the Lostwithiel & Fowey Railway Act. This independent company finally completed its broad-gauge line in 1869, linking the main line with a deep water port at Carne Point, close to Fowey, which could be used for the export of local china clays. In 1874 a rival standard-gauge route was opened to Fowey from Par by the Cornwall Minerals Railway. This launched a price war and resulted in the closure of the Lostwithiel & Fowey's line in 1880 and, ultimately, the dissolution of that company. In 1895 the Cornwall Minerals Railway reopened the line, having rebuilt it to standard gauge, extended it to Fowey, linked the two routes and opened an intermediate station at Golant. China clay remained the primary traffic, though passenger services continued until January 1965. In 1968 the line from Par was closed and made into a road for china clay lorries, but the original Lostwithiel & Fowey route is still in use for the transport of china clay.

△This colourful early 1960s postcard shows a popular view of Fowey from Polruan, across the estuary. A few people are waiting for the ferry to Fowey, some of whom were perhaps hoping to catch the train back to Lostwithiel.

◁In August 1921 GWR Class 1076 No. 1259 waits with its train in Fowey station. There were 266 locomotives in this class, sometimes known as the Buffalo class, built between 1870 and 1881. This example had been rebuilt with pannier tanks the previous year. The last survivor of the class was withdrawn in 1946.

▷After passenger services ended, the branch was kept busy for years with china clay traffic from the quarries. At its peak, the branch was carrying over a million tons of clay per year, much of it being exported from Fowey. It was still busy in the 1980s, when this Class 37 diesel was photographed with its line of hoppers.

◁In the summer of 1960 Fowey was busy with both passenger and goods traffic. Here, a mixed freight headed by 5700 Class No. 8733 has just arrived from St Blazey, while an off-duty driver walks towards the station. At this time there was a camping coach at Fowey, on a siding behind the signal box.

MAP 1

⑩ PRINCETOWN

Railways came early to Dartmoor, with lines being built in the 1820s to transport stone to Plymouth. A long section of one of these, which ran between Sutton Pool and King Tor, was incorporated into a new branch line from Yelverton to Princetown, opened in 1883. This remote line, nominally independent but operated by the GWR, wound its way across bleak and largely inaccessible moorland to connect a series of generally short-lived granite quarries. Passengers, travelling to and from Princetown, were also catered for, along with prisoners bound for Dartmoor. Later, in the 1920s and 1930s, additional minor halts were opened, aimed at quarry workers, walkers and others enjoying the Dartmoor scenery. In the British Railways era, traffic diminished and the line's closure, proposed for 1955, was eventually achieved in March 1956. Today, much of the route survives and is easily explored, offering a magnificent walk across the moor.

△ Yelverton, on the line from Plymouth to Tavistock and Launceston, was the junction for the Princetown branch. Built in stages, the line became a secondary route and closed in 1962.

△ Curiously, prison views were popular with some postcard publishers. This Edwardian card of the prison gates at Dartmoor, near Princetown, shows a work party setting out.

△ The Princetown branch winds its way across a dramatic and desolate landscape. Here, in the early 1950s, the 12.08pm from Princetown approaches the remote Ingra Tor Halt, headed by an elderly Class 4400, No. 4410, a branchline locomotive class that dated back to 1904.

▷ Despite having been closed for over 50 years, the Princetown branch is still largely traceable in the landscape, and its route makes a magnificent moorland walk, as this photograph indicates. Few buildings survive and most of the stations were, in any case, very minimal.

⑪ KINGSBRIDGE

Though authorized in 1863, the Kingsbridge branch was not opened by the GWR until December 1893. The 12-mile route, from the main line at Brent, largely follows the winding valley of the river Avon, crossing it ten times. Extensively wooded, it was famous for its spring flowers, notably primroses. It was built for local freight and the growing holiday traffic, the latter also being the inspiration for a proposed extension to Salcombe that was never to be fulfilled. Busy throughout its life, the line closed in 1963 despite a local battle to save it. Today, much of the route survives, but is largely overgrown and inaccessible. The three intermediate stations, Avonwick, Gara Bridge and Loddiswell, are now private houses. The remains of the terminus station at Kingsbridge survived until 2009; the site is now used by local industry.

▽ Typically, branch lines were built to serve the local economy, so goods traffic was always important. This 1956 view of Kingsbridge station shows sidings filled with various goods wagons, and a van has been driven onto the platform and backed up to the waiting train to ease loading or unloading. Meanwhile, a lady in a long coat chats to the driver.

▷ Loddiswell station has been a private house for decades, but its railway inheritance and history have been carefully preserved. The many period details include the addition of a replica signal box.

△ Much of the route of the branch cannot be traced and, apart from bridges and stations, there is little to see. A surprising survivor is this support for a crossing gate near Gara Bridge.

THE SQUARE AND PROMENADE, KINGSBRIDGE

◁ This postcard, dating from the late 1960s or early 1970s, shows one of the classic views of Kingsbridge, a scene little changed today. The railway had closed by the time this card was published, though the station was still there.

MAP 1

⑯ MORETONHAMPSTEAD

The Moretonhampstead & South Devon Railway completed its route along the Bovey valley to Newton Abbot in 1866. This broad-gauge line made use of earlier transport systems, including the Haytor Granite Tramway of the 1820s and the Stover Canal. Later, it was taken over by the South Devon Railway and then the GWR. In 1903 it was linked to a rural route to Exeter, via Chudleigh. Clay traffic was always important, with several potteries along the route, and this kept part of the branch in use after the end of passenger services in 1959. After a period of closure, the line was reopened in 2011 from Newton Abbot to Heathfield for timber traffic. Plenty survives to be seen along the route, including handsome stone bridges and stations at Bovey and Lustleigh, though the trackbed is often inaccessible. More obvious is the approach to Moretonhampstead across open fields, but only the engine shed is still standing on the station site.

△In 1907 Nellie sent this card to her mother at home in Perranporth to say she had arrived safely in Moretonhampstead. It would have been a slow but easy journey with only a couple of changes.

△Bovey was a typical small country station. Today, the main building remains but, confusingly, a main road now runs along the trackbed and the platform has disappeared.

△Surviving bridges and other structures are in local stone, used in a massive and rustic way that reveals the branch's early date. Typical is the former engine shed at Moretonhampstead, the only part of the station complex still standing, now in a small modern industrial estate.

▷Moretonhampstead station, seen here in May 1952 with the autotrain for Newton Abbot ready to depart, was quite a grand structure with a typical timber train shed. One of the reasons was the GWR's famous and luxurious Manor House Hotel. Both town and hotel were, however, some way from the station.

⑰ SIDMOUTH

Another locally inspired company was the Sidmouth Railway, whose line, via Ottery St Mary, was authorized in 1862 but not completed until 1876. The expansion of holiday traffic was the aim, though the station's position a long way from the centre of Sidmouth and the sea reflected the town's mixed views about the railway. In the event, it flourished, remaining independent until 1923, when it was absorbed into the Southern Railway. At its peak in the 1930s, the line saw 24 trains a day, thanks in part to its connection to Exeter via Budleigh Salterton and Exmouth, opened in 1903. Traffic, including freight, remained busy through the 1950s, and there were some long-distance direct services. However, the rapid decline in traffic in the 1960s brought complete closure in May 1967, when the line to Budleigh and Exmouth also closed. Though sometimes inaccessible, the route can still be followed and plenty survives to be seen, including bridges and Sidmouth station.

△ In an accidental conjunction, this 1960s postcard shows a Ford Anglia splashing through the ford on the river Sid, inland from Sidmouth.

△This classic LSWR box, built high for good visibility over the busy junction at Sidmouth, controlled traffic to Sidmouth and to Exmouth. Sidmouth Junction station was renamed Feniton.

△By 1963, traffic was diminishing rapidly on the branch. The sidings are nearly empty, and the platform is deserted on a wet August day. Two trains are waiting to depart, one for Sidmouth Junction and the other for Exmouth. The long platforms were originally built to cater for the big holiday expresses, by this time increasingly a distant memory. The main station buildings, in the far distance, survive.

◁ The route of the Sidmouth branch can easily be explored, though sections are inaccessible or private. Bridges remain, sometimes almost completely hidden by trees and bushes, and raised sections of track have, as seen so often, been turned into convenient farm access tracks.

21

MAP 1

⑲ HEMYOCK

In Victorian Britain, many small towns wanted their own railway, to connect them to the modern world. The Culm Valley Light Railway was a typical example, built on local optimism and always short of funds. The line finally opened in 1876 and was absorbed into the GWR four years later. It was notable for its rural route along the quiet Devon river valley, and its remarkably slow speeds, with the 7-mile journey often taking up to an hour. Freight was always important, and it was the dairy traffic that kept the line in use until 1975, long after the end of passenger carrying in 1963. There were a couple of intermediate stations, and a few halts were added by the GWR to encourage more use. Today, parts of the route have vanished but plenty remains to be seen, hidden in the gentle valley of the Culm.

▽ There is plenty going on in this view of the line's terminus at Hemyock taken in 1958 – but not much passenger activity. The single-coach train waits at the platform while the driver and guard have a chat, and the locomotive, No. 1449 from the GWR's 1400 Class, introduced in 1932 for branchline work, gently lets off steam. A railwayman cycles away from the goods yard on some errand. For passengers, the way onto the platform is via the traditional kissing gate.

△ A reminder of the Culm Valley Light Railway is the short platform that served as Whitehall Halt but is now a grassy feature in a private garden. Milk trains still passed in the 1970s.

◁ Another little halt was Cold Harbour, photographed here in September 1958 with an active signal box and some rather unkempt flowerbeds. The autotrain is about to depart towards Hemyock.

⑥ CALLINGTON

Originally a mineral line, the Calstock Light Railway was rebuilt and reopened in 1908, linking Callington with the LSWR's main Tavistock-to-Plymouth line at Bere Alston. The most notable feature on the winding and steeply graded route is the famous Calstock viaduct. In 1966 the upper section, from Gunnislake to Callington, was closed. Two years later the main line above Bere Alston was also closed, turning the remainder into a long branch from Plymouth. This, surprisingly, is still open.

△ On an early morning in 1964, the 7.16am from Callington pauses at Chilsworthy. Sadly, there are no passengers to enjoy the magnificent view from the single platform.

◁ Until 1966 Bere Alston was a busy station, serving both mainline services to and from Plymouth and the branch to Gunnislake. With the closure of the main line northwards, the station suddenly became a minor halt on a remote branch line, and decay quickly set in.

⑬ BRIXHAM

The independent Torbay & Brixham Railway opened its short branch from Churston in 1868. Initially a broad-gauge line, it was sold to the GWR in 1883. Famous at first for its distinctive little locomotives, the railway soon became an important part of the local tourist infrastructure and was well used until closure in 1963.

◁ This card, issued soon after the closure of the branch, is a reminder that Brixham remained popular, and was, in the words of the rather feeble poem, 'just like Heaven!'.

△ In this typical late 1950s scene, an autotrain headed by a GWR Class 1400 tank locomotive drops down towards Brixham and the sea, while passengers watch from the open windows.

MAP 1

⑮ ASHBURTON

The branch from Totnes to Ashburton was opened by the Buckfastleigh, Totnes & South Devon Railway in 1872, becoming part of the GWR 25 years later. It remained a local asset until closure to passengers in 1958 and to freight in 1962. The branch was reopened as a heritage line in 1969, but subsequently the section north of Buckfastleigh was closed again and the route was used for road improvements, though the former station at Ashburton survives. Today, the South Devon Railway runs the line.

▽Totnes was the junction for the Ashburton branch. This 1950s view shows the autotrain from Ashburton approaching Totnes, with GWR Class 1400 tank locomotive No. 1470 in charge. Today, steam trains on the South Devon Railway depart from a separate station, adjacent to Totnes mainline station.

△Ashburton station, originally the wooden train shed seen here, survives, along with the nearby stone goods shed, which is now a garage.

⑱ SEATON

The Seaton & Beer Railway opened its short branch from Seaton Junction, on the main line along the Axe valley to Seaton, in 1868 and it became part of the LSWR in 1885. An important section of the region's holiday network, the branch remained in use until 1966. Today, passenger services are operated along part of the route between Colyton and Seaton by the narrow-gauge Seaton Tramway.

△In April 1957 a few passengers and a number of young enthusiasts stand on Colyton platform to watch the approaching train. Today, the station is the terminus for the Seaton Tramway.

◁Though closed in 1966, Seaton Junction survives, with mainline services to and from Waterloo passing every day. The main building is now a private house. The concrete footbridge was used by passengers for the Seaton branch.

⑧ TURNCHAPEL

The LSWR's branch line from Plymouth Friary to Turnchapel via Plymstock was opened in 1897, its main feature being the hand-operated swing-bridge across Hooe Lake. The inspiration for the line was chiefly rivalry between the LSWR and the GWR. Passenger services ceased in 1951 but freight, which had always been important and included military traffic, continued for another ten years.

⑨ YEALMPTON

Another line born out of competition between the LSWR and the GWR, this branch ran from Plymouth Millbay station to Yealmpton via Plymstock. It opened in January 1898, was initially successful, but suffered early from competition with local bus routes offering a faster service. Passenger services ended in 1930, were briefly reinstated during World War II, and then ceased permanently when the line closed in October 1947.

⑳ ILFRACOMBE

The branch from Barnstaple to Ilfracombe, which opened in 1874, was built as a single-track light railway. However, expanding traffic, particularly during the holiday season, caused the LSWR to upgrade and double the whole branch in 1889. Nothing could be done about the fierce climb from Ilfracombe to Mortehoe, so many departing trains were double-headed. From then on, the route attracted many long-distance LSWR and GWR expresses, a pattern that continued until the early 1960s. At that point, the branch was downgraded and cut back to single track again. Freight and through services stopped. From then until closure in 1970, the branch existed as a local line. Much of the route survives, but the bridge over the Taw in Barnstaple has gone.

OPEN & PRESERVED LINES

❶ ST IVES

The scenic branch from the main line at St Erth to St Ives was opened in 1877, inspired by both tourist traffic and local freight, such as fish. Always popular with visitors, the line managed to survive closure, and is now operated as a community railway. It offers one of the best traditional branchline experiences in Britain.

❸ FALMOUTH

Opened in 1863 as a mainline link from Truro to packet boats sailing to and from Falmouth, the railway quickly became the branch line that still operates. The route, along the valley of the Fal, connects a series of busy communities, and its popularity has increased since it became a community railway.

❺ LOOE

This branch, built primarily for the clay trade, was opened in 1860. Its route followed a former canal northwards from Looe to Moorswater. There was no direct connection with the GWR main line at Liskeard until 1901. From that date, the branch's route was from Liskeard to Looe, with the old line to Moorswater, north of the main line, for clay trains only. Though scheduled for closure in the 1960s, the Liskeard-to-Looe line has survived, and it now offers visitors a memorable taste of branchline life.

❼ GUNNISLAKE See **CALLINGTON**, page 23

⑫ KINGSWEAR

The Dartmouth & Torbay Railway opened its line to Kingswear in 1864, and for many years the GWR operated it as a mainline terminus, with its connections for Exeter and London. Reduced to branchline status by British Railways, the Kingswear branch faced closure in 1968. Instead, it was saved, and from 1973 became a heritage line, the Paignton & Dartmouth Steam Railway.

⑭ BUCKFASTLEIGH See **ASHBURTON**, page 24

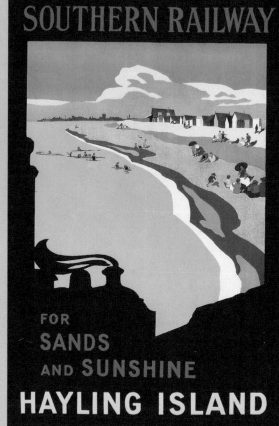

WOODHALL SPA

BROMO-IODINE WATERS   FIRST CLASS GOLF

BOOKLET FROM INFORMATION BUREAU WOODHALL SPA
OR ANY L·N·E·R AGENCY

High Force, Middleton-in-Teesdale

TEESDALE

SEE BRITAIN BY TRAIN

CECIL KING

GLAMIS CASTLE

KIRRIEMUIR

LMS   ITS QUICKER BY RAIL   LNER

Full information from LMS and LNER Offices and Agencies

MAP 2

SOMERSET, DORSET & WILTSHIRE

BRANCH LINES

This is the bay platform for the Bridport branch at Maiden Newton in the 1960s.

Closed branch lines

Closed passenger lines

Open passenger lines

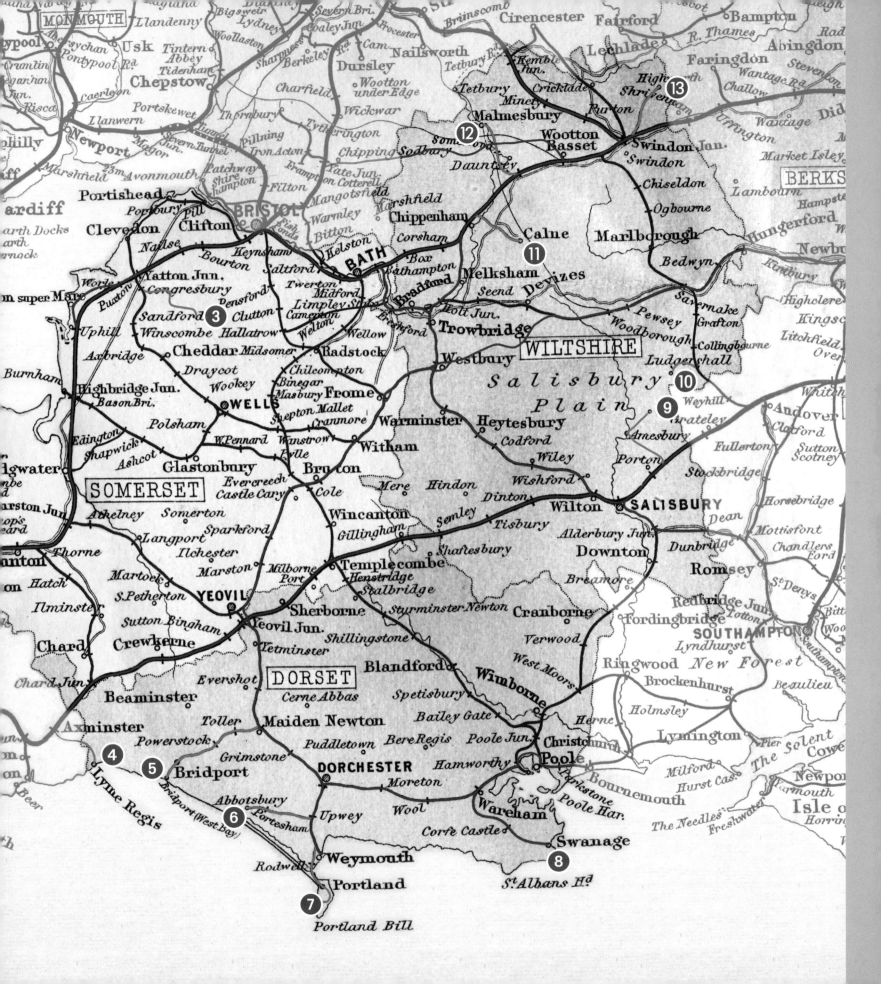

MAP 2

④ LYME REGIS

As a flourishing seaside resort, Lyme Regis tried and failed several times to have its own railway before a route was eventually approved in 1871. Even then, financial problems meant that it was not until 1903 that the branch from Axminster, in Devon, constructed by the Axminster & Lyme Regis Light Railway, was opened. From 1906 the line was operated by the LSWR and subsequently its successors, until closure in November 1965. Lyme Regis station was high above the town and a long way from the beach, but this did not deter visitors, and traffic remained heavy until the 1950s. Today, much of the branch line's route can be explored, although some sections have been lost, and there is plenty to discover in the hilly landscape.

△The branch was famous for its almost exclusive use of the Adams radial tank locomotive, a design from the 1880s. Here, in 1936, one is about to depart from Lyme Regis.

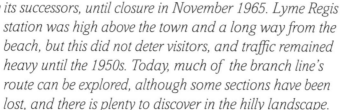

△This card, produced in the early 1900s after the railway arrived and illustrating some of the delights of Lyme Regis, reflects its popularity as a seaside resort.

△The terminus of the branch was Lyme Regis station, far above the town. This photograph shows the station in 1907, shortly after the LSWR took over the route. Visible are the coal yard and the livestock loading bay, along with the station hotel, which survives today. The station now enjoys a new life at the Watercress Line's Alresford station, in Hampshire.

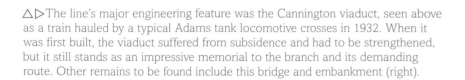

△▷The line's major engineering feature was the Cannington viaduct, seen above as a train hauled by a typical Adams tank locomotive crosses in 1932. When it was first built, the viaduct suffered from subsidence and had to be strengthened, but it still stands as an impressive memorial to the branch and its demanding route. Other remains to be found include this bridge and embankment (right).

⑥ ABBOTSBURY

The exploitation of local iron ore deposits and other mineral traffic inspired the building of the Abbotsbury Railway. The line was first proposed in 1872, but the typical ups and downs faced by small, independent railway companies meant that the line was not opened until 1885. By that time, the GWR was involved and it gradually took over the operation of the line. The hoped-for mineral traffic never materialized, so the branch had to rely on local traffic, agriculture and tourism, and it did so steadily until closure came in 1952. The line left the LSWR's main line to Weymouth at Upwey, in a complicated junction that involved a sharp curve and a platform on a lower level. Today, much of the route can be explored. Stations and platforms survive as private houses at Portesham and Abbotsbury, along with a handsome goods shed. However, there is little to be seen at the Upwey junction.

△Abbotsbury's swannery and grand tithe barn were as popular in Edwardian times, when this card was published, as now. The nesting swans drew many visitors to the town by train.

◁This Edwardian view of Abbotsbury station suggests life on this line was always leisurely. It was sited a mile from the village centre, which must have deterred many travellers. However, agricultural traffic was always important, and there was a dedicated milk platform at Friar Waddon, between Upwey and Coryates.

▷Enthusiasts explore the remains of Upwey's junction platform in the mid-1960s, after the closure of the short goods spur at the end of 1961. This was the departure platform for trains on the Abbotsbury branch, a journey that started with a sharp curve and a rapid descent. The mainline station, on the right, is still in use.

△The stations on the branch were distinctive structures in stone, designed by William Clarke. This is Abbotsbury in the 1960s, long after closure but before it was rebuilt into a private house.

▷Exploring the route of the Abbotsbury branch can be rewarding. A notable survivor is Abbotsbury's stone goods shed, seen here. Nearby, out of view, is the ruined engine shed.

MAP 2

❼ PORTLAND

The railways of Portland have a complicated history that starts early in the 19th century with the construction of tramways to serve the stone trade, notably the original Portland Railway and its incline down to the harbour. In 1865 came a branch line from Weymouth to Portland, jointly operated by the GWR and the LSWR. The Admiralty extended this to a new breakwater, to facilitate coaling of naval ships. Finally, after an extended period of gestation, the Easton & Church Ope Railway took it to Easton, blasting its way through the cliffs on Portland's eastern shore. Passenger services along the whole branch started in 1902, with stations and halts added gradually. Fifty years later, passenger services were withdrawn, but freight continued to 1965, when the whole network closed. Today, much of the Portland branch trackbed is still there, most of it easily explored. The section from Weymouth to Ferrybridge is a cycleway, and other sections are official footpaths.

△The Rodwell Trail is a cycleway along the trackbed from Weymouth to Ferrybridge, just before the start of the causeway to Portland. Several platforms have been retained, with new station nameboards. This is Rodwell, where there was a passing loop.

△Possibly published at about the same time as the card on page 18, this prison view shows the main gate at Portland, with prisoners setting off to the stone quarries. The gate still stands, but the buildings beyond have been redeveloped.

△Shortly before the final closure in 1965, a long special, topped and tailed by Standard Class tank locomotives, ran along the whole route to Easton. Famously, the train stalled on the steeply graded East Weares section, as seen here. This was the most spectacular part of the journey and is today a magnificent walk.

▷The branch started at Melcombe Regis, a separate station adjacent to Weymouth's main station, opened to avoid Portland branch trains having to reverse into Weymouth. From Melcombe, trains went straight onto the steel bridge over the Backwater, seen here in 1960 as enthusiasts watch a passing special.

⑪ CALNE

A railway linking Calne and Chippenham, in Wiltshire, was first promoted in 1860, and the Calne Railway Company opened its line in 1863. The route followed the river Marden and required little expensive engineering. Initially built as a broad-gauge line, it was converted to standard gauge in 1874. The GWR took it over in 1892. The branch enjoyed a long and successful life, with plenty of passenger traffic and freight dominated by Harris's meat products factory, Calne's major employer. The branch was also busy during World War II, thanks to nearby RAF bases, and on two occasions the Germans tried to bomb the line. As usual, the 1960s witnessed a rapid decline and freight services were withdrawn in 1963, unusually in this case before the ending of passenger traffic two years later. In 1972 part of the route was turned into a nature trail, and today most of it is an official cycleway, part of the National Cycle Network.

▽The GWR's Class 1400 tank engines were widely used on branch lines. This is No. 1444, setting off from Calne in September 1964, a year before closure. Passengers watch from the windows while an enthusiast runs to get his photograph. The large yard, developed from the 1890s to handle the expanding freight business, dwarfs the small, single-platform station.

◁This romantic card, posted in Calne on 5 March 1907 to Hilda Hillier, was signed on the back with eight neat kisses.

◁Black Dog Halt, one of two intermediate stations on the branch, was initially a private station for Lord Lansdowne, with its own siding. Later, it was brought into public use and took its place in the timetable. The other intermediate station was Stanley Bridge Halt.

▷The route along the gentle Marden valley is easy to explore. Here, the line crosses the fields on a low embankment, forming a backdrop to these spring lambs enjoying a warm day in March.

MAP 2

❸ BLAGDON

The Wrington Vale Light Railway, opened in 1901, was one of a number of lines that owed their existence to the passing of the Light Railways Act of 1896. This GWR branch line, initially from Yatton and later from Congresbury, ended at Blagdon, where it served a local reservoir development. Traffic was limited because of early competition from buses, and passenger services ceased in 1930. Freight continued to Blagdon until 1950, and then for a further thirteen years to Wrington, the major intermediate station. Some of the trackbed survives, along with the station at Blagdon, now a private house.

△Before freight services were finally withdrawn, the branch was visited by a number of enthusiasts' specials. This is Wrington station, overrun by passengers from the North Somerset Railtour of May 1957.

◁This photograph shows Blagdon station at the time of the branch's opening in 1901. Construction work is still going on, but the nameboard is up, there is a bench on the platform, and the gents' lavatory, a cast-iron building, is ready, The lines of open wagons are for the reservoir works.

❺ BRIDPORT

The Bridport Railway was an independent company set up in 1854 by local people keen to link their town to the national network. The branch, from Maiden Newton on the GWR's line to Weymouth, opened in 1857. Built as a broad-gauge line, it was operated by the GWR, which in due course took control. Conversion to standard gauge came in 1874.

The line continued from Bridport to West Bay, where the GWR hoped to enlarge the harbour and develop a resort. In the event, nothing much happened, but there was a steady trade from West Bay in timber and beach stones. Passenger services to West Bay ended in 1930, while freight continued until 1962. From that point, the branch ended at Bridport. Freight was withdrawn in 1965, but passenger services, though scheduled for closure by Beeching, struggled on until 1975, making Bridport the penultimate Beeching closure in Britain. The route is easily explored, and parts of it can be walked.

▽The station at West Bay, a stone building in a typical local railway style, survived the closure of the Bridport branch and lingered on in a semi-derelict state. It was used for a long period as a boat store, as this 1981 photograph indicates. Now fully restored, and complete with a stretch of track, the former station has a new life as a café.

❾ BULFORD

The Bulford branch was built as a military line, known as the Amesbury & Military Camp Light Railway. It opened for military use in 1901, and passenger traffic, operated by the LSWR, started the following year. Later, further branches serving various military establishments radiated from Bulford, which remained the last stop for passenger traffic until the stations closed and passenger services ended in 1952. Freight continued for another ten years. Today, part of the route is a nature reserve and bird sanctuary.

△ Posted in 1907, this artistic postcard offers a romantic view of the Bulford landscape, probably far from the normal experiences of the many soldiers who used the railway.

▷ This 1930s photograph shows a typically quiet scene at Bulford station, where non-military services terminated.

❿ TIDWORTH

Like the Bulford line (above), the short branch line from Ludgershall to Tidworth opened as a military railway in 1901. Its main function was the movement of troops between camps at either end of the line, and it was part of an extensive development of military railways in the Salisbury Plain area before World War I. A year later, ordinary passenger services started, operated by the Midland & South Western Junction Railway. This company continued to run the line until it was taken over by the GWR in the early 1920s. Military traffic continued to dominate, particularly during World War II, but conventional passenger and freight operations were maintained until 1955, when the War Department closed the line to non-military traffic. The branch then remained in military use until final closure in 1963.

△ Tidworth barracks grew massively during World War I. This postcard, written in 1917, gives an idea of the scale of the camp, at that time served by the railway.

◁ This 1919 view of Tidworth station, the end of the line for public, as opposed to military, use, illustrates the number of staff then involved in operating and maintaining a typical branchline terminus.

MAP 2

⑫ MALMESBURY

There were various plans to bring the railway to Malmesbury, including an elaborate scheme by the Wiltshire & Gloucestershire Railway Company in the 1860s, with both the Midland Railway and the GWR involved. In the end, a simple branch from Dauntsey, on the GWR main line, was built by the Malmesbury Railway Company, being completed in 1877. The GWR was the backer, and soon took control. Though simply built, the line did include one tunnel, on the approach to Malmesbury. In 1933 the branch was connected by a spur to the GWR's main line to South Wales. Despite the railway's benefit to Malmesbury, the branch was an early closure, to passengers in 1951 and to freight in 1962. Today, little remains to be seen, apart from the tunnel.

▽By 1968, six years after closure, little remained to be seen at Malmesbury apart from the station building, its overgrown platform and its goods shed. The station was distinguished by a generous canopy, also seen in the photograph on the left, taken at a time when freight services were still operating on the branch.

△A classic GWR branchline locomotive, No. 5802 from the 5800 Class, waits at the head of an RCTS special while enthusiasts explore Malmesbury station in about 1960.

⑬ HIGHWORTH

There had been various plans to link Highworth to the railway network, but nothing happened until 1879, when the Swindon & Highworth Light Railway Company began to build its short branch line. This company soon ran into financial difficulties, and the line was finally opened in 1883 after being taken over by the GWR. Things then settled down into a pattern of regular passenger and freight use. Traffic expanded during both world wars, thanks to various nearby military installations and factories linked to the war effort. Notable was a Vickers factory near Marston. Industrial traffic declined rapidly in the 1950s and 1960s, prompting the closure of most of the branch in 1962. Some freight traffic continued for a couple more years. Housing and industrial growth have now hidden much of the route.

▽As a light railway, the Highworth branch was cheaply built. There were no significant engineering features, and buildings were fairly basic. This is Highworth station, probably in the 1950s. There is a fine platform lamp adjacent to the minimal signal box. The stationmaster is keeping an eye on the photographer.

❶ WEST SOMERSET MINERAL

The West Somerset Mineral Railway was built in stages from 1856 to carry iron ore from the Brendon Hills to the port at Watchet. The route was complicated: a higher and a lower level were linked by an inclined plane, and there were branches at the top, along the Brendon Ridge to Gupworthy and to a mine at Raleigh Cross. A limited passenger service continued for some years after the mines went out of use in 1880. The railway closed entirely in 1898, was revived between 1907 and 1910, and was then finally abandoned.

OPEN & PRESERVED LINES

❷ MINEHEAD

See also **WEST SOMERSET MINERAL, above**

There were many schemes dating back to the 1840s to bring the railway to Minehead, but in the end it began with a line from Taunton to Watchet built by the West Somerset Railway and opened in 1862. Then, twelve years later, this was extended to Minehead by another company. In due course it all became part of the GWR, which operated it as a long branch line. Over many decades, and into the British Railways era, the line – helped by holiday camps around Minehead – was busy with holiday traffic. Despite this, the branch closed in 1971. Five years later it became a heritage railway, and the whole route has been reopened.

❸ SWANAGE

The branch from Wareham to Swanage was built by the Swanage Railway Company and opened in 1885. It was operated from the start by the LSWR, which subsequently took control, and it later passed to the Southern Railway and thence to British Railways. Although popular with holidaymakers, the branch was listed for closure in the 1960s. Fierce local opposition delayed this, but the end came early in 1972, apart from the surviving freight line to Furzebrook, used by clay and oil trains. Within a few years the branch became a heritage railway. The route has gradually been reopened, and there is now the possibility of passengers being offered a full branchline service from Wareham to Swanage.

△On a winter's morning, frost marks the route of the Bridport branch (*see also* page 34) near Maiden Newton.

Branchline stations

↑ Portland's original station, completed in 1864 as the terminus of the branch from Weymouth, in Dorset, was replaced when the line was extended to Easton.

↑ The GWR station at Dartmouth, Devon, had no railway. Opened in 1880, it was the terminus for the ferry from Kingswear station. It is now a café.

↑ Blake Hall station, on the Epping-to-Ongar branch, in Essex, was built by the Eastern Counties Railway in 1865 in the domestic style of that time.

↑ The Hawkhurst branch, which opened in 1893, was distinguished by unusually tall station houses, some of which survive. This is Goudhurst, in Kent.

↑ This is Wilby station, on the Laxfield branch, in Suffolk. The wagon body and corrugated iron shed were typical of basic stations on light railways.

↑The Llanfyllin branch, Montgomeryshire, had large combined station and station houses. This is Llansantffraid, opened in the 1860s, now a restaurant.

↑Opened in 1884, Tregarth, on the Bethesda branch in Carnarvonshire, was a classic timber rural branchline station.

↑The terminus station at New Radnor, opened in 1875, reflects in its detail the pride of small local railways. It survives, looking sad, in a caravan park.

MAP 3

HAMPSHIRE & BERKSHIRE

BRANCH LINES

❶ **Lymington Pier**
Hampshire (page 47)

❷ **Fawley**
Hampshire (page 41)

❸ **Lee-on-the-Solent**
Hampshire (page 46)

❹ **Stokes Bay**
Hampshire (page 47)

❺ **Bembridge**
Hampshire (page 46)

❻ **Hayling Island**
Hampshire (page 42)

❼ **Bishop's Waltham**
Hampshire (page 43)

❽ **Bordon**
Hampshire (page 44)

❾ **Lambourn**
Berkshire (page 45)

❿ **Faringdon**
Berkshire (page 47)

⓫ **Wantage**
Berkshire (page 47)

⓬ **Abingdon**
Berkshire (page 47)

⓭ **Wallingford**
Berkshire (page 47)

Windsor & Eton
See **Map 9** (pages 106–7)

Closed branch lines

Closed passenger lines

Open passenger lines

② FAWLEY

Approval was given for a branch line serving the western shore of Southampton Water in 1903, but nothing happened until the early 1920s, when the Totton, Hythe & Fawley Light Railway took over the scheme. In the end, the Southern Railway took control and opened the line in 1925. Traffic greatly increased after Britain's biggest oil refinery was opened at Fawley and, although passenger services continued until 1966, this became the mainstay of the line. Freight traffic, serving the refinery and Marshwood Military Port, has continued ever since. The result is a kind of time warp, with all the stations and infrastructure in place, including manually operated crossing gates and semaphore signals. Proposals published in 2009 to reopen the branch to passengers, along with all the former stations and a new one south of the mainline junction at Totton, are awaiting a decision.

△The Hythe pier tramway, shown in this 1950s card, is a delightful survival. The pier dates from the 1880s, while the electric tramway, connecting with ferries to Southampton, goes back to 1922. The electric locos are even older.

△In 1958 a former LSWR Class M7 tank locomotive, No. 30033, a veteran dating back to the late Victorian era, pauses to take water just outside Hythe station. The pebble-dashed building, a bit run down, reveals the economical approach used by the Southern Railway when building the branch in the mid-1920s. Today, the stations, and the line, are still intact, making reopening a realistic proposition.

▷On a summer's day in 2012, a Class 66 diesel, No. 66059, takes a couple of closed wagons through Marshwood station, on its way to Didcot from the Marshwood military base. These, and the refinery trains – usually just two or three a day – make up the modern traffic on the branch.

MAP 3

❻ HAYLING ISLAND

A typical Victorian rural line, the Hayling Island branch was built by the LB&SCR and opened fully in 1867. As was the case with many lines constructed with holiday traffic in mind, trains were busy during the summer and often empty out of season, a pattern little altered throughout the life of the branch. The major engineering features, which caused problems during construction and subsequent operation, were the embankment and bridge across Langstone harbour. Indeed, it was the decayed state of this swing-bridge that prompted the closure of the branch in 1963, British Railways having decided that the cost of its replacement could not be justified. Various attempts were made to keep the branch open, but the track was finally lifted in 1966. Today, much of the route is a footpath and cycleway, named the Hayling Billy Trail after the popular name for the line.

△This 1907 card shows one of Hayling Island's more famous hotels, The Grand. It was sent by a lady staying not in the hotel but in a local cottage to a friend in Ballachulish, Scotland.

▷While two women and a child set off to do some shopping in Havant, the driver and fireman look after their charge, an elderly Class A1X Terrier tank locomotive, No. 32678, making sure it is ready for the next journey along the Hayling branch. Weight restrictions on the bridge over Langstone harbour meant these small locomotives operated the route from the end of the 19th century to closure in 1963; two of this former LB&SCR class hauled the last train on the branch, on Sunday 3 November.

▽Crossing the embankment and swing-bridge over Langstone harbour was the high point of the journey. Here, on a sunny October day in 1962, the driver enjoys the view as he takes his Terrier over the water. The cream cabin on the bridge controls the opening section.

▷A battered signal post is a famous survivor on the route. Originally the signal controlled the harbour crossing. The concrete supports for the embankment can still be seen, along with the remains of the bridge mechanism. The trackbed can be walked or cycled from here to the former station yard in Hayling.

❼ BISHOP'S WALTHAM

Bishop's Waltham was at the centre of a number of ambitious mainline plans during the 1860s, but in the end all the Bishop's Waltham Railway managed to build was its short branch line from Botley, opened in 1863. The owners had to take out further loans to complete the terminus station and goods yard, but financial problems continued and in the end the railway was forced to sell to the company operating it, the LSWR, which took control in 1881. The branch, always lightly used by both passenger and goods traffic, was busy only during the brief strawberry season, when special trains were organized to transport this famous Hampshire product to the London markets. Low passenger numbers also encouraged the LSWR to try out early railmotors on the branch, with limited success. The line closed to passengers in 1932 and to goods traffic 30 years later.

△ Jack posted this card from Portsmouth to Norfolk in December 1907 and, judging by the message, spent most of his time travelling and eating out. The carefully posed view of Bishop's Waltham High Street is full of interesting details.

◁ The Bishop's Waltham Railway was always short of money, yet the directors managed to build themselves a substantial terminus station, perhaps in the vain hope that they would one day be able to continue the line to the northeast to make a mainline connection. Today, nothing remains except a pair of crossing gates at the start of a short trackbed footpath.

▽ The branch's route can be followed along the valley of the river Hamble, though it is mostly overgrown and sometimes inaccessible. A number of bridges survive, along with occasional trackside details. This overgrown bridge, near Dursley Mill, is typical of what the dedicated explorer can find.

△ This view, taken shortly before the line's closure to passenger traffic in 1932, shows an unusually crowded platform at the Bishop's Waltham terminus, perhaps the result of an excursion. Goods traffic, in evidence here, was to continue until 1962.

43

MAP 3

⑧ BORDON

Between the Boer War and World War I a number of military camps were built or expanded, many needing railway connections to facilitate the movement of men and equipment. Typical was a new camp at Bordon, developed from 1903. In conjunction with the War Department, the LSWR built a branch to link this to the main line at Bentley, with an intermediate station at Kingsley. It opened in December 1905, soon after the start of the construction of the Longmoor Military Railway, connecting Bordon to Longmoor Camp and ultimately to the Portsmouth line at Liss, although as a purely military line this never carried regular passenger traffic. The Bordon branch was largely dependent on the army camp, and its role, like that of the camp, diminished after World War II. In 1959 passenger-carrying ended, and when army freight traffic ceased in 1966 the branch was closed and lifted. The Longmoor Military Railway closed in 1969. In 2009 the Bentley-to-Liss route was on a list of lines that could usefully be reopened to passengers; the decision is still awaited.

△This Edwardian card, showing the infantry married quarters at Bordon Camp, was sent to Guernsey, perhaps by a soldier's wife writing to her son. The houses were then newly built.

▷The Bordon branch was lightly engineered and made little impact on the landscape, but some sections of the route can still be traced. This view, of a former level crossing, is typical of what remains to be found.

△Two boys in cub scout uniform pose on the buffers at Bordon station. It is the 1950s, probably soon after the ending of passenger services on the branch. The long platform was built to serve troop trains.

△In May 1934 a Southern Railway service pauses at Bentley, the junction for what the nameboard calls the Bordon Light Railway.

⑨ LAMBOURN

The Lambourn Valley Railway had a long period of gestation. Authorized in 1883, the branch from Newbury was not opened until April 1898. For the first few years this small, independent company used its own locomotives ('Aelfred', 'Eahlswith' and 'Eadweade') and rolling stock. However, all were sold in 1904, replaced by railmotors hired from the GWR, which took over the railway the following year. At the start, there were seven intermediate stations along the very rural route, and the GWR added one more. Racehorse traffic was important, thanks to the many stables on the Downs. A spur linking the branch to RAF Welford was added in the 1950s, and this kept the Newbury-to-Welford section open until 1973, the remainder having closed in 1960. Today, some stretches have been lost, but the route can be explored and the Lambourn Valley Way partly follows the railway.

▽This photograph was taken on the railway's opening day in April 1898. Much of the LVR's rolling stock is on display, along with one of the company's three locomotives.

◁In August 1959 a typical Lambourn branch train comprising a single carriage and a former GWR Class 2251 0-6-0 locomotive, No. 2214, slowly makes its way along the line near East Garston station. The fireman and a couple of passengers lean out to enjoy the sunshine.

△Posted from Lambourn to Coventry in May 1908, this card shows the town's famous 15th-century market cross. The sender writes: 'Lovely day here. Hope you are having a good time.'

▽Following the route today is quite hard as some sections have been lost and others are inaccessible. However, there are places where the line can be clearly seen. Here, the trackbed describes a straight line separating the grassy foreground from the wheat field that climbs towards the sky – a downland landscape characteristic of the former branch.

MAP 3

❸ LEE-ON-THE-SOLENT

*This short branch line had a rather chequered career. It was built
with some difficulty by an independent company, the Lee-on-
the-Solent Light Railway, from a junction near Fort Brockhurst
on the Gosport line, and opened in May 1894. There were three
intermediate halts. For the first fifteen years the line was run by
the contractor, and then the LSWR became the branch's operator.
However, the railway remained independent until 1923, when the
Southern Railway absorbed it, albeit with some reluctance. It then
proceeded to close the branch, to passengers in 1931 and then to
freight four years later. The route has subsequently been buried
under later development, with the result
that there is little to be seen today. Lee-on-
the-Solent station survives, however, in use
as an amusement arcade.*

▷The developing popularity of Lee-on-the-
Solent as a resort was one of the reasons for
the building of the railway. This postcard was
sent in September 1907 by a visitor who may
well have stayed in the building depicted,
having arrived by train.

△ Having tried its best to make the branch
pay, the Southern Railway was well on the
way to giving up by the time this photograph
was taken in August 1930, and closure was
only five months away. The branchline train,
headed by a Class 02 locomotive, waits at Fort
Brockhurst, while everyone on board watches
the photographer.

❺ BEMBRIDGE

*The Isle of Wight Railway opened its short branch from Brading to Bembridge in May
1882, a route made possible when Brading Marshes were drained during improvements to
Brading harbour. The line was popular with holidaymakers and yachtsmen, and in summer
Bembridge station was often packed, and the turntable in constant use. After World War II,
the whole Isle of Wight network was in decline, and the Bembridge branch, an early
casualty, closed in 1953. Bembridge station was demolished in the 1970s and the site
redeveloped, but parts of the route can be walked. St Helen's station is a private house.*

△A popular sailing centre since the Victorian
era, Bembridge has long had the benefit of two
yacht clubs. This 1913 card shows the buildings
of the Bembridge Yacht Club, founded in 1886.
The railway ran to the rear of the buildings.

◁Bembridge station had one long platform,
two long sidings, a signal box and a cramped
turntable at the buffer end of the platform. The
station building was quite grand, enriched with
bargeboarding and Tudor-style chimneys. In
September 1953, with closure imminent, a train
waits to depart, headed by one of the island's
characteristic Class 02 tank locomotives.

⑩ FARINGDON

The Faringdon Railway's short branch from the GWR main line at Uffington was opened in June 1864. It was built as a broad-gauge line and operated from the start by the GWR, which finally took control of it in 1876, converting it to standard gauge two years later. The branch was initially successful with farmers and local industry, and well used in the Edwardian era, but traffic then declined steadily and the GWR was making losses through the 1920s and 1930s. The branch survived into the British Railways era, but passenger services were withdrawn in 1951 and total closure came in 1963.

△This multiview card was posted in 1963, the year the Faringdon branch line was finally closed. The sender came by car and had a difficult journey: 'At long last I arrived OK.'

◁In April 1959 an RTC (Railway Touring Club) special waits to depart from Faringdon, headed by a former GWR Class 1361 saddle tank locomotive, No. 1365, a class designed in about 1910 for dock shunting.

④ STOKES BAY

The Stokes Bay Railway & Pier Company was set up in 1855 with a plan to construct a pier for Isle of Wight steamers served by a short branch from Gosport. It was all open by 1863. Trains ran along the pier to the steamers, as at Ryde. The LSWR bought it in 1875, but the already limited trade soon declined. The last train ran on the pier in 1915. The Admiralty took over much of the branch. (See also the GWR leaflet on page 114.)

⑪ WANTAGE

Opened in 1875, the Wantage Tramway was a 2-mile roadside branch line connecting Wantage with Wantage Road station on the GWR main line. Tram-style steam locomotives hauled passengers and freight. Passenger carrying ended in 1925, freight in 1945.

⑫ ABINGDON

The Abingdon Railway opened its branch in 1856. It was built as a broad-gauge line, linking the town to the main line near Culham. The GWR operated it from the start, and acquired it fully in 1904. In the 1870s it was converted to standard gauge and extended to meet the main line at Radley. Passenger services ceased in 1963, but freight, mostly for the MG car factory, continued until 1984.

OPEN & PRESERVED LINES

① LYMINGTON PIER

Built by the independent Lymington Railway and opened in 1858, the Lymington branch was designed both to connect the town to the national network and to offer a direct ferry link to the Isle of Wight, via Yarmouth. It was taken over by the LSWR in 1878. Initially not as popular as Portsmouth-to-Ryde, the route had a slow start but eventually became established. Today, the single-track branch is operated by modern electric trains, but it remains a traditional branch line, with passengers changing for the local train at Brockenhurst.

⑬ WALLINGFORD

The Wallingford branch has its origins in the Wallingford & Watlington Railway of 1864, conceived as part of a through route to Princes Risborough. However, construction stopped at Wallingford, and the line was opened as a branch in 1866. It became part of the GWR network six years later. Passenger services ceased in 1959 but freight, serving a maltings near Wallingford, continued until 1981. The line was then taken over by a preservation society and reopened in stages from 1985 as the Cholsey & Wallingford Railway.

Lost line legacy

MAP 4

SUSSEX, SURREY & KENT

BRANCH LINES

Closed branch lines

Closed passenger lines

Open passenger lines

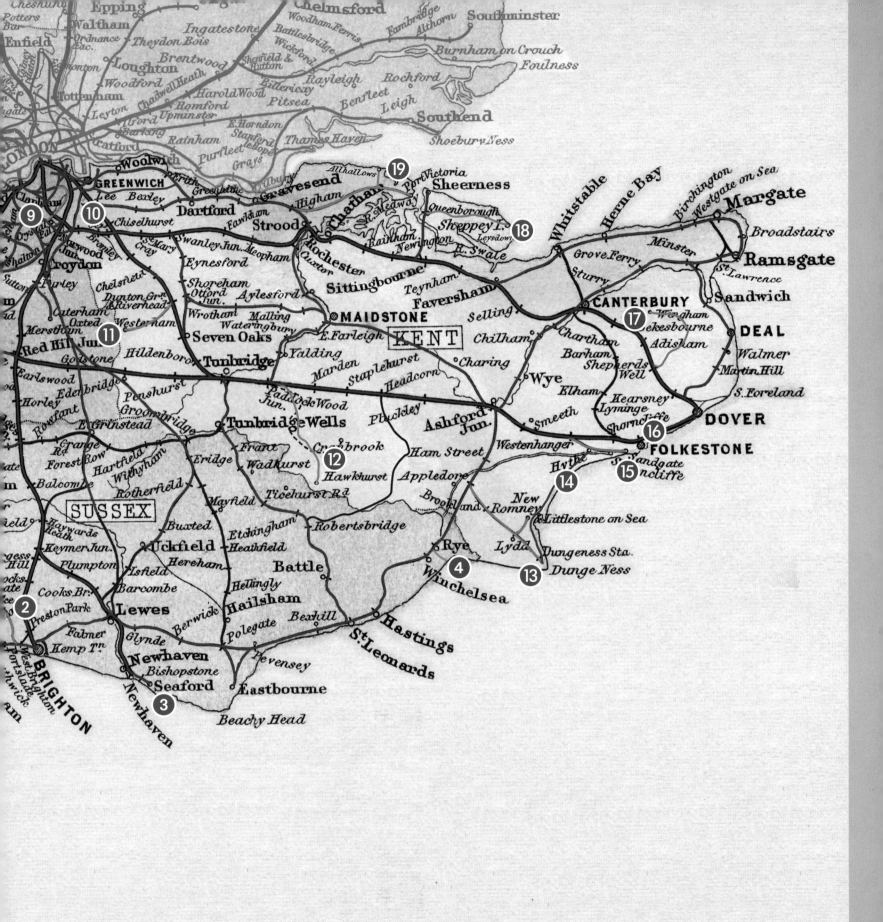

MAP 4

❶ SELSEY

The light railway that linked Chichester and Selsey, known originally as the Hundred of Manhood & Selsey Tramway, opened in 1897. It was a lightly built line whose major engineering feature was the lifting bridge that carried the track over the Chichester Canal. It served a number of isolated communities and became popular before World War I thanks to expanding holiday traffic. This traffic also inspired a short-lived extension to Selsey beach, and this proved to be the high point in the history of the line, which by then was known as the West Sussex Railway. Serious flooding in 1911 significantly damaged the line's finances, and it struggled to recover from this setback. In the 1920s, when the Southern Railway decided not to take control of it, the line joined Colonel Stephens' light railway empire, and under his control it featured some rather unusual custom-built, petrol-driven railcars. Despite these economies, the railway could not compete with quicker, more efficient road services, and it closed in January 1935. Being lightly built, much of the route quickly disappeared, along with the timber station buildings. Short stretches can be explored, including a section near Hunston that is an official footpath, but the most obvious survival is the remains of the supports for the lifting bridge over the canal.

△Most of the railway's route vanished soon after closure in 1935, but short stretches can still be identified, including a couple of sections that are now footpaths. A pair of ducks are enjoying a walk along this well-manicured stretch near Hunston.

△In the railway's heyday before World War I, it was popular with summer visitors keen to explore this remote region of Sussex. Here, in about 1910, a group of passengers and railway staff chat on the platform at Selsey, perhaps enticed by the many information and advertising boards on display. A smartly dressed small boy poses by the locomotive, one of the fleet of mostly elderly Manning Wardle, Peckett, Neilson and Hudswell Clarke hand-me-downs that operated the railway.

△This card was posted in the 1950s, twenty years after the tramway's closure, but the unchanging appeal of Selsey is revealed by the lack of cars and the group of horses being ridden through the centre of the village. Before World War I, all the shops would have been supplied by the West Sussex Railway.

② BRIGHTON DYKE

At the end of the 19th century, the Devil's Dyke, high on the South Downs above Brighton, was very popular with visitors enjoying the landscape, the bandstands and the fairground rides. A branch line, built by the Brighton & Dyke Railway, opened in 1887 and contributed massively to the area's popularity. The steeply graded line, climbing to within 200ft of the Dyke's summit, carried thousands of people keen to enjoy the walking, the views and the tea and cakes on sale at the rather basic terminus station. The branch closed in 1917, was reopened in 1920, and soon became part of the Southern Railway. Busy trains continued to carry visitors to and from the Dyke until increasing competition from buses brought it all to an end in 1939. Today, much of the route can still be traced, but not all is accessible. One section, from Hangleton Way to the Brighton & Hove Golf Club, is the Dyke Railway Trail. The former junction station for the branch is now called Aldrington.

△ This card, posted in 1908 by a visitor who had just arrived at the Dyke, shows the simple, very exposed station, as well as the long trains in use. The converted railway carriage on the left housed the tea shop.

◁ Two Southern Railway tank locomotives work hard together to draw their long train up towards the Dyke station, and the branch's terminus. The carriages are packed, with many passengers leaning out of the windows. At this time, in the 1920s, the Dyke was still a popular tourist attraction, best reached by train.

▽ The railway's route is still visible as a big sweeping curve over the Downs, indicated by the line of thick bushes and trees across the open fields. The Dyke station was off to the right of this photograph.

▽ This flowery farm track is the route of the branch as it approaches the site of the Dyke station terminus. Nothing survives from the railway or the station, but the location is quite close to that shown in the 1920s picture above.

MAP 4

⑨ CRYSTAL PALACE

In 1854 Paxton's Great Exhibition building of 1851, now known as the Crystal Palace, was reopened as an exhibition and concert hall in South London. It became apparent that it needed a direct rail link, so the Crystal Palace & South London Junction Railway's branch line from Nunhead was opened in 1865. There was a grand terminus station, designed by EM Barry and known as Crystal Palace High Level. Later, several intermediate stops were added to the route, one of which, Lordship Lane, features in a famous Camille Pissarro painting of 1871. For decades the branch was very successful, carrying hundreds of thousands of people to and from events at the Palace, as well as growing commuter traffic. This pattern continued after World War I and in 1925 the branch was electrified. When the Palace burnt down in 1936, traffic immediately declined, leading to the closure of the branch in 1954. Since then, much of the route has been built over, though tunnels survive. Barry's station has gone and houses stand on the site, but the subway to the Palace lives on.

△The writer of this 1909 card says that he passed the building, but did not go in. This is the famous view of the rebuilt and enlarged Crystal Palace in its park, a major South London feature from 1854 to 1936.

△The surviving pedestrian subway that linked the High Level station to the Crystal Palace hints at the magnificence of Barry's original building. Polychrome brick pillars, in a style that has echoes of the Middle East, were a fashionable look in London in the 1860s. Now restored and listed, the subway is opened from time to time for visits.

△The High Level station was a classic Victorian terminus building, with a glazed iron roof supported by arches in coloured brick. Its scale indicated the density of traffic using the branch, particularly during major events taking place at the Crystal Palace. This photograph shows it in the late 19th century.

▷ The intermediate stations were a later addition to the branch, reflecting the growth in commuter traffic. This is Honor Oak in the early 1920s, shortly before the line was electrified by the Southern Railway.

⑪ WESTERHAM

After a complicated gestation period, the short branch from Dunton Green, on the main line, to Westerham was finally completed in 1881. The original plan to continue the line to Oxted was never fulfilled. The branch was built by the independent Westerham Valley Railway, but it was operated, and soon owned, by the South Eastern Railway. By the mid-1950s, after an uneventful life, the branch was making a steady loss. It was scheduled for closure and, after a battle, closed in 1961. There followed a long struggle by local residents and others to reopen the line as a combined commuter and heritage line. This ended in failure in 1965, and two years later the track was lifted to pave the way for the M25 to be built over some of the route. As a result, little remains to be seen today, but a stretch from Dunton Green towards the motorway can still be identified as it crosses the fields.

△ Dunton Green, on the main line from Charing Cross to Sevenoaks, was the junction for the Westerham branch. This Southern Railway direction sign was still hanging there when the branch was closed in 1961.

◁ Posted in 1906, this card shows the green at the centre of Westerham. Nowadays, the scene is dominated by a statue, erected in 1911, of General James Wolfe, born here in 1727.

▽ The dense hedge crossing the fields marks the route of the branch line soon after it left Dunton Green. The remains of the branch platform have only recently disappeared beneath new buildings.

△ In a classic scene from the Westerham branch line, the 2.50pm from Dunton Green pauses at Brasted Halt, one of the two intermediate stations. It is August 1961 and closure is imminent. The locomotive, a regular on the line, is a Class H, No. 31308, a Wainwright design dating back to 1904. Also veteran are the SER platform lamp and the timberclad station building. The fireman and guard are watching, but no one gets on or off the train. The trains were busy only at commuting times.

MAP 4

⑫ HAWKHURST

Though incorporated in 1877, the Cranbrook & Paddock Wood Railway did not complete its branch until 1893. There had been other plans, including through routes, but none were fulfilled, leaving the branch to end at the remote village of Hawkhurst. The line was operated from the start by the South Eastern & Chatham Railway, which took it over a few years later. Passenger traffic was always light – the branch served only a few small towns and villages – but there was plenty of freight, mainly fruit, timber and coal. Notable were hop pickers' specials, the mainstay of the route during the season, and when this trade diminished, the writing was on the wall for the branch. It closed quietly in 1961. Much of the route survives and can be explored, while Cranbrook and Horsemonden stations live on as private houses.

▷Hawkhurst station is now an industrial site. Some railway buildings survive, including the goods shed and the engine shed, adapted for modern use. However, this well-maintained signal box, seen in its original form in the old photograph below, was demolished in 2012.

▷The branch's terminus station was a basic affair, some way from the village, and a legacy of the plans to continue the line beyond Hawkhurst. Here, in September 1958, a typical push-pull unit waits to depart towards the main line at Paddock Wood. The shortage of passengers that characterized the route throughout its life is apparent.

△A familiar stalwart of Kent branch lines was the Class H tank locomotive, a design dating back to 1904. This is No. 31177, waiting with its train at Goudhurst in the summer of 1961, during the last months of the line's existence. The tall station building is typical of the branch.

△Priscilla's Parlour was a local 15th-century guest house in Hawkhurst. The senders of this card stayed here in April 1936, having arrived by train. They told the recipient they had to go up the stairs on the left to their bedroom.

⑱ LEYSDOWN

In August 1901 the Sheppey Light Railway was opened. Its route, from Queenborough, on the main Sheerness line, to Leysdown-on-Sea, was designed to open up the hitherto remote regions of the Isle of Sheppey, particularly to holiday traffic. In the event, the line was never busy, and from the early days various railmotors were used on the branch. During World War I a link was built to serve the naval air station at Eastchurch, and military traffic became important in both world wars. After World War II, the roads improved and the slow branch, with its many level crossings, stations and halts, could not compete. Closure came in December 1950. Since then, much of the line has vanished, leaving only a few stretches to be seen.

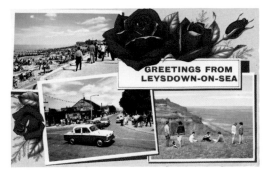

△ This card was sent in 1968, by a couple from London having 'a nice rest and plenty to eat'. By then the railway, originally built with holidaymakers in mind, was a distant memory.

▷ The drive leading to the suitably named Sheppey Light Farm is actually the former trackbed, one of the few surviving sections of the route that can be easily identified. An original concrete crossing-gate post is also visible.

△ There is little to see in Leysdown, but just outside the town a line of bushes starting near a former level crossing marks the branch's slightly raised route, visible across the fields but not easily accessible.

◁ An early Wainwright design still in branchline use into the British Railways era was the Class R-1 tank locomotive. Here No. 31705 waits at Queenborough with a Leysdown service on the last day of the branch in December 1950. A solitary enthusiast and the driver focus their attention on the photographer.

MAP 4

❻ BISLEY

The history of the Bisley branch line is inextricably part of the story of the National Rifle Association of the United Kingdom, which was founded in 1859. The incentive for it came both from the spread of the volunteer militias of the Victorian period and from the increasingly fashionable status of competitive shooting, among both men and women. Established first at Wimbledon, the NRA moved its camp to Bisley in Surrey in 1890. The principal ranges used today are based largely on those of the 1890s. From the start, it was realized that a railway connection was vital, so a short branch was opened by the LSWR from Brookwood to serve the new camp. It was built as a light tramway and always operated with weight restrictions and a speed limit. The major engineering feature was a bridge over the Basingstoke Canal. Services operated, somewhat erratically, until closure in 1952. The station building survives, with a different use.

▽ The speed restrictions gave the branchline train the ironic but suitable nickname, the Bisley Bullet. When this Railway Correspondence and Travel Society special visited the branch in 1952, closure was imminent. The simple timber buildings are indicative of the line's basic nature, but it did offer goods and parcels services.

⓭ NEW ROMNEY & DUNGENESS

The Lydd Railway was a small company set up in 1881 to build a branch from Appledore, on the SER's main line, to Dungeness. This opened in 1883, and a year later a separate short branch serving New Romney was completed. In 1895 the SER absorbed it all. The driving force was the possibility of a cross-Channel port at Dungeness and, later, the potential for holiday development around New Romney and Littlestone-on-Sea. In the event, they were little-used branches serving a rather remote area. Passenger services ceased on the Dungeness branch in 1937, but part of the route still exists to serve the nuclear power station. New Romney & Littlestone-on-Sea station, to give it its full name, survived until 1967.

▽ As the junction station for the two branches, Lydd supported a substantial staff, photographed here in about 1910. As ever, the men's uniforms define seniority and status.

▷ The line's terminus, seen here in the 1950s, was a small brick station with two platforms, a little goods yard and a siding to deliver coal to the Romney, Hythe & Dymchurch Light Railway (see page 61). Nothing remains.

⑮ SANDGATE

A branch line from Sandling, on the SER's Dover line, to Sandgate, was proposed in 1864, with the aim of extending it to Folkestone in order to avoid the existing route's steep climb through the town. The branch was eventually opened in 1874, by which time the Folkestone plans had largely been abandoned, involving as they did the building of an expensive tunnel underneath the town. As a result, the branch, serving Hythe and Sandgate, was always little used, despite a splendid and grand Arts & Crafts style, Tudor revival station at Sandling Junction, completed in 1888. Closure began early, with the Hythe-to-Sandgate section of the branch disappearing in 1931. The rest of the line followed in 1951. However, Sandling's interesting station building has survived, along with its original lattice footbridge.

△This Edwardian postcard shows the extensive Sandling Junction station. The platforms for the Sandgate branch are on the right.

▷The Sandgate Tramway was a horse-drawn network designed to link Hythe and Sandgate. The section along the front, shown here, was opened in 1891, its development linked to the building of the esplanade and Sandgate's emergence as a resort. The tramway closed in 1921.

⑯ FOLKESTONE HARBOUR

Folkestone harbour was the creation of the SER, so the harbour branch was an early development, opening in 1843 and extended six years later to a new quayside station. The line crossed the harbour on a low viaduct, which included a swing-bridge section, and then ran along the pier. Steeply graded to the main line above the town, the branch often featured heavy boat trains with as many as four banking locomotives at the rear. There was also busy freight traffic until the 1960s. Electrified in 1961, the branch was in regular use until 2001, when it closed to normal traffic. Special trains, notably the Pullmans of the Venice Simplon Orient Express, continued to use the line until 2009 to allow passengers direct quayside access. Negotiations are under way to reopen the line as a heritage railway.

△ Posted in Folkestone in 1912, this card was sent by Genevieve to her friend Renée in Paris. The view shows the pier, with the station in the background. A number of goods wagons indicate the importance of freight at this time.

◁The steeply graded line through the town must have added interest, and noise and smoke, to the lives of the people whose houses flanked the branch. In June 1960 a former GWR tank locomotive struggles up the hill at the head of a boat train, helped by three or four other engines at the rear. This familiar daily scene is about to disappear, however, for electrification is on its way, with the chairs to carry the third, electric rail already in place.

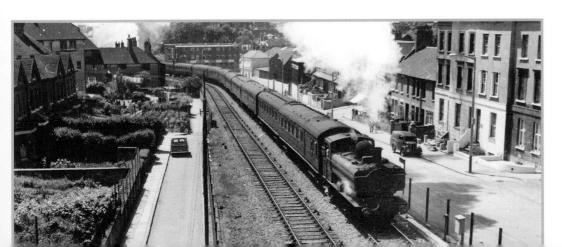

MAP 4

⑲ PORT VICTORIA & ALLHALLOWS-ON-SEA

Born out of LCDR and SER competition for North Sea trade, the Hundred of Hoo Railway was established in 1879. Its line to a new harbour at the end of the Hoo peninsula, Port Victoria, was opened in 1882. With its pier regularly damaged by storms and marine worms, the port never prospered, though its relative remoteness made it popular with the royal family. A steady decline brought about Port Victoria's closure in 1951, although – long after passenger traffic had vanished – subsequent development of an oil refinery, cement works and other industry has kept the line that served the port open for freight. In the 1920s expanding holiday traffic in the region prompted the Southern Railway to build a new branch, to Allhallows-on-Sea. Opened in 1932, it closed in 1961.

▽ This Edwardian view of Port Victoria's simple wooden pier reveals ambitions that were never to be fulfilled, though North Sea services continued to operate until the 1930s. Nothing remains today.

The Pier, Port Victoria, Kent. Pub. by F.R.Lawrence, Lower Stoke.

▷ Headed by a typical H Class tank locomotive, a Gravesend service waits at Allhallows-on-Sea in October 1961, two months before the branch's closure.

⑤ BROOKWOOD CEMETERY

Established from 1849 in response to overcrowding in the capital's graveyards, the London Necropolis Company built at Brookwood what was then the world's largest cemetery. Consecrated and opened in 1854, the cemetery was to see over 235,000 burials. Later, from 1917, military cemeteries were also developed. From the start, coffins and mourners were transported by train, with scheduled services from a dedicated section of Waterloo station. At Brookwood the funeral trains reversed onto a short branch line that served the cemetery and its two stations, one for Anglicans, one for Non-Conformists and others. The trains catered for about 2,500 burials a year, well below the promoters' expectations. In 1941 bombing closed the departure station at Waterloo, though occasional funeral trains operated for a while longer from other platforms. After World War II the branch closed and most of the buildings were removed or given other uses. Today, both station sites can be identified, with a Russian Orthodox monastery and a shrine to King Edward the Martyr occupying the former Anglican station buildings.

④ RYE & CAMBER

The Rye & Camber Tramway, whose short 3ft gauge line opened in 1895, was a typical product of the expansion of leisure activities in that era. The engineer was Holman Stephens, later famous for his light railway empire. The inspiration came from the holiday trade, and more particularly from golf, with the line serving Camber Sands as well as the local links. Trains, at first hauled by steam and later by petrol locomotive, were popular in the 1920s and 1930s. The line was taken over for military use in World War II and never reopened.

⑰ WINGHAM

The East Kent Light Railway, designed primarily to serve the Kent coalfield, was built in a random way from 1911. Passenger services operated to Wingham from 1916, but the planned extension to Canterbury never happened. A coal port, opened at Richborough, was not a success. Passenger traffic ceased in 1948 and freight shortly after, except for the line to Tilmanstone colliery, which was busy until the end of the Kent coal industry in the early 1980s.

OPEN & PRESERVED LINES

❸ SEAFORD

The Seaford branch, opened in 1864, was built primarily to serve the port of Newhaven, then being greatly expanded for cross-Channel services. The line, from Lewes, also serves Bishopstone, and originally there were three stations at Newhaven. One of them, Marine, a dedicated spur for ferry services, has been closed since 2006. The line was electrified in 1935, and at the same time the Southern Railway added Art Deco touches to some stations.

❼ HAMPTON COURT

The short branch from Surbiton to Hampton Court via Thames Ditton was opened in 1849. At the start, services were horse-drawn. The original station buildings at Hampton Court, which included a goods shed, were built in a Tudor style to reflect the grandeur of Hampton Court itself.

❽ CHESSINGTON

Planned in the late 1930s by the Southern Railway as a commuter route to link Motspur Park with Leatherhead, the line was terminated at Chessington South in 1939 by the outbreak of World War II. Work never resumed, so it remained a branch. Electrified from the start, it featured a sequence of modernist Art Deco concrete stations, which survive to give the branch a distinct period quality.

❿ BROMLEY NORTH

Rivalry between the LCDR and the SER led to the building of the short branch to Bromley North by the nominally independent Bromley Direct Railway. Opened in 1878, it was soon taken over by the SER, to enable it to challenge the LCDR's dominance in the area. The SER named it Bromley North. When the line was electrified in 1926, a new station was built in a decorative Baroque style, designed by JR Scott. Today, it is a classic branch line, operated by a shuttle from Grove Park.

⑭ ROMNEY, HYTHE & DYMCHURCH

Opened in 1927, and often called the world's smallest public railway, the Romney, Hythe & Dymchurch Light Railway embodied the dreams and ambitions of two wealthy racing drivers, Count Louis Zborowski and Captain JEP Howey, both of whom were also miniature railway aficionados. The 15in gauge line also reflected the enthusiasm of that era for miniature passenger-carrying lines. It runs for more than 13 miles along the Kent coast and has always been both a tourist railway and a public service route, carrying over 100,000 passengers each year. Until 1967 there was a connection with the national network at New Romney, but the railway now operates in isolation.

Military & hospital branches

↑ On the Longmoor Military Railway, in Hampshire, a group of soldiers pose beside 2-10-0 'Kitchener' after their driver training, probably in the 1950s.

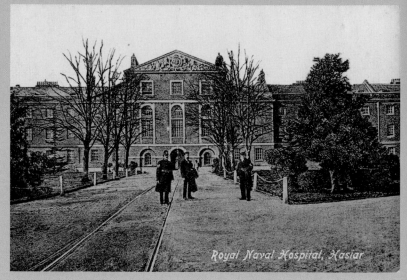

Royal Naval Hospital, Haslar

↑ Opened in 1753, the Navy's Royal Hospital Haslar, Hampshire, seen here on a postcard of about 1910, had its own railway connection from Gosport.

↑ The depot on the Longmoor Military Railway reveals the scale of this training operation. In 1949 the LMR had a fleet of 27 locomotives.

↑ After World War I several airfields and RAF depots had their own railway systems and locomotives. The RAF's last locomotive was retired in 1983.

↑ The private Whittingham Hospital Railway, in Lancashire, was 2 miles long with a station at each end. This typical train is at Grimsargh. See also far right, top.

↑ The Royal Victoria, a military hospital at Netley, Hampshire, opened in 1863 and from 1902 until the 1960s had its own station, seen here in 1955.

↑ The Whittingham opened in 1873 as a psychiatric hospital. The branch line between Grimsargh and Whittingham (above) operated from 1889 to 1957.

↑ An electrified branch line serving the local psychiatric hospital from 1903 to 1959 met the main line at Hellingly station, in Sussex.

WALES

TOP LEFT: *The locomotive crew and a single passenger watch the photographer at Bethesda station in the early 1950s.*

BOTTOM LEFT: *In October 1963, with Snowdon as a backdrop, a double-headed special waits in the platform at Llanberis.*

TOP RIGHT: *Enthusiasts from a railtour crowd the platform at Blaengarw in 1960, in a landscape dominated by coal.*

BOTTOM RIGHT: *While the locomotive runs round its train at Llanfyllin in 1956, the stationmaster and the guard load milk crates.*

MAP 5

PEMBROKESHIRE, CARMARTHENSHIRE, GLAMORGANSHIRE & BRECKNOCKSHIRE

BRANCH LINES

Closed branch lines

Closed passenger lines

Open passenger lines

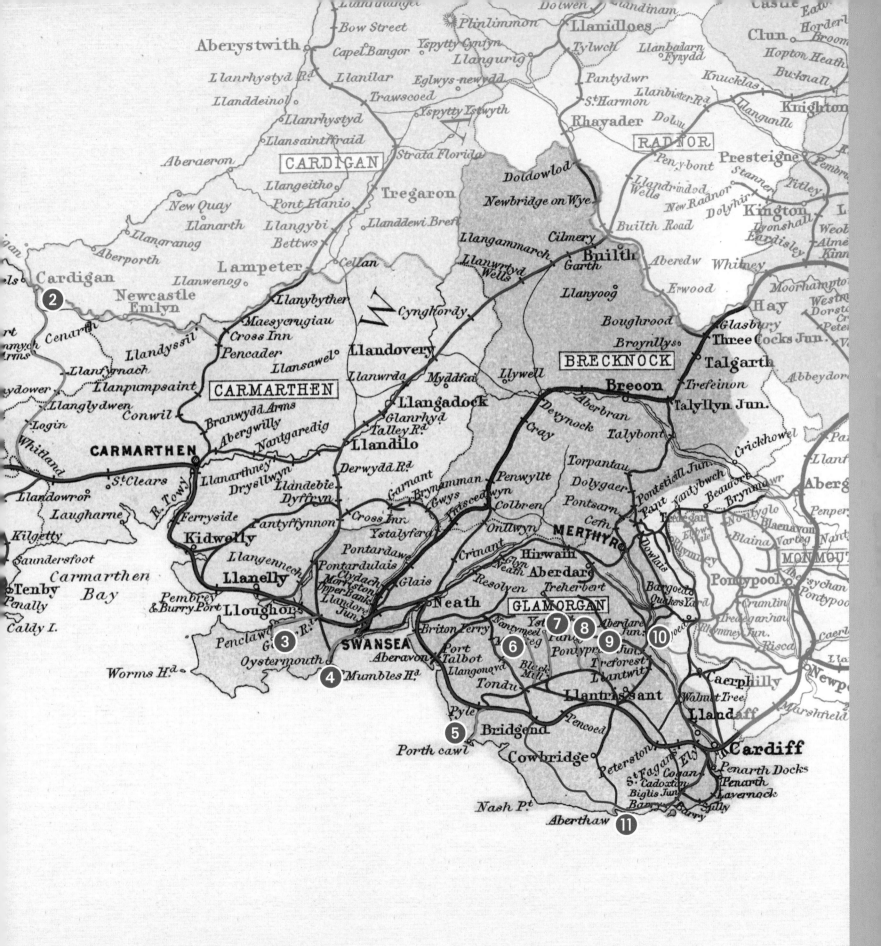

MAP 5

② CARDIGAN

Cardigan, though a busy port and an important market town with a powerful history, remained isolated from the railway network until 1886, the year in which the long and winding route of the Whitland & Cardigan Railway was finally completed. There had been a number of earlier schemes, all of which had come to nothing. The arrival of the railway brought benefits to Cardigan and the villages along the 27-mile branch, but it was a slow, leisurely journey from the junction at Whitland through rural Carmarthenshire and Pembrokeshire, with nine intermediate stations, and Whitland was still a long way from Carmarthen. The branch was never busy, though freight traffic was significant. The GWR took control two years after the opening of the line, having operated it from the start, and set a pattern that was to be largely unaltered until the early 1960s, by which time the service had been reduced to three or four little-used trains on weekdays. It was no surprise when passenger services were ended in September 1962, and not many people turned up to see the final train. Freight continued for a short while longer and then, after the track was lifted, much of the branch sank quietly back into oblivion. Today, some of the route is remote and inaccessible, but there are discoveries to be made and enjoyed, including the remains of stations and bridges. Nearing Cardigan, there is a footpath by the river Teifi and a nature reserve.

△ This shows a classic view of Cardigan's 18th-century bridge over the Teifi. The river was the county boundary, so Cardigan station, on the south side, was in Pembrokeshire, while most of the town, on the north side, was in Cardiganshire.

△ Boncath, seen here near the end of its days, was typical of the little stations along the Cardigan branch, basic structures serving remote places. The nameboard looks handwritten. There is no one to be seen, and the bicycle probably belongs to the photographer. A bicycle would have been a more effective way of exploring the line than waiting for a train.

◁ Much of the route is hidden and inaccessible, and where traces do remain, they sometimes look like relics from the Dark Ages rather than bits of railway history. It is hard to believe that trains crossed the river here as late as 1962.

⑤ PORTHCAWL

Porthcawl was a major coal port long before it became a holiday resort, and railways were active in the area in the 1820s. In fact, it was the Duffryn, Llynvi & Porthcawl Railway that first developed the harbour in 1825. Gradually, these local lines came together, ultimately as part of the GWR. By the end of the century, Porthcawl had been eclipsed by Barry as an industrial port, and the GWR closed the harbour in 1906. However, the railway lived on as the holiday trade was becoming increasingly well established, and in 1916 the GWR opened a new station for the resort. The 1920s and 1930s were the golden era for the town of Porthcawl, aided by a sequence of decorative railway posters promoting its beaches, but its short branch line, from Pyle junction, remained busy until 1961, when there were still 26 trains each way on weekdays. The decline then came quickly, and the branch was closed to passengers in 1963 and to freight two years later. Today, much of what was only a short branch line has been lost, particularly in and around Porthcawl, but the trackbed can be traced in the farmland to the north of the town.

△ As this postcard from the early 1960s shows, Porthcawl's Coney Beach had all the attractions of a traditional railway-inspired seaside resort, including a rollercoaster and donkey rides along the sands.

◁ Nottage Halt was the only intermediate station on the branch, serving little more than a cluster of farms and houses. Surprisingly, the single platform survives, though – as is so often the case with lost branch lines – the trackbed has become an informal farm access lane.

△ Porthcawl station was built by the GWR, from 1916, with the long platforms and extensive carriage sidings that were typical of a holiday destination. However, by the time this photograph was taken, perhaps in the early 1960s, there was already a sense of disuse and decay.

MAP 5

❻ BLAENGARW

The rich coal seams in the Valleys of South Wales inspired the building of a dense railway network during the second half of the 19th century. Typical was the Garw valley, a relatively inaccessible region until the GWR opened a branch from Bridgend along the valley to Blaengarw in 1876. Eventually there were five major collieries at work, one of which was producing 1,000 tons of coal a day, along with many smaller concerns and drift mines. Vast quantities of Garw valley coal were exported all over the world. By the 1960s the South Wales coalfield had passed its peak, and the 1970s saw the start of a steady decline. The last mine in the Garw valley, Ocean colliery, closed in 1985, and with it the Blaengarw branch line, though it was reopened briefly in the 1990s to remove the vast spoil tips from the head of the valley. Passenger services to the four stations along the route had ceased long before, in 1953. Today, the line is a kind of time warp, with track and infrastructure all left in place since the last train ran in 1997.

△The decline of the South Wales coal industry went hand in hand with the closure of railway lines, prompting many enthusiasts' specials to tour the region. This one visited Blaengarw in May 1973, when the branch was still working.

◁As the branch is still, in effect, a complete railway, there are plenty of interesting relics to be seen along the route. This van body, now abandoned, was probably used as a trackside tool store.

△In 1985 another special came up the branch to Pontycymer, by then the head of the line as the last mile and the area around Blaengarw station had been redeveloped. This photograph shows the special passing the remains of Pontycymer station and platform.

◁ Exploring the Blaengarw branch is easy because the track and most of the infrastructure are still in place, including warning signs at level crossings. For some of the route, there is also a parallel cycle track, which is useful as the track is often overgrown. Today, the branch, and the valley as a whole, are very green, making it hard to envisage a working coalfield here. A heritage organization, the Garw Valley Railway, is working to reopen the branch.

⑧ MAERDY

In the mid-1800s several small, independent colliery lines were brought together by the Taff Vale Railway to form a branch line from Porth to Maerdy. There were four intermediate stations, the most important being Ferndale and Tylorstown, which were also served by a street tramway. However, passenger traffic was never significant and railmotors were used in the early 1900s. In 1923 the Taff Vale Railway was merged into the GWR, which continued to operate the Maerdy branch as a major coalfield line. Most of the traffic came from the Maerdy colliery, which was famous as a centre of political radicalism and militancy until the closure of the mine in 1986. Maerdy was also the site of a disaster in 1885, when an underground explosion left 81 miners dead. Passenger services on the branch ended in June 1964, but coal trains continued to run until 1986. From then on, coal from Maerdy was extracted via the nearby Tower colliery, served by a different line. The track was lifted in 1987 and part of the route was used for the Taff Trail cycle route. Much can still be explored on foot and plenty remains to be seen, though access is not always easy, with the route often on the side of the valley. The section above Porth and around Ynyshir has disappeared under a relief road.

△ In 1962 Ferndale shed, a sub-shed of Treherbert, 88F, was still busy. On 13 May that year, it housed at least one member of Class 5600, designed by the GWR in 1924 specifically for heavy coal trains in the Welsh Valleys.

▽ Having been closed relatively recently, the Maerdy branch still had plenty to offer in 2012. This bridge carries the trackbed southwards along the valley from Maerdy station, the cleared site of which is behind the camera.

◁ The Maerdy branch attracted its share of enthusiasts' specials. This one, organized by the RCTS (Railway Correspondence and Travel Society) in 1973, has paused at Porth before setting off along the branch.

MAP 5

7 NANTYMOEL

△This 1950s view of Nantymoel shows a typical Welsh Valleys station surrounded by hills and overlooked by lines of terraced houses. The train has the right away and is about to set off on its way down the Ogmore valley.

The Ogmore Valley Railway, later the Llynvi & Ogmore Railway, was one of a number of independent lines constructed around the 1860s to access the collieries in the Welsh Valleys. Most, through various mergers, ended up as components of the GWR. The OVR's line, from Nantymoel to Tondu, and then on to Pyle and Porthcawl's coal harbour, was opened in 1865. North of Brynmenyn it was joined by the Blaengarw branch. Primarily a colliery line, the Nantymoel branch also served, with four intermediate stations, the towns and villages of the Ogmore valley. This traffic continued until May 1958, when British Railways withdrew passenger services. Along with other railways in the region, the branch continued to carry coal, remaining in use after other lines had closed for the transport of coal to the Ogmore Vale coal washery.

9 YNYSYBWL

A remote South Wales farming village in the Clydach valley with 200 inhabitants was turned into a large coal town of 7,000 by the opening in the 1880s of the Lady Windsor colliery which, at its peak, employed around 1,500 people. The branch line to Ynysybwl,

built and operated by the Taff Vale Railway, opened in 1887 to serve the colliery. At Coedpenmaen it joined the dense network of the TVR. This was one of the largest of the Valleys' coal railways, its axis being Pontypridd, the meeting point of three valleys. Passenger services were introduced on the branch, and there were several intermediate stations. Later, it became part of the GWR network. Passenger traffic survived into the British Railways era, finally being withdrawn in 1953. The Lady Windsor colliery closed in 1988, and the remains of the branch line disappeared with it, as did most of the former Taff Vale Railway empire.

▽The last station on the branch was Old Ynysybwl Halt, a remote spot in the middle of nowhere. This photograph shows this, and hints at the rural nature of the Clydach valley before the coming of coal. Here, on a summer's day in about 1950, the autotrain's crew relax in the sun and watch the photographer.

⑩ SENGHENYDD

The Rhymney Railway's 4-mile Senghenydd branch from Aber was opened in February 1894, primarily to serve local collieries but also to operate passenger services along the valley, and to Caerphilly. The branch had three intermediate stations. There were several collieries in the area but the Senghenydd name will always be associated with the Universal colliery, the site of Britain's worst coal-mining disaster. An underground explosion on 14 October 1913 killed 439 men and boys. This was the second disaster to engulf Universal and the Senghenydd community; an earlier explosion, on 24 May 1901, had killed 81 people. At this time, the South Wales collieries were at peak production, so a number of disasters were caused by careless work practices and inadequate management. The Universal colliery was closed in 1928, but the shafts were left open for ventilation purposes until 1985. The branch line closed in 1964.

▽Rows of miners' cottages and pit-head winding gear set the scene around Senghenydd station, which seems completely deserted in this 1950s photograph. A single lorry loading coal from a single wagon is the only sign of life, yet the local collieries were still at full production at this time. Perhaps it was a Sunday.

① NEYLAND

Brunel's ambition to link the GWR to Ireland gave rise to the development of a new harbour at Neyland. This, with its railway, was opened in 1856 as Milford Haven, but was soon renamed Neyland, and then New Milford. Built by the South Wales Railway, a GWR associate, it was initially successful, but was later eclipsed by Fishguard, which had a more direct route. In 1906 the name reverted to Neyland and this was used until closure in 1964.

④ MUMBLES

Famous as the world's first railway to carry fare-paying passengers, the Swansea & Mumbles, or Oystermouth, Railway can trace its origins back to 1804. During a long and complex history, the railway used every known form of traction, including sail. Two other railways were built along a similar route, but it was the Mumbles line that the Swansea public took to their hearts. Operated as an electric tramway from 1928, it closed in 1960.

③ LLANMORLAIS

The Llanelly Railway & Dock Company was one of the most ambitious operating in South West Wales in the first part of the 19th century. Its tentacles reached in many directions, including the building of a short branch on the north of the Gower peninsula, from Gowerton to Penclawydd, to serve both coal mines and the local shellfish trade. In 1877 this branch was extended to Llanmorlais. It was closed to passengers in January 1931, but short sections remained in industrial use until 1964.

⑪ ABERTHAW

The independent Cowbridge Railway opened a branch line from Llantrisant to Cowbridge in 1865, and in 1892 this was extended to Aberthaw. Here there were two stations: Low Level, which was the terminus of the branch, and High Level, on the Cardiff-to-Bridgend main line. The branch was little used, and passenger services ended in 1930. Later, another, much shorter branch was built to serve the power station at Aberthaw.

Branchline business

South Eastern and Chatham Railway.

Braxted STATION. June 30th 00

Receive the following Cans containing Milk, and forward at rate, subject to the undermentioned conditions.

Signature *K Spink*

CONDITIONS.

The following Conditions apply to Milk Traffic, and Rates are only quoted on these conditions.

EAST KENT RAILWAY.

Please quote this reference No.

Your reference No.

8th December 192 2   To   Mr E.J.Grey.

Memo. from the........ Traffic .... Dept.   51, Strond Street,

.... Shepherdswell .... Station.   .....Dover.

Dear Sir,

Passenger Tickets.

Herewith collected tickets for the month of November 1922.

Yours truly,
J. Akhurst
per

T. 2357).

FISH WAY-BILL.

NORTH EASTERN RAILWAY.

From HULL (Goods) Station, Cranbrook

CARRIED BETWEEN HULL (GOODS) AND DONCASTER STN., &c., FISH TRAIN.

NOTICE TO GUARDS.—The Guard of the Train must see that the entries on this bill correspond with the packages delivered to and given up by him. Care must be taken not to obliterate the details of the Way-Bill.

INSERT DETAILS IN BLOCK LETTERS

BRITISH RAILWAYS   O. 6014 (G)

GOODS DEPT. 20-4-   19

From SILVERTOWN

TO BUNTINGFORD

Region GE   Secn.

Via

Owner and No. of Wagon   Sheets in or on Wagon

134066   **3**

Consignee   SILLOCK

BARRY RAILWAY.

Not to be used for Miscellaneous Traffic.

(407D)   Guards' Signatures.

PARCELS WAY BILL.   From CARDIFF (Riverside) to Barry Island

No._____   Via

Departure _____ o'clock Train, ____ day of

Waterlow & Sons Limited, Printers, Dunstable and London.

No.	Description	Name.	Destination.	Weight. lbs.	Paid on. £ s. d.	TO PAY. £ s. d.	Paid. £ s. d.	Excess Luggage. £ s. d.	Sender.
1		Parkes		5					
2									
3									
4									
5									

N.B.—The Guard of the Train must see that the Entries on this Bill correspond with the Parcels delivered to and given up by him.

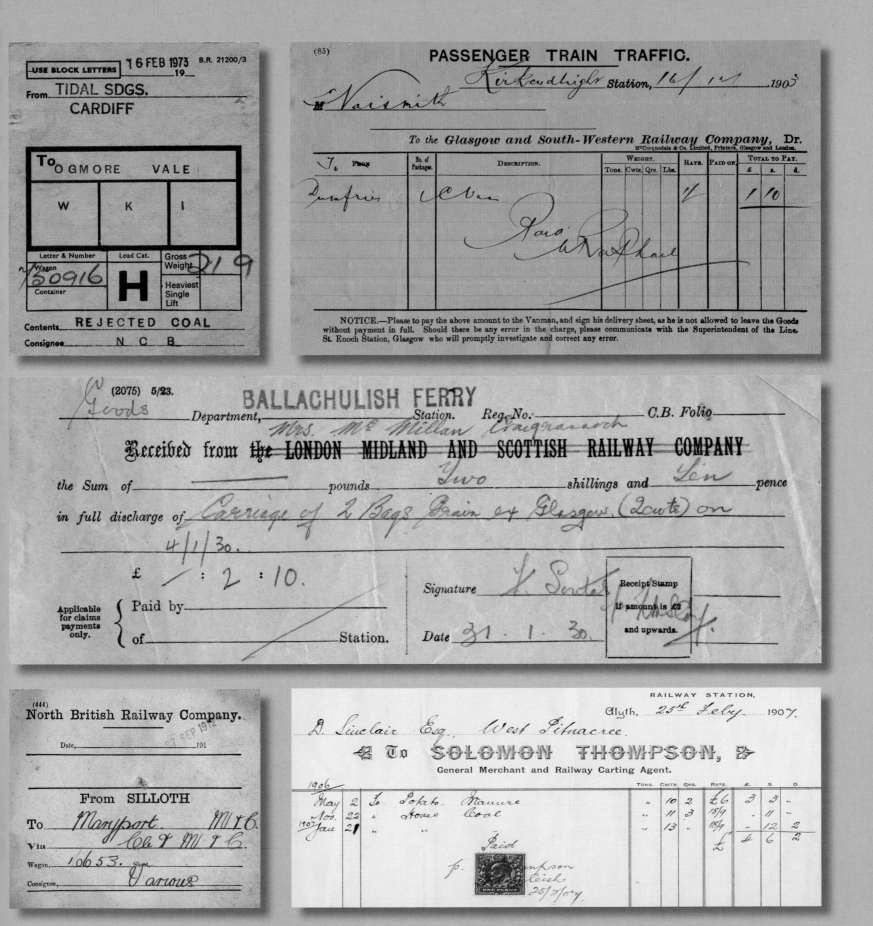

MAP 6

CARDIGANSHIRE, RADNORSHIRE, MONTGOMERYSHIRE & MERIONETHSHIRE

BRANCH LINES

This is the site of Aberangell station, on the Dinas Mawddwy branch.

Closed branch lines

Closed passenger lines

Open passenger lines

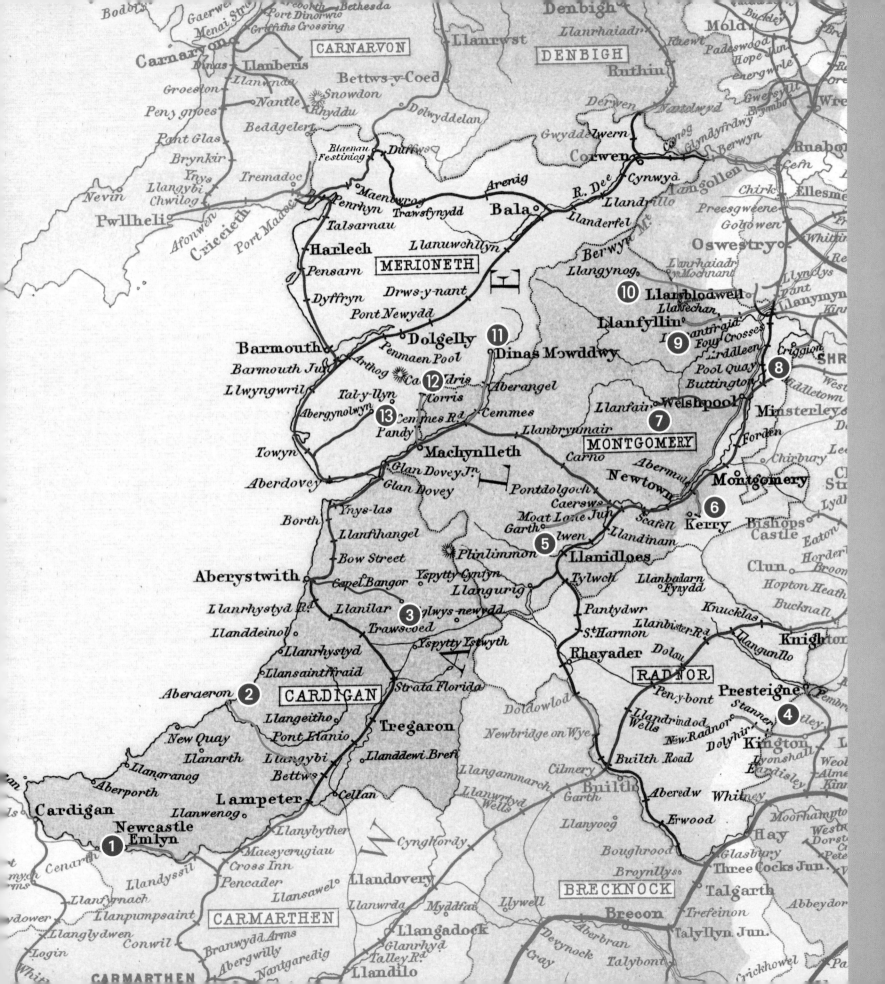

MAP 6

❶ NEWCASTLE EMLYN

In 1854 the Carmarthen & Cardigan Railway launched its grand plan to link those two towns with a line that passed through Newcastle Emlyn. Work started and by 1860 the first section, from Carmarthen to Conwil, was open. The money then ran out and, although the line was later extended to Llandyssil, constant financial problems brought it all to a halt. In 1881 the GWR, which had been operating the line, reluctantly took control and, faced with a branch that ended in the middle of nowhere, took it on to Newcastle Emlyn. So in 1895 the town finally had its own station, not on a through route as planned but at the end of a long rural branch from Pencader.

And so it remained for the next 60 years, a branch fulfilling the limited needs of the local community. In September 1952 British Railways bowed to the inevitable and withdrew passenger services. Freight continued until 1973. Today, much of the route has gone back to the quiet landscape of the Teifi and Tyweli, leaving little to explore. Most visible is the section from Henllan towards Newcastle Emlyn, now the narrow-gauge Teifi Valley Railway.

▽The long association between the river Teifi and the traditional Welsh coracle is celebrated in this 1930s postcard. The coracle men were local fishermen.

▽The local dairy industry kept freight traffic alive on the branch until the early 1970s, so the line was popular with enthusiasts' specials. This one, organized by the Stephenson Locomotive Society, visited before the track was lifted in 1976.

△It is near the end. The station buildings have gone and everything looks run down. A few milk tankers are just keeping the branch alive.

▷ Much of the route along the river valleys is hidden and inaccessible, though adjacent roads sometimes give views of low embankments in the woods or, occasionally, more significant remains, such as this half-demolished iron bridge, left looking like a piece of sculpture.

② ABERAERON

A product of the 1896 Light Railways Act, the Lampeter, Aberayron & New Quay Light Railway was an independent local enterprise authorized in 1906. Work started in 1908 and the line opened as far as Aberaeron in 1911. There it ended, and neither the planned extension to New Quay nor the line to the harbour were ever built. The GWR ran it, but did not take full control until 1923. Through the 1920s and 1930s the branch, a single-track line with one intermediate station, Felin Fach, and six minor halts, catered adequately for local needs. Freight traffic, primarily agricultural, was limited by the company's failure to complete the line to the harbour, though the building of an expensive iron bridge over the Aeron just outside the town indicated an intention to do this. In 1951, as so often when faced with uneconomical minor lines, British Railways took the decision to withdraw passenger services. However, freight lived on and was given a boost by the opening near Felin Fach of a new creamery, which kept much of the branch alive until 1973. The branch was a cheaply built local line, so sections have inevitably disappeared, but there is still plenty to see and explore. North of Lampeter a footpath follows the route, and platforms survive at Silian and Talsarn. At Aberaeron, the iron river bridge is still in use.

▽Aberaeron is a delightful town and harbour, distinguished by handsome terraces of houses, visible in this 1960s card.

△This is Ciliau Aeron, a typical minor halt on the branch, built cheaply from wood and using an old van body. A fisherman, a young girl and a railwayman are in conversation, perhaps about the next train.

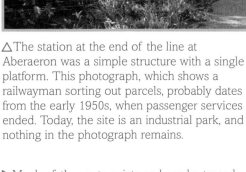

△The station at the end of the line at Aberaeron was a simple structure with a single platform. This photograph, which shows a railwayman sorting out parcels, probably dates from the early 1950s, when passenger services ended. Today, the site is an industrial park, and nothing in the photograph remains.

▷Much of the route exists and can be traced, though it is not always accessible. Here, the trackbed, now used as a farm path, crosses the hills near Felin Fach.

MAP 6

⑨ LLANFYLLIN

The branch to Llanfyllin was built by the Cambrian Railways to access the limestone quarries in the area. It opened in 1863. The route started at Llanymynech Junction, on the Oswestry & Newtown Railway's main line. This was an area of dense railway activity, with connections between the Cambrian, the Tanat Valley, and the Potteries, Shrewsbury & North Wales railways, as well as the Oswestry & Newtown. Also present at the junction was the Ellesmere Canal. Once the branch was clear of the complicated junction, there were three intermediate stations, all serving rural communities but with passenger services secondary to the stone traffic. In the 1920s the GWR took control and everything carried on as normal until the formation of British Railways, when a boundary change put the branch into the London Midland Region. Rationalization under the Beeching plan brought about the closure in 1965 of the old Oswestry & Newtown main line and with it the Llanfyllin branch. Today, much of the trackbed has gone, but there are stations and bridges to mark the route.

△This artistic Edwardian card, sent to Essex, indicates in a rather romantic way the quality of the landscape that surrounds the branch. Llansantffraid was one of the intermediate stations, and survives today as a restaurant.

△This stretch of embankment across the fields near Llansantffraid is one of several features that survive to identify the route of the Llanfyllin branch along winding river valleys.

▷In 1962 Llanfyllin was still a classic branchline terminus, at the centre of local life. While the train prepares to depart, a porter wheels a trolley laden with parcels and packages towards the guard's compartment. Until the branch closed in 1965, parcel traffic helped keep passenger services alive.

④ NEW RADNOR & PRESTEIGNE

Railway history is littered with ambitious schemes destined never to be fulfilled. Typical was the proposed line from Leominster to Aberystwyth. It started with the Leominster & Kington Railway, which opened in 1857. And that was that. The line progressed no further, except for the addition of two branches opened in the 1870s, from Titley to Presteigne, and from Kington to New Radnor, conceived originally as another step towards Aberystwyth. The GWR took control and then, under British Railways, the closures began. Passenger services ended on both branches in 1951, but freight continued for another ten years, helped at New Radnor by a local quarry. Today, both branches have left plenty of traces, though access is often difficult. Bridges and stations survive, with Titley station carefully preserved as a private house.

△The qualities of both New Radnor and Presteigne as traditional market towns are well known. This 1960s card, sent by one CB radio ham to another, gives a good idea.

◁ A surprising survivor is Stanner station, on the New Radnor branch. Now looking neglected and uncared for, this handsome stone building stands on its platform alongside a main road.

△New Radnor station, seen here in 1949 with the Leominster train about to depart, was built as a through station, not a terminus, but the line was never extended. This small stone building still stands, surrounded by caravans.

▽As so often, a stretch of identifiable trackbed survives because it is now in use as a farm access path or private drive. This section runs from the site of a level crossing into the distant woods, where a bridge takes it over a little river.

△Kington station was originally built as a terminus, and then a new building was erected when the line continued towards New Radnor. This classic branchline scene, rich in period detail, mostly GWR, dates from about 1950, shortly before passenger services ceased on both branches.

MAP 6

⓫ DINAS MAWDDWY

Slate was the inspiration behind a number of Welsh railways, including the Mawddwy branch. This opened in 1867 to connect local slate quarries to the Cambrian Railways' main line at Cemmaes Road. After a somewhat erratic existence, it closed in 1908, only to be reopened three years later under the Light Railways legislation. Some quarry links were maintained, but in essence the Mawddwy Railway became a conventional rural branch line, trying to serve local needs and interests, albeit limited by the remoteness of the route and all the stations, including the terminus at Dinas Mawddwy. The GWR took control, quickly appreciated the line's problems and ended passenger traffic in 1931. Freight kept going for another twenty years. The terminus station and goods shed survive in private use.

▽This charming 1950s view shows the terminus at Dinas Mawddwy at about the time of the branch's final closure. An old man and a child enjoy their picnic, surrounded by chickens, while the visiting photographer has left his motorcycle by the station. Today, the main building is a well-maintained private house, and a woollen mill operates from the goods shed.

◁Sent in 1974, when the branch was a distant memory, this card shows the landscape around Dinas Mawddwy. Elaine writes to a friend: 'It's sunny here but not in the same class as Cannes.'

⓬ CORRIS

It opened in 1859 as a narrow-gauge branch connecting the main line at Machynlleth with slate quarries around Aberllefenni and the Dulas valley, but from the 1880s the Corris Railway turned itself into a passenger-carrying tourist line. The slate traffic continued, but at a steadily decreasing rate. A number of connecting bus routes were also developed. After various changes of ownership, the Corris ended up with the GWR. Passenger carrying ended in 1931, freight in 1948. A section is now open as a heritage railway.

❿ LLANGYNOG

The Tanat Valley Light Railway opened its 15-mile branch from Blodwel Junction to Llangynog in 1904. Primarily a mineral line, the railway also served a series of small villages along the Tanat valley and, via its connections, made it possible to travel to Oswestry, Gobowen, Chirk and Wrexham. In 1921 debts resulted in the company being sold to the Cambrian Railways, which were absorbed by the GWR two years later. Passenger services ceased in 1951, and most of the branch was closed the following year.

❺ GARTH & VAN

A notably obscure branch was built by the Van Railway from Caersws, on the Cambrian Railways' main line, to lead mines 6 miles to the west. It opened in 1871 and carried passengers from 1873 to 1879. Closed in 1895, it later reopened to supply ballast.

❻ KERRY

A short branch from Abermule, on the Cambrian Railways' main line, to Kerry was opened in 1863. As so often, a lack of money meant that the line stopped well short of its intended destination. Passenger traffic ended in 1931 and freight in 1956.

❽ CRIGGION

The 1860s saw the opening of the Criggion branch by the Potteries, Shrewsbury & North Wales Railway. Stone was the reason, though passengers were carried, particularly after the line and the branch were taken over by Colonel Stephens. All traffic ceased in 1933.

OPEN & PRESERVED LINES

❸ VALE OF RHEIDOL

Opened in 1902, at first for mineral traffic but really as a narrow-gauge tourist line, the Vale of Rheidol Light Railway has been an important part of the Great Little Trains of Wales ever since. The route, from Aberystwyth to Devil's Bridge, is perennially popular. During its long life it has been operated by Cambrian Railways, the GWR and British Railways, and now runs independently.

⓭ TALYLLYN

Opened in 1866, the narrow-gauge Talyllyn Railway was built to connect slate quarries around Bryn Eglwys to the harbour at Tywyn. Passenger carrying started at the same time, and later the railway became an important tourist line. Privately owned up to 1950, the Talyllyn became Britain's first heritage railway in 1951.

❼ WELSHPOOL & LLANFAIR

After a false start, the Welshpool & Llanfair Light Railway opened its narrow-gauge line linking the two towns in 1903. Worked initially by the Cambrian Railways, it later became part of the GWR. Closed to passengers in 1931 and to freight in 1956, the line has since been reopened as a heritage railway.

△ The grassy mound across this field is the trackbed of the Llanfyllin branch (*see also* page 80).

Railcars & multiple units

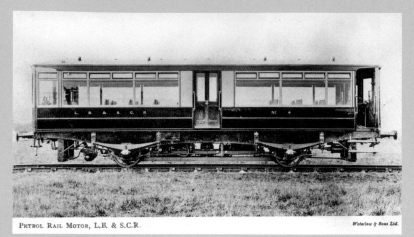

Petrol Rail Motor, L.B. & S.C.R.   Waterlow & Sons Ltd.

↑ In about 1905 the London, Brighton & South Coast Railway introduced for a short time some Dick, Kerr & Co petrol railcars for branchline use.

↑ The rubber-tyred Michelin railcar was tried out by the GWR on a number of routes in the 1930s, but the experiment was not a success.

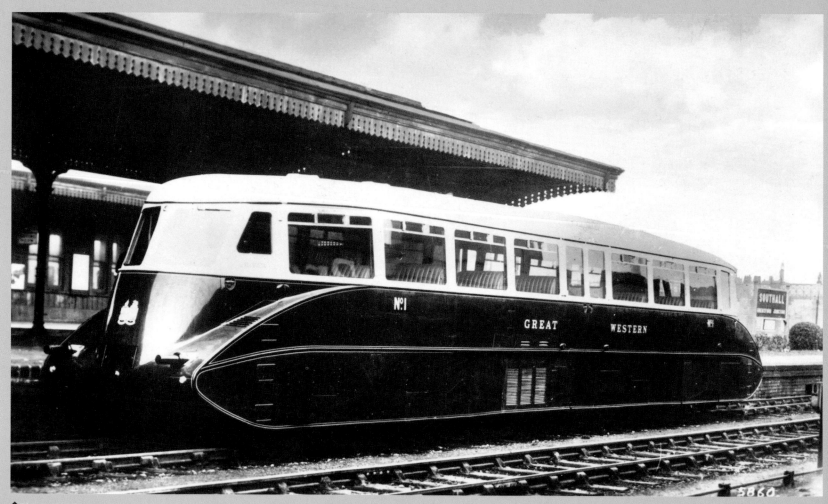

↑ This is the first GWR diesel railcar, introduced from 1934. The fashionably streamlined bodywork led it to be nicknamed the 'flying banana'.

↑ The production models of the GWR railcar had a more angular body. Some examples from the 38 built survived in service until the early 1960s.

↑ British Railways began to introduce various single and multiple diesel units and sets in the late 1950s. This is a typical example of an early single-car unit.

↑ Here, in 1965, a two-car DMU set, one of over 30 DMU classes, is in use on the Sidmouth branch, in Devon, shortly before the line's closure.

↑ Single-car units, of the kind seen here in 1984, were built for country and branchline use. Some were built specifically for the transportation of parcels.

↑ A two-car DMU set, preparing to work the Windermere branch, is setting back from Oxenhope, in Cumberland, in June 1976.

↑ From the 1960s to the end of British Rail in the 1990s, DMUs were a common sight everywhere. This is Washwood Heath, Birmingham, in May 1981.

MAP 7

ANGLESEY, CARNARVONSHIRE, FLINTSHIRE & DENBIGHSHIRE

BRANCH LINES

❶ **Amlwch & Red Wharf Bay**
Anglesey (pages 88–9)

❷ **Llanbedrog**
Carnarvonshire (page 93)

❸ **Blaenau Ffestiniog**
Carnarvonshire (page 94)
See also **Map 6** (pages 76–7)

❹ **Nantlle**
Carnarvonshire (page 93)

❺ **Bryngwyn**
Carnarvonshire (page 93)

❻ **Snowdon Mountain**
Carnarvonshire (page 94)

❼ **Llanberis**
Carnarvonshire (page 92)

❽ **Bethesda**
Carnarvonshire (page 90)

❾ **Llandudno**
Carnarvonshire (page 94)

❿ **Dyserth**
Flintshire (page 91)

⓫ **Holywell Town**
Flintshire (page 92)

⓬ **Minera**
Denbighshire (page 93)

⓭ **Glyn Valley**
Denbighshire (page 93)

Holyhea

Passenger facilities at the Dyserth terminus were somewhat limited.

Closed branch lines

Closed passenger lines

Open passenger lines

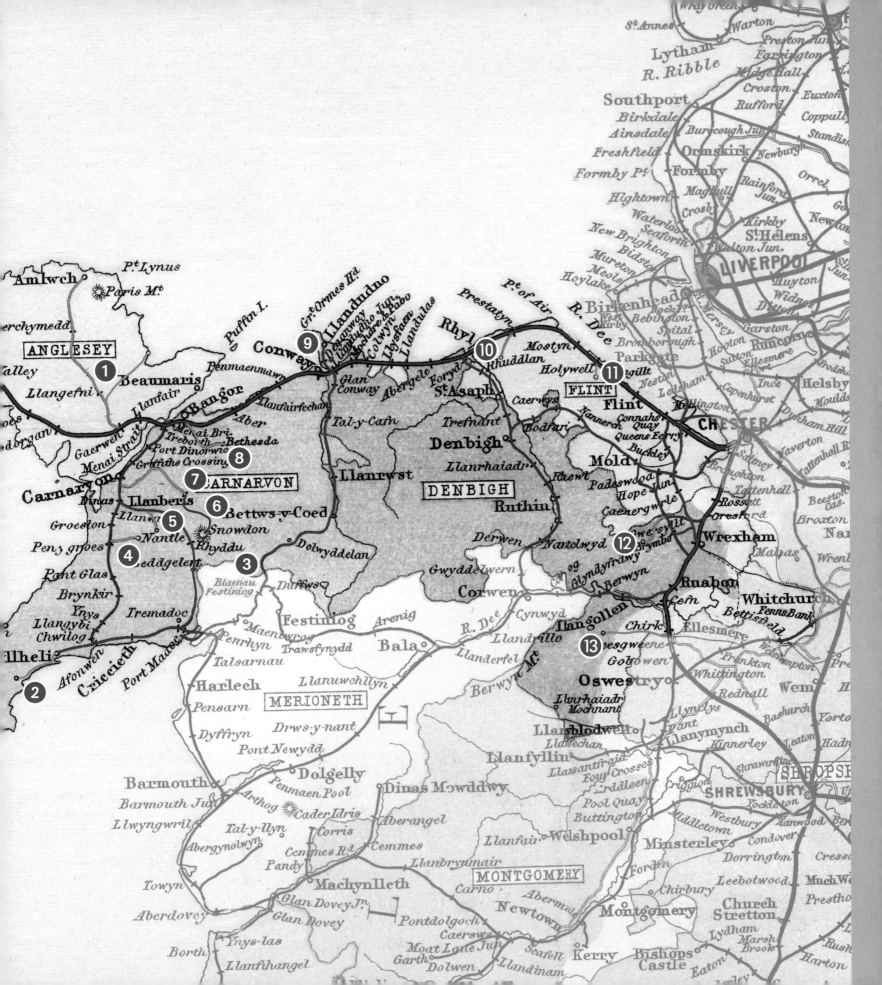

MAP 7

❶ AMLWCH & RED WHARF BAY

By 1850 the Chester & Holyhead's pioneering main line was open and the Irish Mail had taken its place in the railway timetable. This route soon became the backbone from which other lines grew. One of these was the Anglesey Central Railway, whose line from Gaerwen to Amlwch was opened in 1867. Nine years later the line was taken over by the LNWR, which was instrumental in opening a second branch in 1909. Built to light railway standards, this ran from a junction at Holland Arms to Red Wharf Bay. Amlwch had developed into a popular resort, known for its beaches and the sea baths at Bull Bay, and it was hoped that Red Wharf Bay would follow suit. Sadly, it did not, so the LMS, which had taken over in 1923, withdrew passenger services in 1930. Freight, which included the carriage of herrings, continued to 1950. Amlwch was a different story, with full passenger services continuing until 1964. Thanks to a chemical factory near Amlwch, freight continued on the branch through to 1993. When this ended, the branch was closed, but track, signals and infrastructure were left in place. As a result, the route, easy to follow and explore, has a kind of 'sleeping beauty' atmosphere, with the railway there but extensively overgrown. The reawakening of all or part of the branch as a heritage railway and/ or cycle path looks likely. The line to Red Wharf Bay is another matter, with much of the route lost in the landscape.

△Amlwch's harbour, presented in a decorative manner on this Edwardian card, was one of the reasons for the branch being built. This was sent as a Christmas card to someone in Banff.

△Until 1993 British Rail continued to operate regular freight services to the Octel chemical factory at the end of the line in Amlwch. This 1980s photograph captures a scene familiar to anyone living near the railway. With the track left in place after closure, the reopening of the branch either to Llangefni or all the way to Amlwch is a possibility.

▷Amlwch station, which does not survive, was always well cared for and decorative, with plenty of platform planting. This 1963 photograph shows a Bangor train ready to depart, headed by a British Railways Standard Class 2MT, No. 84001, looking a bit tatty although only ten years old.

◁The former station at Red Wharf Bay, a basic timber structure painted in LMS colours, remained standing long after the branch had closed in 1950. This photograph is taken from the buffers, and the goods yard was on the left.

△Much of the Red Wharf Bay branch has disappeared, but sections can be traced on embankments and, as seen here, in a clearing through the woods.

△Nature may have taken over, but the Amlwch branch is all there still. Here, on the approach to the former mainline junction at Gaerwen, the signal seems ready to give the road to a train approaching from the Amlwch direction.

MAP 7

8 BETHESDA

The rivalry in North Wales between the LNWR and the GWR was intensified by competition over the slate industry, and this resulted in the construction of a number of branch lines and industrial railways. Typical was the Bethesda branch line, sponsored by the LNWR and opened in 1884. The route, from Port Penrhyn Junction on the main line from Bangor, included intermediate stations at Felin Hen and Tregarth, some rock cuttings, a tunnel and a quantity of bridges. With hindsight, it is easy to see that branches like this, born out of competition and expensive to build, could never have paid their way. Once open, the story of the Bethesda branch followed a predictable pattern: railmotors were introduced in 1905 to save money, then the LNWR was replaced by the LMS, and in due course by British Railways, whose attitude to costing and rationalization was much more ruthless. As a result, the branch was closed to passenger traffic in 1951 and to freight in 1963. One of the last trains on the branch was, inevitably, an enthusiasts' special. Today, sections of the line can be followed. Around Tregarth, a cycle track uses some of the trackbed. Bridges can be seen, along with stretches of embankment, but survival is, as so often, random.

△Posted in September 1910 from Bethesda to Welshpool, this card captures the flavour of the North Wales town: well-kept terraces, prominent chapels, tidy gardens and a dramatic landscape setting.

▽There is not much to see in Bethesda but on the outskirts of the town the railway comes to life in the form of a well-defined stretch of embankment, overlooked by powerful hills that hint at the expensive engineering required.

△Stretches of trackbed exist in the landscape, but finding them can be hindered by recent changes and modern development. As a rule, trackbed will be removed if it is worth the effort or in the way. This iron accommodation bridge, with its decorative lattice railings, still stands near Felin Hen, partly hidden by a new road.

△Bethesda had a surprisingly grand station, with a long platform, seen here in a ruinous state after the branch had been closed in 1963. Nothing remains of this today.

⑩ DYSERTH

The history of the short Dyserth branch goes back to the early 1860s, when local quarry owners began to campaign for the building of a railway. Initial plans were quite complicated and included a loop connecting several quarries. These were simplified by the LNWR, which opened the branch from Prestatyn to Dyserth in 1869. It then remained a mineral line until passenger services, along with a number of intermediate stations, were introduced by the LNWR in September 1905. This was the result of a long campaign, driven both by local residents and by the increase of tourism in North Wales – attractions near Dyserth included a waterfall and the viewpoint and hillfort on the dominant Moel Hiraddug. As a company, the LNWR was particularly responsive to the appeal of tourism and, famously, published hundreds of postcards publicizing the scenic qualities of its routes. From the start, the LNWR operated services on the branch with a new kind of steam railmotor, and a set of postcards was issued to promote this. Similar railmotors were introduced to other branch lines around this time. When the LMS took over, it was more cautious, and passenger services were ended in 1930. The branch then reverted to its original mineral status and continued to serve the quarry until 1973. The route is now a footpath and cycleway, part of the North Wales Path.

△This postcard, showing the new Meliden station and one of the railmotors, is from the set introduced by the LNWR in 1905 to promote passenger services on the branch. The station building survives.

▷After the end of passenger services in 1930, the branch continued to serve quarries and other local interests such as the Vale of Clwyd Farmers Ltd. The passenger station, little more than a wooden hut, thought to be one of the smallest in Britain, was beyond the warehouse.

▽Today, the branch is an enjoyable path and cycleway, with a secluded and protected route through the landscape. A number of bridges survive, including a short viaduct.

△As the branch switched quite quickly from an operating railway to an official footpath, a number of items from its days as a freight line were left in place, including a loading gauge at Meliden and this goods yard crane, which is now incorporated into a bench.

MAP 7

❼ LLANBERIS

▷The habit of posting cards at the summit of Snowdon began in the early 1900s. This 1950s example bears the Snowdon Summit mark.

Though nominally independent, the Carnarvon & Llanberis Railway was set up with the backing of the LNWR in the 1860s, with the aim of building a 9-mile branch to connect villages at the foot of Snowdon to the main line. Following a period of complex ownership discussions, the line was completed in 1869 and taken over by the LNWR the next year. Initially, traffic was light, but the opening in 1897 of the Snowdon Mountain Railway, with which it connected, greatly increased its usage by tourists prior to World War I. Decline in the 1920s brought an end to regular passenger services in 1930, but summer excursions continued to 1962 and freight until 1964. Llanberis station is now a craft centre, and bits of trackbed survive, notably beside the river Seiont.

▷In the summer of 1926 the Llanberis branch was still quite busy with tourist traffic. The train in the foreground is the regular Caernarfon service, while the older LNWR carriages behind are probably an excursion.

⓫ HOLYWELL TOWN

▽The train crew and the platform staff wait at Holywell Town's minimal station, all eyes on the photographer. Closure, in 1954, is approaching, and the single carriage, fitted for push-pull operation, is ample for the branch by that time. The locomotive is a former LMS Class 2MT, No. 41276, built in 1950.

An early Christian martyr, St Winefride, was the origin of Holywell, long a place of pilgrimage. This might have inspired the independent Holywell Railway to build its short branch from the main line to the town and its holy well, in 1867. However, it was not a success and closed a few years later. The branch lay unused and derelict until about 1911, when it was bought by the LNWR, rebuilt and reopened. The steeply graded, single-track line continued to operate until 1954, when passenger carrying ceased. Freight, mostly to a local textile mill, continued until August 1957. Today, the trackbed is a footpath and the site of Holywell Town station is a tidy park. The grand Italianate mainline station at Holywell Junction, opened in 1848, survives.

▷Percy sent this card to Win in 1922. He writes: 'Lovely day, rather windy', but the angle of the stamp is code for something else, namely 'my heart is yours'.

⑫ MINERA

The Minera branch was part of a dense network to the west of Wrexham. It was built by the Wrexham & Minera Railway with the backing of the LNWR and the GWR, to serve the lead mines, quarries and limeworks around Minera. An earlier mineral railway, dating from the 1840s, was absorbed into the route. Also significant was the Brymbo steelworks. In May 1882, in response to local pressure, the GWR started a passenger service. There were several stations and halts, with the terminus at Berwig Halt, a remote spot east of the Minera limeworks. This service was finally withdrawn by British Railways in 1950. The Minera limeworks kept the line between Brymbo and Minera open for freight until the early 1970s, while the section from Wrexham to the steelworks stayed open until the 1980s. Over the 100-year life of the quarry and limeworks, 8 million tons of limestone were moved by train. Limekilns can still be seen at Minera.

▽This photograph, taken in May 1969, shows an enthusiasts' special waiting at Minera, alongside a rake of loaded limestone wagons, while members of the group explore the site. A number of similar railtours visited the branch, starting in the early 1950s, soon after the end of regular passenger carrying.

② LLANBEDROG

A 2-mile horse tramway was opened in 1894 westwards along the shore from Pwllheli, primarily to transport stone from a quarry but also to carry passengers. Completely rebuilt after storm damage in 1896, it was extended to Llanbedrog, where the tramway's owner, Solomon Andrews, had purchased a mansion, which he opened as an art gallery. Services were reduced before World War I but recovered in the 1920s. In October 1927 a storm washed away long stretches of the tramway and it was never rebuilt.

⑤ BRYNGWYN

In 1877 a 2-mile branch to Bryngwyn was built from Tryfan Junction on the North Wales Narrow Gauge Railways, which later became part of the Welsh Highland Railway. Mainly a slate line, the Bryngwyn branch was connected to quarries above Bryngwyn by a double-track inclined plane. Passengers were carried as far as Bryngwyn station from about 1877 to 1916, but the slate traffic continued until complete closure in 1936. The trackbed has been turned into a footpath.

④ NANTLLE

Opened in 1828 to connect slate quarries in the Nantlle valley to Penygroes and Caernarfon, the Nantlle Railway was a narrow-gauge line engineered by Robert Stephenson. From 1867 much of it was converted to standard gauge, but the quarry sections remained narrow gauge and horse drawn until 1963. The retirement of the Nantlle horses in that year represented the end of British Rail's use of horse-drawn vehicles. Passengers were carried at various times between Penygroes and Caernarfon until 1932.

⑬ GLYN VALLEY

The Glyn Valley Tramway opened its narrow-gauge line between Chirk and Glyn Ceiriog in 1873. Initially horse drawn, the tramway switched to steam in 1888. Connections were built in 1878 to local quarries. The passenger service that had operated during the horse-drawn period was put on a more regular basis in 1891. This continued until increasing road competition forced the tramway to give up passenger carrying in 1933 and, two years later, to close completely.

MAP 7

OPEN & PRESERVED LINES

❸ BLAENAU FFESTINIOG

The first railway to reach the slate quarries of Blaenau Ffestiniog was the Festiniog's narrow-gauge line, in 1836. Next came the Conway & Llanrwst's standard-gauge line southwards from Llandudno. Work started in 1860 but was not completed until 1881, by which time the LNWR was in control. The third line, the GWR's long meandering branch from Bala, arrived in 1883, too late for the slate industry, which was by then in decline. The result was that the small town of Blaenau Ffestiniog had three independent railways. First to cease operation was the Festiniog, but this has reopened as a famous heritage railway. The GWR's Bala line closed in 1961, but the Conwy Valley line, though often threatened with closure, is still there, sharing its station with the reinvigorated Ffestiniog. The journey from Llandudno Junction, one of Britain's best branch lines, is a memorable exploration of the landscape of North Wales as the line follows the Conwy to Betws-y-Coed and into Snowdonia. The train then climbs the steep and rocky Lledr valley before emerging from a famously long tunnel into the slate mountains that surround Blaenau.

❻ SNOWDON MOUNTAIN

Opened in 1897, the narrow-gauge Snowdon Mountain Railway is the UK's only rack and pinion-operated line. Its 5-mile route climbs from Llanberis to the summit station, near the top of Wales's highest mountain. The railway has operated successfully for well over a century, and the journey is an essential part of any Welsh experience. Some of the original locomotives are still in use.

❾ LLANDUDNO

Though Llandudno has a long history, it was the coming of the railway that turned it into a major seaside resort. The first station, opened in 1858, was the end of a branch line from Conwy, on the Chester-to-Holyhead main line. Following the completion of Llandudno Junction, a new and grander station was opened in Llandudno in 1892. Today, this station is much diminished, but it continues to be the terminus of a branch line, and a major refurbishment is due for completion in 2014.

△No trains have run on the Amlwch branch since 1993, but the track and some of the infrastructure are still in place (*see also* page 88).

Branchline tickets

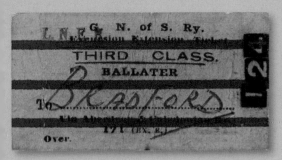

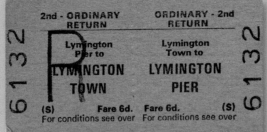

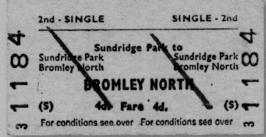

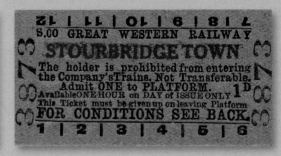

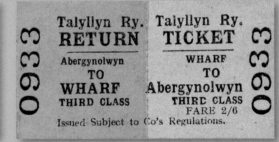

CENTRAL
&
EASTERN
ENGLAND

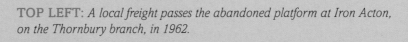

TOP LEFT: *A local freight passes the abandoned platform at Iron Acton, on the Thornbury branch, in 1962.*

BOTTOM LEFT: *In 1954 an RCTS special, headed by Class J6 No. 64199, waits in the platform at Spilsby.*

TOP RIGHT: *In 1956 passengers from the Suffolk Venturer, an enthusiasts' special, crowd the platform at Hadleigh.*

BOTTOM RIGHT: *An early DMU drifts past the signal box and into the terminus at Aldeburgh in 1961.*

MAP 8

MONMOUTHSHIRE, HEREFORDSHIRE, GLOUCESTERSHIRE, WARWICKSHIRE & WORCESTERSHIRE

BRANCH LINES

❶ **Thornbury**
Gloucestershire (page 103)

❷ **Dursley**
Gloucestershire (page 103)

❸ **Nailsworth**
Gloucestershire (page 100)

❹ **Tetbury**
Gloucestershire (page 101)

❺ **Fairford**
Gloucestershire (page 102)
See also **Map 9** (pages 106–7)

❻ **Shipston-on-Stour**
Warwickshire (page 103)

❼ **Harborne**
Warwickshire (page 103)

❽ **Stourbridge Town**
Worcestershire (page 103)

New Radnor & Presteigne
See **Map 6** (pages 76–7)

Longdon Road for Ilmington was a long name for this minor station on the GWR's Shipston-on-Stour branch.

Closed branch lines

Closed passenger lines

Open passenger lines

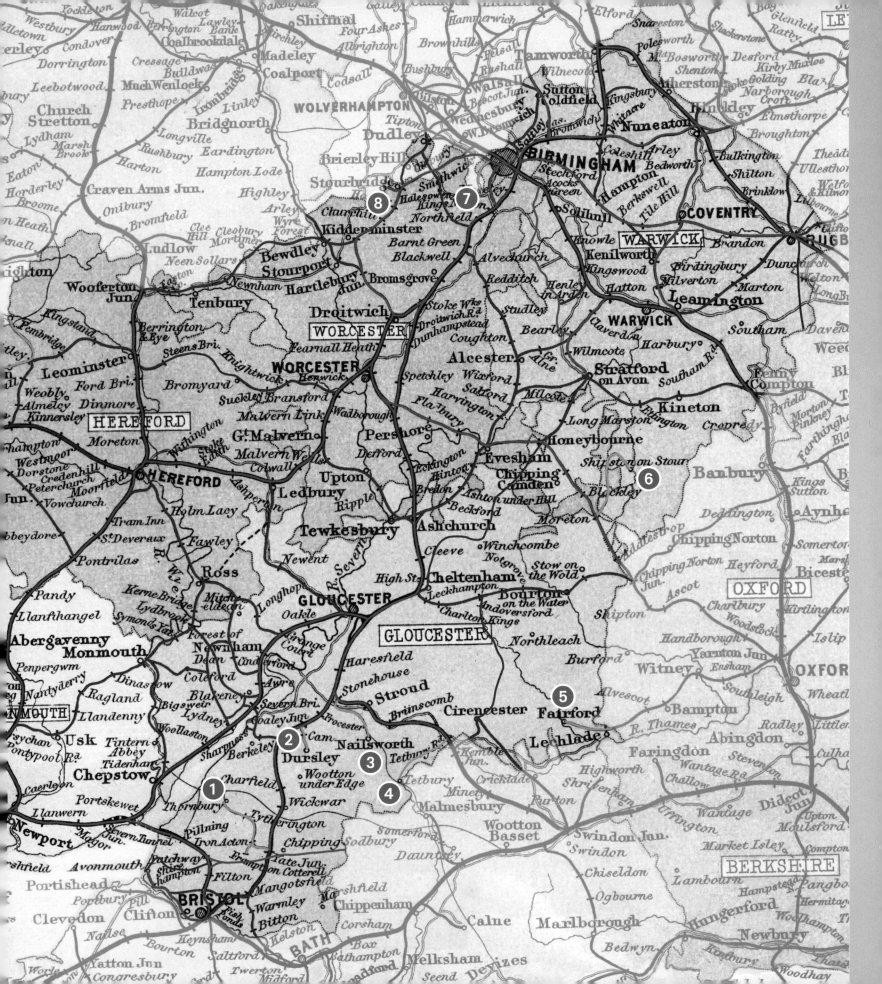

MAP 8

❸ NAILSWORTH

The Stonehouse & Nailsworth Railway, a short branch line inspired by local ambitions, was authorized in 1863 and opened four years later. Financial problems, not helped by a difficult route and extravagant stations, started immediately. However, the branch staggered on until 1878, when it was bought by the Midland Railway, which saw it as a useful first stage in its planned route southwards to Southampton. In the event, this never happened, so the branch settled down as a quiet rural line whose main function was to carry freight to and from the local textile mills. This, and other freight traffic, was to keep the branch alive until 1966, passenger services having ended in 1949. Today, the route is a footpath and cycle track, along a valley protected by trees from roads and encroaching development. Impressive stations and other buildings also survive, now mostly private houses.

△ Posted in 1908, this card of Watledge, near Nailsworth, was sent to Dora in Birmingham by her French friend Henri. It shows the steep-sided valley in which Nailsworth lies.

▽ Designed by Sir George Barclay Bruce, Nailsworth station is a High Victorian Gothic extravaganza in Cotswold stone and brick, with a splendid porte cochère.

▷ Today, Nailsworth station is a private house, complete with platform, and can be seen from the trackbed footpath. The remains of a hotel and an impressive goods yard are also visible.

④ TETBURY

Kemble, now a handsome 1872 station on the main Swindon-to-Gloucester Golden Valley Line, used to be the junction for two GWR branch lines, one eastwards to Cirencester Town and the other westwards to Tetbury. The latter, opened in 1889, left Kemble from a bay platform beneath the massive water tower that still dominates the station. Initially there was only one intermediate station, Culkerton, but four opened later, mostly halts serving small communities and destined never to generate enough traffic for the branch. One of the larger places, Rodmarton, was quite a way from its station, while Jackament's Bridge was open only during World War II, to serve a local airfield. Nevertheless, the line somehow survived the GWR era into the time of British Railways, which tried hard to keep the branch going. Maintenance was kept to a minimum, and railbuses were introduced, designed in the late 1950s specifically for use on rural branches. However, it all came to an end when the branch closed in April 1964. Today, much of the route of this rural branch can be explored, and most of the trackbed survives, often hidden by trees and sometimes offering unofficial walks enjoyed by locals. There are no stations and little infrastructure to be found, but at Tetbury the goods shed still stands, a mass of dark brick beside the car park that has taken over the station site, set in the valley below the town.

△ This Edwardian card shows Westonbirt House, now a school. It was designed by Lewis Vulliamy in the 1860s for Robert Holford, founder of the famous arboretum. Tetbury was the closest station.

△ Contrasting methods of transport sit at Tetbury station in about 1960. The four-wheel railbus is one of a group of 22 introduced by British Railways in 1958. They were built by various manufacturers in Britain and Germany, and all were withdrawn as the branches they worked on were closed. The station looks a bit untidy, but the Rolls Royce raises the tone.

◁ Much of the route of the Tetbury branch is visible as a line of trees curving across the undulating countryside, interspersed by low embankments and cuttings. Even without bridges and stations, the branch has left a permanent mark on the landscape.

MAP 8

❺ FAIRFORD

The long branch to Fairford was built in two stages. First came the Witney Railway's line from Yarnton on the main line north of Oxford, opened in 1861. Next came the East Gloucestershire Railway, which planned to build a through route on from Witney to Cheltenham, with the support of the GWR. The GWR lost interest and, when the line was opened as far as Fairford in 1873, the East Gloucestershire gave up, though a short stretch was partially built beyond Fairford. The GWR took it all over in 1890. The 23-mile rural route across Oxfordshire and into Gloucestershire connected some reasonable sized towns, including Eynsham, Witney and Lechlade, but traffic was always light. Local industry was, as usual, the mainstay of the branch. Passenger traffic eventually ended in 1962 and British Railways closed completely the section east of Witney. Freight then continued to serve Witney until 1970. Since closure, much has been lost, particularly near Witney. The trackbed can be seen heading west in the direction of Fairford, but it is often inaccessible. There are other reminders, such as bridges, to be spotted.

△This 1930s postcard celebrates the glorious set of 28 medieval stained-glass windows in Fairford church. Never posted, the card must have been bought as a souvenir by a visitor.

▷In May 1959 the drivers of two former GWR tank locomotives prepare to pass at Brize Norton & Bampton station and exchange greetings. The station was right by the airfield, hence the security fencing.

▽This 1932 photograph of Fairford station has plenty of interesting detail, including the typical GWR pagoda-style cycle store and the signal box's unusual roof. The goods shed is busy, keeping the branch alive. The line was originally planned to continue to Cheltenham, so Fairford was built as a through station, not as a terminus.

▷The site of Kelmscott station has been cleared, but the concrete platform lamp post still stands among flowers that were once part of the station garden. It is fascinating to think of William Morris getting off the train here and walking down the lane to Kelmscott Manor, perhaps to join his wife, Jane, and Dante Gabriel Rossetti for dinner.

❶ THORNBURY

The Midland Railway opened its 7-mile branch from Yate to Thornbury in 1872. There were two intermediate stations, Iron Acton and Tytherington. The inspiration came from stone quarries and coal mines, but most of these were soon out of use, making the branch dependent upon local traffic. Apparently, the greatest day in the line's history was in 1885, when thousands travelled to Thornbury in the hope of seeing a stranded whale at Littleton Wharf. The LMS took over in 1923, and ended passenger services in 1944. Freight continued, helped by the building of the Severn bridge and Oldbury power station in the 1960s. The line was then closed, but reopened to serve Tytherington quarry, and is still in occasional use. Some things remain along the route, including tunnels, the platform at Iron Acton station, and the stationmaster's house at Tytherington. A supermarket stands on the site of Thornbury station.

▽It is March 1962 and a local mixed goods drifts through Tytherington station, headed by an old 1920s Midland Railway 0-6-0 locomotive, No. 44553. Although it closed to passengers in 1944, the wooden station looks intact, lacking only its nameboards.

❷ DURSLEY

The Dursley & Midland Junction Railway opened its short branch from Coaley Junction on the Midland's Bristol-to-Gloucester line in 1856. The Midland operated it, and took control from 1861. The original builders were responsible for all the stations, at Dursley, Cam and Coaley. Passenger trains on the branch were familiarly known as the Dursley Donkey, and services continued until 1962. The ever-expanding Lister factory supplied much of the freight traffic until closure in 1970. A couple of bridges are the only relics.

❼ HARBORNE

The short branch opened in 1874 by the Harborne Railway was part of a larger scheme to build a connecting line to link the GWR and the LNWR. This was abandoned and the truncated branch became a successful Birmingham commuter route with up to 27 services each way on weekdays. Independent until the LMS took over, the branch was closed in 1934 owing to road competition. Freight traffic, notably for the brewery, lived on until 1964.

❻ SHIPSTON-ON-STOUR

This 6-mile branch from Moreton-in-Marsh began life in 1836 as part of the horse-drawn Stratford & Moreton Tramway. It was converted into a conventional railway in 1859, but for legal reasons had to remain horse powered. The GWR bought the line in the 1860s, and the prohibition against the use of steam was removed in 1889. The branch then ran normally until passenger services ended in 1929 and freight in 1960.

OPEN & PRESERVED LINES

❽ STOURBRIDGE TOWN

What may be Europe's shortest passenger branch line (0.8 miles) opened in 1879, primarily as a freight link to Stourbridge basin. The route still operates, using Parry People Movers, as a traditional branch line from Stourbridge Junction to Stourbridge Town.

Modern branches — as they were

↑ In the 1950s the Liskeard-to-Looe branch, in Cornwall, was steam hauled. Here, a train pauses at Causeland to pick up a couple of passengers.

↑ In 1960 a Falmouth branch train headed by a GWR pannier tank arrives in Truro station, Cornwall, while a freight waits at the signal on the main line.

↑ In the early 1960s Gunnislake, in Cornwall, was an intermediate station on the Calstock branch. Now it is the line's much more basic terminus.

↑In 1963 the Lymington branch from Brockenhurst, Hampshire, was steam operated. Here, a typical train leaves Lymington Town for Lymington Pier.

↑In the late 1950s the Art Deco stations on the Chessington branch, in Surrey, were not looking their best and were still carrying SR target nameplates.

↑Today, Watchet is served by the heritage West Somerset Railway's steam trains. This is 1962, when it was on the British Railways network.

↑Seaford station, Sussex, seen here in the 1970s, is a classic branchline terminus. The buildings date from the 1860s, when the line opened.

MAP 9

OXFORDSHIRE, BUCKINGHAMSHIRE, BEDFORDSHIRE, NORTHAMPTONSHIRE & HUNTINGDONSHIRE

BRANCH LINES

❶ **Blenheim & Woodstock**
Oxfordshire (page 108)

❷ **Watlington**
Oxfordshire (page 109)

❸ **Henley-on-Thames**
Oxfordshire (page 113)

❹ **Marlow**
Buckinghamshire (page 113)

❺ **Windsor & Eton**
Berkshire (page 113)
See also **Map 3** (page 40)

❻ **Brill**
Buckinghamshire (page 110)

❼ **Newport Pagnell**
Buckinghamshire (page 111)

❽ **Higham Ferrers**
Northamptonshire (page 111)

❾ **Ramsey North**
Huntingdonshire (page 112)

❿ **Ramsey East**
Huntingdonshire (page 112)

Fairford
See **Map 8** (pages 98–9)

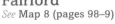
Closed branch lines

Closed passenger lines

Open passenger lines

Aston Rowant station, on the Watlington branch, and its ground frame are looking run-down following closure in 1961.

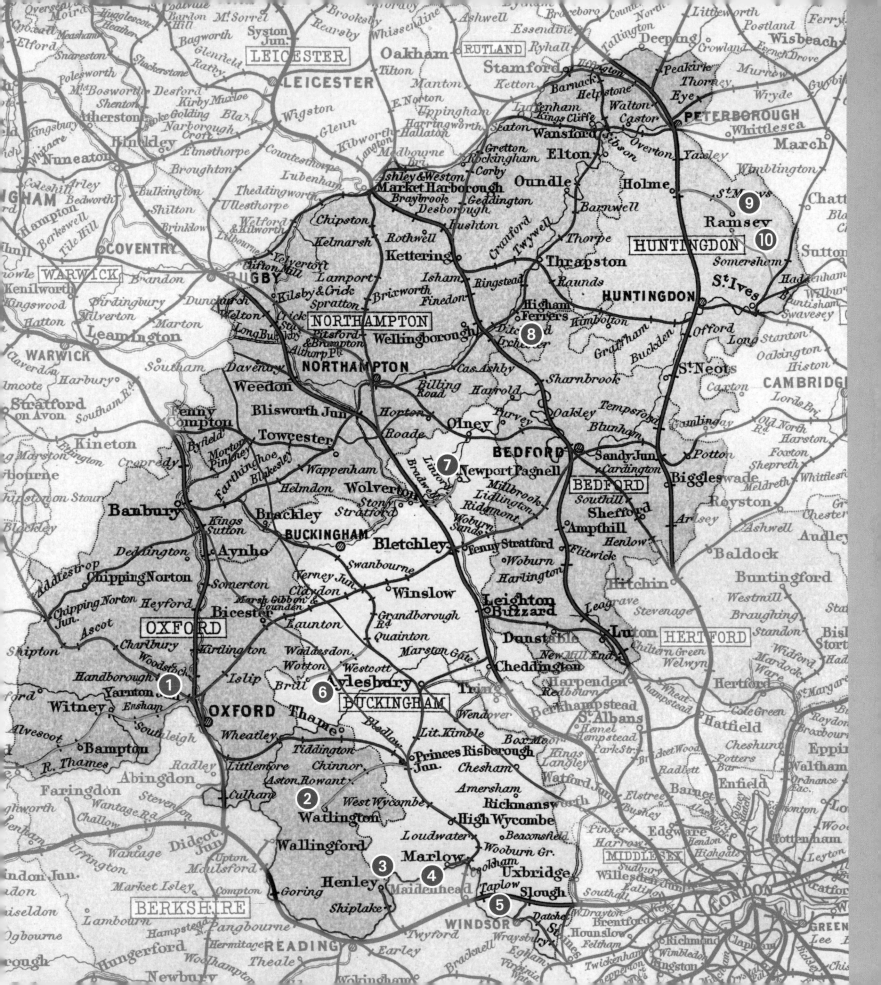

MAP 9

❶ BLENHEIM & WOODSTOCK

The original sponsor of the Woodstock branch was the Duke of Marlborough, keen to have a railway link to his house, Blenheim Palace. The 4-mile branch opened in May 1890, initially to a junction north of Kidlington on the main line. The GWR extended the line to the south, to make the junction at Kidlington station, and took control in 1897. One intermediate halt, Shipton-on-Cherwell, was opened in 1929 for the cement works, and the branch enjoyed an uneventful life until it was closed by British Railways in 1954. The line was cheaply built across the fields, and the only significant piece of engineering was an embankment leading to a bridge across the Banbury road. This, and the bridge's abutments, have survived. Elsewhere short stretches of the route are now a footpath and nature reserve, but the rest has mostly been removed or infilled, or is otherwise inaccessible.

▽This card was sent in 1907 by a visitor to Blenheim Palace. Having arrived by train, he would have walked up through the town and entered by this gate.

△Blenheim & Woodstock station was a simple stone building rather inconveniently sited well to the east of the town centre and a long walk from Blenheim Palace. Judging by the vehicles parked in front of the station building, this photograph was taken on a sunny day in the early 1950s.

▷The station building still stands, surrounded by modern housing development. It has gone through various changes of usage and for a long time was a garage and petrol station, as seen here, probably in the late 1960s.

△The embankment that carried the line to the Banbury road bridge is an eerily silent, secret world. A section of trackbed lies hidden among trees and bushes.

❷ WATLINGTON

Railway routes had been planned but came to nothing, and it was not until 1872 that a 9-mile branch line finally opened, built by the Watlington & Princes Risborough Railway. Like so many local lines, the railway faced immediate financial problems and the branch was sold to the GWR in 1883. With several intermediate stations, the branch was able to operate adequately as a local railway, at least until World War II. For example, in 1925 trains on the branch carried over 29,000 milk churns – an indication of the importance of this traffic to countless rural branch lines. The 1920s also saw the opening of the cement works at Chinnor, which greatly increased the line's freight traffic. The branch lived on into the British Railways era, but declining traffic brought about the end of passenger carrying in 1957. The section from Chinnor to Watlington was closed completely, but the lower section, from Chinnor to Princes Risborough, was kept open by the cement works until 1989. At that point a preservation society stepped in, and this section is now open as a heritage line, the Chinnor & Princes Risborough Railway. Today, the upper section is largely lost and inaccessible, though stretches can be identified and a few buildings and structures survive. All traces of Watlington station have gone, other than some overgrown remains of the wooden goods shed.

△This Edwardian comic postcard was issued all over Britain and could be overprinted with the name of the local railway or station. This example was never posted.

△Taken with some difficulty from the window of the carriage, this 1957 photograph shows the former GWR autotrain preparing to stop at Bledlow Bridge Halt, shortly before the end of passenger services. A note on the back, written later, says that the platform is still there, minus the hut. Today, although the halt is on the heritage route, it is not in use as the platform is too low.

△In July 1956 the train has arrived at Watlington. Today, nothing remains of the station, which was inconveniently sited away from the town. The goods shed on the right of this photograph survives as a ruin hidden in trees.

▷The site of Watlington station is a cleared area, with the trackbed disappearing into the distance. The station buildings (seen above, on the left) lived on in a dilapidated state for many years.

MAP 9

❻ BRILL

The 6-mile branch line to Brill enjoyed a complicated and eccentric history. Built by the Duke of Buckingham in 1871 for his own use, the horse-drawn line first carried passengers in 1872. Plans in the 1880s to extend the line to Oxford caused it to be renamed the Oxford & Aylesbury Tramroad. Nothing happened, and in due course it was bought by the Metropolitan Railway and rebuilt to a more modern standard in 1910. Traffic was still limited, with local freight keeping the branch alive. In 1933 the Metropolitan Railway became part of London Transport, so the Brill branch became an extremely remote and rather inconvenient corner of this urban underground network. With no real development potential, the branch was closed in 1935 and all the infrastructure removed and sold. Today, very little remains to be seen, other than the former junction at Quainton Road.

▽A month before the line's closure in July 1935, a typical Brill train, headed by a Metropolitan Railway A Class locomotive, makes its slow way along the branch.

△This postcard of Quainton was sent on 6 May 1907, in the evening, from Woolwich to Plumstead, but the message has nothing to do with Quainton, or Brill. It confirmed the time of a lesson due to take place the following day.

△Another A Class tank locomotive waits in vain for passengers at Brill, shortly before the closure of the branch. The line's chequered history meant that the infrastructure was basic, albeit considerably improved after the reconstruction of 1910. The LNER has made its presence felt on the noticeboard at this remote spot, and the stationmaster keeps his eye on things.

◁A modern Chiltern train on the High Wycombe-to-Bicester line races past the abutments of the bridge that carried the Brill tramway near Wood Siding. This is one of the most visible relics of the branch, apart from the junction platform at Quainton Road, now home to the Buckinghamshire Railway Centre.

❼ NEWPORT PAGNELL

After several failed attempts to bring the railway to Newport Pagnell, the 4-mile branch linking the town to the LNWR main line at Wolverton was opened by the Newport Pagnell Railway in 1867. An extension was planned to Olney, and then on to Wellingborough, but this was abandoned after some preliminary construction work. The LNWR took control in 1875, and briefly considered the electrification of the branch at a later date. Competitive bus routes opened early, but the branch was well supported – except by local housewives in the Bradwell area, who found that the railway took their water supply on washing day. After the usual decline in the 1950s, closure to passengers came in 1964 and freight two years later. Today, platforms exist at Bradwell and Great Linford, and some of the route is a cycleway, part of the Milton Keynes network.

△The grand church of St Peter & St Paul, seen in this Edwardian card, dates back to the 14th century and is the town's most imposing building.

▽The last train on the branch was the 5.34pm from Newport Pagnell on 5 September 1964. Seen here pausing at Bradwell, the train was packed with locals and enthusiasts who had fought in vain to keep the line open.

❽ HIGHAM FERRERS

In 1894 a 5-mile branch was opened to link Rushden and Higham Ferrers to the Midland Railway's main line at Wellingborough. In common with other short branch lines, there was an abortive plan to extend the line, in this case to meet the Kettering-to-Huntingdon line at Raunds. Apart from catering for local passenger traffic, the branch was used extensively by the shoe industry and for the carriage of minerals. This helped to keep it open until 1969, ten years after the ending of passenger services. Until 1964, August Bank Holiday specials continued to use the branch, maintaining local connections to Blackpool and other Lancashire coast resorts. Today, much of the trackbed can still be explored, and Rushden station, after a period of abandonment, has been completely restored as a transport museum. Some track has been relaid and there are plans to reopen the whole branch.

△This is Rushden station, probably in the 1980s, soon after its rescue from dereliction. It is now home to the Rushden Transport Museum, housing collections of rail and road vehicles.

◁In May 1959, shortly before the end of passenger services, a British Railways Standard Class 2MT, No. 84006, rests at the head of its short train in the sunny but deserted platform at Higham Ferrers. The station has since been demolished, and nothing remains on the site.

MAP 9

⑨ RAMSEY NORTH

A small market town, formerly in Huntingdonshire and now in Cambridgeshire, Ramsey grew up in the shadow of its Benedictine abbey. Little of the abbey survives, but the grand church underlines the town's monastic history. The town was unusual in having two railway stations. The first was built by the independent Ramsey Railway, a 5-mile branch from Holme on the GNR's Huntingdon-to-Peterborough line. It opened in 1863 and in 1875 was bought by the GER, which planned to extend it to Somersham on the St Ives-to-March line. This plan was abandoned, and the branch reverted to the GNR. Later, another branch was opened to Ramsey from Somersham, but the two lines were never connected. When the LNER took over in 1923, it found itself with two stations in Ramsey, neither very convenient for the town, so it renamed them North and East. Passenger services to Ramsey North ended in 1947, just before the British Railways era, but freight lasted until 1973. The station has not survived.

▽Ramsey North enjoyed quite a long life as a freight depot after the ending of passenger services, and this photograph dates from that period. Only the lamp hints at the station's former life, and the needs of passengers. Since the mid-1970s, all the station buildings have gradually disappeared.

⑩ RAMSEY EAST

△ Ramsey East was always the smaller of Ramsey's two stations, with fewer buildings. One of these was an old wagon body, just sitting on the platform. This view probably dates from the 1950s, long after the ending of passenger traffic. The station survived in a derelict state until the late 1960s, but nothing now remains.

Although the plan to build a railway to connect Holme and Somersham via Ramsey never came to anything, a separate branch line was opened to Ramsey from Somersham in 1885. This was operated jointly by the GNR and the GER. The station, initially called Ramsey High Street, was renamed Ramsey East by the LNER which, finding that it did not need two separate branches to the town, closed this one to passengers in 1930. Occasional holiday excursions continued to run from Ramsey East, taking large numbers of visitors to Clacton via Cambridge and Colchester until 1957, when the upper section was closed. Freight on the lower section of the line, between Warboys and Somersham, continued until 1964. Ramsey East, like so many other disused stations, was bulldozed, and industrial units now occupy the site.

OPEN & PRESERVED LINES

❸ HENLEY-ON-THAMES

Running from Twyford on the main line, the Henley branch was built by the GWR and opened in 1857. At first there was one intermediate station, Shiplake, but later Wargrave was added. The link with the Royal Regatta has helped to maintain the line's popularity, and its operation as a traditional branch.

❹ MARLOW

The origins of the Marlow branch lie in the GWR line from Maidenhead to High Wycombe, opened in 1854. A short branch from Bourne End to Marlow was added in 1873, built by the independent Great Marlow Railway. The GWR took control in 1897. In 1970 the line to High Wycombe was closed, so a longer Marlow branch now runs from Maidenhead.

❺ WINDSOR & ETON

The GWR's short branch from Slough opened in 1849, despite objections from Eton College. The line, much of which is on a low viaduct, was built partly to satisfy the needs of the royal family, and the station, originally a timber structure facing the Castle, was rebuilt in 1897 to mark Queen Victoria's Diamond Jubilee. At first named Windsor, the station was renamed Windsor & Eton, then Windsor & Eton Central.

The GWR's great rival, the LSWR, opened its own, longer, branch from Waterloo to Windsor, also in 1849. The grand Tudor-style station, Windsor & Eton Riverside, was not completed until 1851. The location, by the Thames, was not as central as the GWR's, but the route served more places. Electrified in 1930, the branch has retained its popularity as a commuter route.

△The firm surface of the cycleway that has replaced the Newport Pagnell branch (*see also* page 111) is lightened by snow on the canal bridge.

LMS

1933   C 402.R

"A Pilgrimage to Snowdon"

WITH AN OPPORTUNITY OF

ASCENDING MOUNT SNOWDON

AT NIGHT

Saturday, September 10th

SPECIAL RESTAURANT CAR DAY EXCURSION

TO

LLANBERIS

(FOR MOUNT SNOWDON)

AS UNDER—

FROM	TIMES OF DEPARTURE	THIRD CLASS RETURN FARES
	p.m.	s. d.
LONDON (EUSTON)	4 40	18 0
NORTHAMPTON (CASTLE)	4A47	14 9
RUGBY	5 10	13 9
COVENTRY	5B23	12 6
BIRMINGHAM (NEW STREET)	5C50	12 0
WOLVERHAMPTON	6C18	11 0
LLANBERIS Arrive	p.m. 10 29	

A—Passengers change at Rugby on outward journey only.
B—Passengers change at Rugby on outward journey and Birmingham (New Street) on the return.
C—Passengers change at Stafford in each direction.

RETURN ARRANGEMENTS

Passengers return on Sunday, September 11th by Special Train leaving Llanberis at 2.18 p.m., Caernarvon at 2.38 p.m., Bangor at 2.58 p.m., due Wolverhampton at 6.41 p.m., Birmingham at 7.20 p.m., Coventry at 8.38 p.m., Rugby at 7.0 p.m., Northampton (Castle) 7.32 p.m., and London (Euston) at 8.55 p.m.

A RESTAURANT CAR will be provided for the service of Supper on the outward journey, and Luncheon on the return, at a charge of 2s. 9d. each meal, including gratuities; also Light Refreshments will be supplied at popular prices.

The Snowdon Mountain Railway Refreshment Rooms at Llanberis and also at Snowdon Summit will be opened specially for passengers arriving by this Excursion. Breakfast at 3s. per head will also be obtainable at the Royal Victoria Hotel, Llanberis, on the Sunday morning, but a definite order must be given for this meal, not later than Friday, September 9th, when purchasing Rail Tickets.

BOOKINGS FROM LONDON SUBURBAN STATIONS

Tickets at the London Fares may be obtained at Suburban Stations, and holders of such tickets will be allowed to travel (by any route pure) L.M.S) by any ordinary train to Euston, or St. Pancras without extra charge for the purpose of joining the Excursion Train, provided a train service exists. A similar availability will also apply on the return journey provided a train service exists.

RESERVATION OF SEATS AND COMPARTMENTS

Seats and Compartments may be reserved on the outward journey by passengers joining the Special Train at Euston on payment in advance of a booking fee of 1s. per Seat, or 5s. per Compartment (six passengers), on application to the Enquiry Bureau, Great Hall, Euston, provided notice is given within a reasonable time before departure of the train.

Reservations can also be made at numerous Suburban Stations, Town Offices, and Auxiliary Agencies.

FOR PARTICULARS AND DIRECTIONS FOR THE ASCENT OF MOUNT SNOWDON SEE OTHER SIDE

E506/27,000   Mercury Press, Northampton.

SATURDAYS, 25th AUGUST to 22nd SEPTEMBER

for 8 or 15 Days

EXCURSIONS

TO

BARNARD CASTLE	REDCAR
BISHOP AUCKLAND	SALTBURN
DARLINGTON	SOUTH SHIELDS
DURHAM	STOCKTON
FERRYHILL	SUNDERLAND
HORNSEA	THIRSK
HULL	THORNABY
†MALTON	TYNEMOUTH
MIDDLESBROUGH	WEST HARTLEPOOL
NEWCASTLE	WHITLEY BAY
NORTHALLERTON	WITHERNSEA
†PICKERING	†YORK

† No bookings to Malton, Pickering and York on August 25th.

TICKETS WILL BE ISSUED IN ADVANCE, AND PASSENGERS ARE REQUESTED TO OBTAIN THEM BEFORE THE DATE OF THE JOURNEY.

For Departure times, Fares, &c., see pages 2, 3 and 4.

Communications respecting the running of Excursions, and the issue of Weekend or Pleasure Party Tickets, should be addressed to the District Passenger Manager, 99, Wellington Street, Leeds (Telephone No. : Leeds 29615), or to the Company's Town Offices.

LNER

No. 2382

THE ENGLISH LAKES

FOR YOUR 1962 HOLIDAY

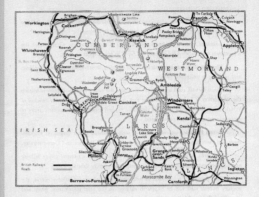

COMBINED RAIL ROAD AND LAKE TOURS HOLIDAY RUNABOUT TICKETS

EVERYTHING FOR YOUR HOLIDAY

LONDON MIDLAND

TROSSACHS

VIA

ABERFOYLE

No. 2

LONDON & NORTH EASTERN RAILWAY

WEEKLY HOLIDAY SEASON TICKETS

FOR RUN-ABOUT HOLIDAYS
IN NORTH-EAST SCOTLAND

1st Class	3rd Class
11/-	7/6

Issued from June to September inclusive.

All Stations between Boat of Garten, Lossiemouth and Spey Bay, via Craigellachie and Elgin.

The territory covered by this ticket contains some of the most picturesque scenery of moor, hills and the torrential River Spey.

Elgin, with its famous Cathedral and glorious climate, also Lossiemouth, the Northern Outpost of the London and North Eastern Railway.

Visitors from places south of Aberdeen can obtain Weekly Season Tickets available in the Sections shown on the map below, on production of the Return Halves of their Ordinary, Tourist or Holiday Return Tickets.

These Holiday Season Tickets are available by any train including Day and Half-Day Excursion Trains advertised between any Stations within the Areas covered by the Tickets.

The Tickets can be obtained on application at any Station within the limits set out, on two days' notice being given.

Children under 14 years of age are charged half fare.

1st Class	3rd Class
15/-	10/-

Issued from June to September inclusive.

All Stations between Huntly, Banff, Lossiemouth and Elgin, via Coast or Craigellachie routes.

The features of the countryside over which this ticket is available are the same as described for Ticket No. 1, but with the added charm of the Moray Firth Coast from Lossiemouth to Cullen. On a clear day, the hills of Caithness are visible, also the Sutors at Cromarty, the natural harbour of the Fleet.

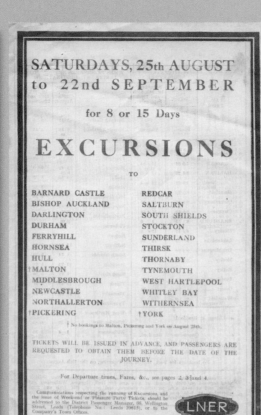

TRAVEL AS OFTEN AS YOU LIKE

CHEAPEST FORM OF HOLIDAY TRAVEL

1st Class	15/-
3rd Class	10/-

Issued from 11th July to 15th August, inclusive.

All Stations between Aberdeen and Ballater, Alford, Insch, Kyvie and Boddam.

A new Holiday Ticket covering the magnificent valley of the Dee, with Braemar, Balmoral Castle and Lochnagar. On Donside, the scenery is also of the grandest, and "Benachie" (1698 feet), from which a grand view of the surrounding country can be obtained, can be easily climbed from Kemnay or Oyne Stations.

March 1932   LONDON AND NORTH EASTERN RAILWAY   (20-M)   (G. 3555)

MAP 10

MIDDLESEX, HERTFORDSHIRE & ESSEX

BRANCH LINES

Enthusiasts explore Mill Road's short platform, on the Thaxted branch.

Closed branch lines

Closed passenger lines

Open passenger lines

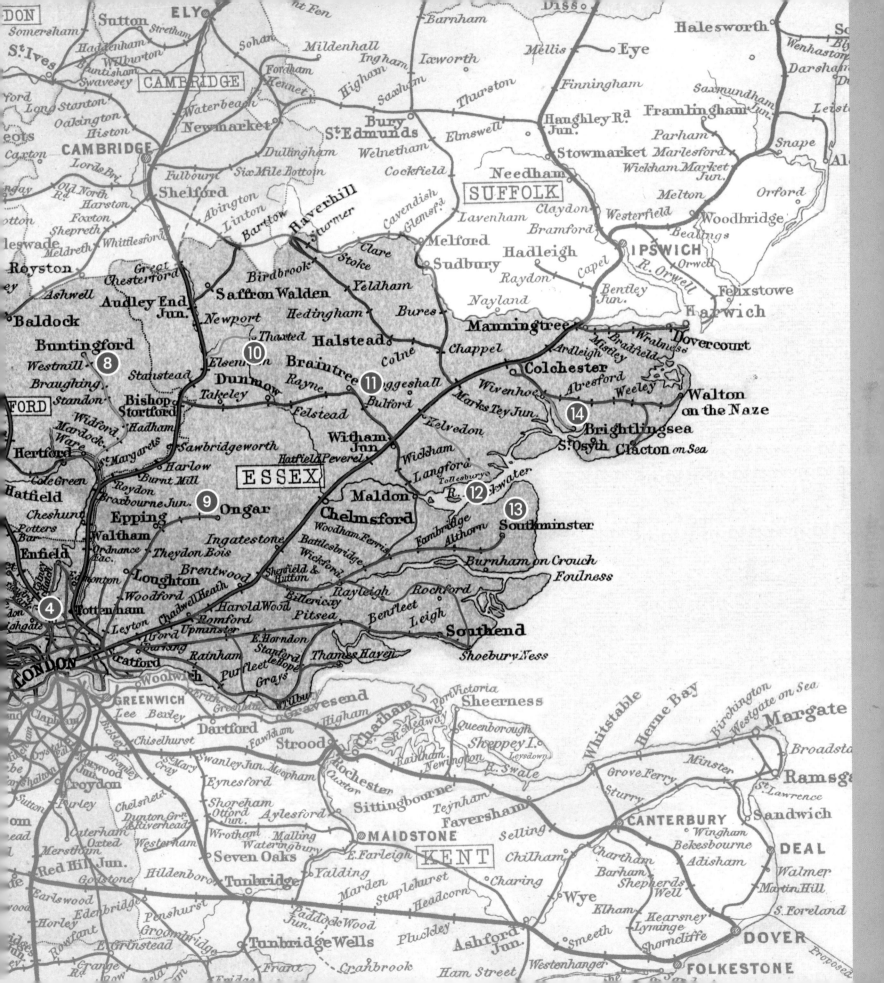

MAP 10

⑧ BUNTINGFORD

This branch was built, with some difficulties, by the Ware, Hadham & Buntingford Railway. With help from the Eastern Counties Railway and later the GER, it finally opened in 1863, but went to St Margaret's rather than Ware. The GER took control in 1868, and the branch settled down to a steady life, serving commuters and local businesses. There were through trains to London until the late 1950s, and then it all began to change. DMUs took over, and it became a local branch line, increasingly unable to compete with other lines and the rise of the motor car. Closure to passengers came in November 1964, and freight a year later. In its day, the branch was famous for its many bridges, eight of which were river crossings. Some of these survive and, while sections of the route have disappeared, there are parts that can be explored. Some stations, notably Buntingford and Braughing, are now private houses.

△ In July 1906 JR sent this card to Miss Chapman of Dunmow, Essex, to tell her that he had moved to Hormead Rectory, Buntingford, and he looked forward to seeing her in August.

◁ On what looks like a typical summer's day at Buntingford in the late 1950s, the train for St Margaret's waits, but there are no passengers to be seen. The fireman is off to get a flask of tea.

▽ The most remarkable sight on the Buntingford branch today is Braughing station, whose owner has painstakingly created a detailed replica around the surviving buildings and platforms. The trackbed has become a neat lawn, and there is even a carriage resting on a short section of track.

⑩ THAXTED

The Elsenham & Thaxted Railway was a typical product of the Light Railways Act of 1896. Authorized in 1906, the 5-mile branch took seven years to build, and then stopped short of Thaxted, despite financial support from the government and the GER, which operated the line from the start. It was a classic case of too little, too late, so the railway played only a small part in Thaxted's history. However, it lived on through the LNER era and into the days of British Railways, which disposed of it fairly quickly, withdrawing passenger services in September 1952 and closing the branch completely nine months later. The line was built cheaply, without significant engineering, and with station buildings made from timber or old carriages. As a result, although parts of the route can be traced, there is not much to be seen today.

▽ While the crew pose for the photographer, the old Class J69 tank locomotive, No. 68579, rests before taking its train back to Elsenham. This is Thaxted station shortly before the branch's closure in 1952. As is apparent from the setting, it was a long way from the town, something that contributed to the line's rather dismal history. The locomotive survived until 1960.

△This Edwardian card shows the classic view of Thaxted high street: the guildhall, other medieval and later buildings, and the tall church spire.

▽The most visible reminder of the branch's short life is a footpath on a stretch of embankment alongside fields, near the site of Sibley's for Chickney & Broxted station.

△Closure is imminent and Henham Halt is not looking its best. The carriage-body shelter is falling apart, the lamp has gone and grass is growing over the platform.

MAP 10

⑫ TOLLESBURY

This 9-mile branch through Essex backwaters, inspired by the Light Railways Act, was opened by the Kelvedon, Tiptree & Tollesbury Railway in 1904. It was cheaply built and cheaply operated, with basic stations and secondhand rolling stock. In 1907 the line was extended to Tollesbury Pier, giving it access to the local shellfish trade. The other major activity was the transport of jam from Wilkinson's factory in Tiptree, and this continued until final closure in 1962. Passenger services had ceased in 1951. Today, there is little to hint at the existence of the route, much having been ploughed away.

△The old timber boat stores are a famous feature of Tollesbury and have often been depicted on postcards. The railway's route to the pier was nearby, but all traces were obliterated by floods in 1953.

▷Tolleshunt D'Arcy was one of five intermediate stations. This view, taken in 1952, a year after closure, shows the basic timber structures built by the railway to save money.

△The branch did not start at Kelvedon's mainline station but at a separate one on a lower level. Notices such as this were therefore necessary to guide people changing trains. The signs lived on long after the GER era.

△A typical Tollesbury branch train was made up of an old engine, a few goods wagons and some secondhand carriages. This example, photographed in 1951 just before closure, features a pair of four-wheeled carriages with an elderly and rather tired-looking Class J69 tank locomotive, No. 68578. The GER design dates back to 1900.

▷It is hard today to find traces of the railway. Having been built with minimal engineering, it quickly vanished back into the landscape after closure. This section, more like a country footpath than a railway trackbed, survives near Tolleshunt D'Arcy.

⑭ BRIGHTLINGSEA

Like many of the branch lines in this area, this was built by an independent company, the Wivenhoe & Brightlingsea Railway, an associate of the Tendring Hundred Railway, which had built the line from Colchester to Wivenhoe. Authorized in 1861, the railway was opened in 1866 and was operated by the GER, which took over completely in 1893. It took 40 per cent of the receipts which, thanks in part to the traffic in oysters and fish, were satisfactory for many years, and the branch was run successfully until the 1950s. Much of the route was along an embankment flanking the tidal estuary of the river Colne, and the only major structure was the iron swing-bridge that carried the line over Alresford Creek on the approach to Wivenhoe. The cost of maintaining this bridge, essential for the passage of sand and gravel boats, was given as the reason for the eventual closure of the branch in 1964. Today, apart from the bridge, which was demolished soon after closure, virtually the entire route of the line survives to be explored on foot or by bicycle.

△This 1950s postcard is a reminder that Brightlingsea, long a busy fishing port, was also popular with yachtsmen and holidaymakers visiting the quiet estuaries of the Essex coast.

△Walking or cycling along the embankment that carries the trackbed all the way to the remains of the Alresford Creek bridge is delightful, and popular with local people and their dogs. It is also excellent for birdwatching.

△The trackbed is almost entirely on an embankment alongside the Colne estuary and offers magnificent views in all directions. This is near Brightlingsea, with bathing huts flanking the beach and the town beyond. The station was just off the photograph to the left.

▷The Wivenhoe & Brightlingsea Railway built a substantial terminus station, on an elevated site overlooking the beach and convenient for the town. It is shown in this early 1960s view with the local DMU waiting to depart. The station was demolished in 1968.

MAP 10

❸ STANMORE

The steady expansion of suburban London in the latter part of the Victorian period, and the rise of commuting, encouraged the building of many new railways, often by competing companies. Typical was the LNWR's branch line from Harrow & Wealdstone to Stanmore, which opened in 1890. Initially successful, the line carried both passengers and freight, though the mainline connection at Harrow precluded trains on the branch from running direct to London. In 1932 the Metropolitan Line opened a station at Stanmore, which offered a much quicker service to London and direct Underground links. The LNWR's response was to open a new, and better-placed, intermediate station to the south of Stanmore, at Belmont. This took the bulk of the commuter traffic and resulted in the end of passenger carrying on the Belmont-to-Stanmore section in 1952. Freight continued for a while, then the rest of the branch closed in 1964.

▽ Stanmore station, seen here in about 1910, had a single platform graced with an elegant canopy. The main building, at the far end, was built to resemble a church, with a tower and spire, visible here above the canopy. The reason, apparently, was to make it harmonize with surrounding village architecture.

❷ UXBRIDGE BRANCHES

The GWR built two branches to Uxbridge. The first, a line northwards from West Drayton to Vine Street, was opened in 1856 and closed in 1964. The second, known as High Street, was a shorter line from the north, designed to meet the Vine Street line and form a loop. It opened in 1907 but the connection was never made, so High Street became a terminus. It closed to passengers in 1939.

❹ ALEXANDRA PALACE

The Muswell Hill Railway's branch from Highgate to Alexandra Palace opened, with the palace, in 1873. Two weeks after opening, the palace burnt down, and the line was closed for two years while it was rebuilt. The GNR took control in 1911. Plans made in 1935 to merge the line into the London Transport network were brought to an end by World War II. The line closed in 1956. Alexandra Palace station survives, and part of the route is a footpath.

❺ CROXLEY GREEN

In 1912 the LNWR opened a branch to Croxley Green from its Watford and Rickmansworth line, mainly driven by the desire to keep its great rival, the Metropolitan Railway, at bay. Despite its minor status, the branch remained open until 1996. Track is still in place, along with the remains of the station. Under the new Croxley Rail Link plan, parts of the branch will be reopened, with a new connection to London Underground's Watford line.

❻ HEATH PARK

In 1877 a branch line to Hemel Hempstead was opened from Harpenden, on the Midland Railway's main line. Originally, this was planned to join the LNWR main line at Boxmoor but, although a connection was made for freight, it was never used for passengers and was cut by 1916. Meanwhile, a new terminus for the branch was built at Heath Park in 1905 and services improved for a while. By the 1920s the branch was in decline, thanks to more efficient competition, and passenger services ended in 1947.

OPEN & PRESERVED LINES

❶ SHEPPERTON

The grandly named Thames Valley Railway was set up in 1862 to build a branch line from Strawberry Hill to Shepperton. There was originally a scheme to carry on across the Thames to Chertsey, but this was soon abandoned. The branch opened in 1864 and a few months later the LSWR took over. Always a busy commuter line, the branch was electrified in 1916.

❼ ST ALBANS ABBEY

The LNWR's branch from Watford, which opened in 1858, was the first railway to reach St Albans. Mainline stations followed, but somehow the branch survived. The terminus was renamed St Albans Abbey in 1924. There have been many closure threats but the line, now electrified, seems secure and may even be extended. It operates as a true rural branch line.

❾ ONGAR

The GER opened its line to Ongar in 1865 and it continued to operate as a through route until 1949, when it was taken over by London Transport. At that point, the Epping-to-Ongar line became a true branch, with its own shuttle trains, at first steam and then electric tube stock. The branch was closed by London Transport in 1994, but has since been reopened as a heritage line.

⑪ BRAINTREE

In 1848 a railway was opened from Maldon to Braintree via Witham, and twenty years later another line was opened, westwards from Braintree to Bishop's Stortford. This was closed to passengers in 1952, followed by the Witham-to-Maldon section in 1964. Thus the Witham to Braintree line remains as a branch.

⑬ SOUTHMINSTER

The Southminster branch, commonly known as the Crouch Valley Line, was opened by the GER from Wickford on the Southend line in 1889. Threatened with closure in the 1960s, the line was saved by expanding commuter traffic and the carriage of nuclear materials for Bradwell power station. The branch was electrified in 1986, though it is still largely single track.

△It looks like a sea wall, but the raised embankment along the Colne estuary is actually the route of the Brightlingsea branch (*see also* page 121).

Branchline locomotives

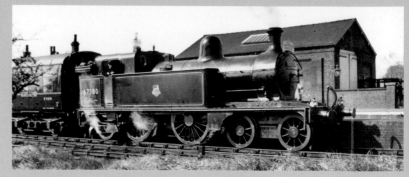

↑ Photographed at Holme, Huntingdonshire, in April 1957, this Ivatt-designed 4-4-2, No. 67380, was built for the Great Northern Railway in about 1898.

↑ Built to a Reid design for the North British Railway in about 1904, this Class J88 short wheelbase 0-6-0, No. 68325, was still at work in the 1950s.

↑ A Midland Railway design, this Class 3F, No. 47432, built in about 1924 for the LMS, was based at Kentish Town, London, when the photograph was taken.

↑ In the mid-1920s LNER Class D51, No. 10425, is at work at Edinburgh Waverley. This North British Railway design dated back to 1900.

↑ A Drummond design of 1905 for the Highland Railway, this Class 1P, No. 55051, is about to leave Dornoch, in Sutherland, in May 1952.

↑ The London, Brighton & South Coast Railway's D1 Class was introduced in 1873. 'Hilsea', No. 249, was built in 1881 and withdrawn in 1938.

↑ Adams radial tanks were built for the London & South Western Railway from 1882. In 1959 No. 30582 was working on the Lyme Regis branch, in Dorset.

↑ Seen here at Torquay, Devon, in 1957, this is No. 5503 of the Churchward-designed GWR 4500 Class, introduced from 1906.

MAP 11

CAMBRIDGESHIRE, SUFFOLK & NORFOLK

BRANCH LINES

A train dating from the Great Eastern era leaves Mildenhall in 1946.

Closed branch lines

Closed passenger lines

Open passenger lines

Firsby
Skegness
Thorpe Cowbank
Culvert Croftbank
stville Wainfleet
ake

Hunstanton ⑩ Burnham Wells Blakeney Sheringham Cromer
Holt
Heacham Stanhoe Docking Mundesley
Sedgeford Walsingham Gunton
Snettisham Thursford Melton Flemingham N. Walsham Happisburgh
Dersingham Fakenham Constable Aylsham Honing Ruston
Wolferton Sandringham Hindol- Corpusty Guestwick Buxton Worstead Stalham
Long Sutton Wootton N. vestone Ryburgh Lammas Coltishall Catfield
Sutton bridge Cas. Rising Barnham Reepham Cawston Winterton
Lynn Grimston Park Foulsham NORFOLK Wroxham Martham Hemsby
Middleton Hillington Massingham N. Elmham Lenwade Attlebridge Salhouse Ormesby
Walpole East Winch Fransham Dereham Drayton Witlingham Jun. Caistor
Terrington Narborough Wendling Yaxham NORWICH Brundall Acle
Clenchwarton W. Lynn Castle Hellesdon Thorpe Lingwood YARMOUTH
Middle Magdalen Rd. Acre Dunham Thuxton Hethersett Trowse Buckenham Cantley
Drove Watlington Swaffham Hardingham Kimberley Swainsthorpe Belton
Smeeth Rd. Stow Holm Hale Hingham Reedham Somerleyton
Emneth ⑨ Downham Watton Wymondham Flordon Haddiscoe Mutford
Coldh. Ilpwell ⑧ Stoke Ferry Stow Bedon Long St. Olaves Jun. Lowestoft
Hilgay Attleborough Forncett Stratton Ellingham Aldeby Carlton Colville
Stones Brandon Wretham Eccles Rd. Earsham Bungay Beccles
Manea Littleport Harling Rd. Tivetshall Pulham Homersfield Brampton
teris Lakenheath Roudham Jun. Jun. Burston
ack Bank Thetford Burnham Harleston ⑦
Chittisham Diss Halesworth Southwold
ELY Barnham Eye Blythburgh
Stretham Soham Mildenhall Mellis Laxfield Wenhaston Darsham
ton Fordham Ingham Ixworth Finningham Saxmundham Dunwich
CAMBRIDGE Kennet Higham Thurston Haughley Rd. Framlingham Jun. Leiston
Waterbeach Sawham Jun. Parham ⑤
Newmarket Bury Elmswell Stowmarket Marlesford Snape
Dullingham St. Edmunds Wickham Market Jun. Aldeburgh
GE Six Mile Bottom Welnetham Needham Melton Orford ⑥
Fulbourn Cockfield SUFFOLK Westerfield Orfordness
Shelford Abington Cavendish Claydon Woodbridge
Linton Haverhill Glemsf'd Lavenham Bramford Bealings
sford Barnow Shimer Melford Sudbury Hadleigh Capel IPSWICH Orwell Felixstowe
Saffron Walden Birdbrook Stoke Kersey Bentley R. Orwell Harwich
y End Newport Hedingham Clare Nayland Jun.
Jun. Thaxted Halstead Bures Manningtree Wrabness Dovercourt
stead Dunmow Braintree Colne Chappel Ardleigh Bradfield Mistley Walton on the Naze
shop Takeley Rayne Coggeshall Colchester Wivenhoe Abresford Weeley
rtford Felstead Bulford Marks Tey Jun. Kelvedon
adham Brightlingsea

MAP 11

❶ MILDENHALL

One of many lines conceived as part of a larger plan, the Mildenhall branch was built by the GER as the first section of a diversionary route from Cambridge to Norwich via Mildenhall and Thetford. This much was completed in 1885, then the GER decided to proceed no further, leaving the branch as a rural line in a remote agricultural region. In fact, most of the traffic came from agriculture, as the branch served a sparsely populated area of northeast Cambridgeshire. A halt for the local golf club added interest, but few passengers. RAF Mildenhall helped to keep the line open during World War II, but the decline was rapid in the 1950s, leading to the end of passenger services in 1962 and freight in 1964. Today, much of the route is invisible, taken back into the flat landscape. Fordham station, the junction for the branch on the Ely-to-Newmarket line, exists in a derelict state. Mildenhall station and goods shed survive in private hands. Other features to be found include a bridge near Isleham.

△ This card, probably from the 1920s, suggests that Mildenhall enjoyed some tourist trade, to which the railway may have contributed.

▷ Exploration of the Mildenhall branch is hard because so much of the route has been ploughed out. A rare survival is this bridge, built of engineering bricks, alongside a crossroads near Isleham. The substantial structure seems in good condition and stands in isolation, hidden by trees and bushes.

▽ The end cannot have been far away when this photograph was taken at Mildenhall, but everything is in good order. The station is tidy, with fire buckets in place, and some decorative gardening is going on in the foreground. A small boy, perhaps with the photographer, walks towards the Cambridge-bound DMU, which may well be waiting in vain for passengers.

△ Fordham, the junction station for the branch, is boarded up, and nature is taking over.

② HADLEIGH

As is sometimes the case with branch lines, the Hadleigh branch was in fact a relic of a much grander scheme. It started in 1846 with the ambitious plans of the Eastern Union & Hadleigh Junction Railway, whose line opened the next year, although many stations and buildings were incomplete. In the event, the connections that would have made the line a through route never materialized, so it settled down as a branch from Bentley to Hadleigh. Traffic was always limited and, with the advent of buses after World War I, the line was no longer viable. Passenger services ceased in 1932, but freight lingered on until 1965. Today, parts of the route can be traced, and a 2-mile section is an official footpath and cycleway. Stations also survive as private houses, including Hadleigh's 1847 terminus.

◁This card of Hadleigh Castle was sent from Guildford to Derby in 1906 at 8pm. Its message, about a visit early the next day, tells of the reliability of the postal service at this time. With several deliveries a day, postcards were often used as a rapid means of communication.

▷The Hadleigh Railway Walk follows the line from Hadleigh to Raydon Wood. A Sustrans sculpture marks its junction with a national cycle route.

△The grand ambitions that lay behind the Hadleigh branch meant that stations and other structures were built to a high standard. The Eastern Union Railway, later the GER, was behind the scheme, as seen in the architecture. Typical is the grand station at Raydon Wood, photographed perhaps in the 1950s.

▷Though a bit of a ruin, Raydon Wood station still stands. Its Italianate style, careful detailing and elegant symmetry reflect the architectural fashions of the late 1840s, while Hadleigh station, by contrast, has a more Jacobean look.

MAP 11

❸ EYE

The short branch line to Eye was built by the Mellis & Eye Railway, a small independent company promoted by local merchants. It opened in April 1867, with an intermediate halt at Yaxley, midway between Mellis and Eye, but traffic soon indicated that it would probably never pay its way – a familiar story with short, independent branch lines. The GER operated the branch from the start and eventually, in 1898, it reluctantly took it over, mainly for the freight business generated by Eye's brewery, maltings and cattle market. The branch survived into the LNER era, but passenger services ceased in 1931. Freight continued until 1964. Today, there is not much to be seen. The stations at Mellis, on the main line, and Eye have both disappeared, and much of the trackbed has been ploughed out or otherwise lost. Elsewhere, there are a few traces to be discovered, including a bridge.

△ The cars suggest this postcard view of the marketplace at Eye dates from the 1930s. The memorial, erected in 1888, is to Sir Edward Kerrison, a general of the Napoleonic era who was later MP for Eye.

▷ Near Yaxley, a section of trackbed leads to a powerful-looking bridge in engineering brick. Bare fields beyond it show no evidence of the railway ever having continued any further.

△ At one point on the route there is a stretch of low embankment that can be recognized, but it comes to an abrupt end halfway across a field.

▷ This photograph shows Eye station in the 1920s. On what is probably a typical day on the branch line, the staff are preparing to load some parcels onto the waiting train, but otherwise not much is going on. Nothing of this scene has survived.

❻ ALDEBURGH

The Aldeburgh branch was one of a number constructed by ambitious East Anglian railway companies in the mid-19th century. In this case it was the Eastern Counties Railway that opened the branch, from Saxmundham to Leiston, in 1859, and then extended it a year later to Aldeburgh. The GER, keen to promote holiday traffic, took over in 1862, and in due course through trains from London and excursions began to visit Aldeburgh, which by now boasted a substantial covered station. Thorpeness was also developed as a holiday and golf resort. Freight was important, notably for Garrett's engineering works at Leiston. In the British Railways era, passenger traffic declined rapidly, despite the increasing popularity of the region for visitors, and the branch closed in 1966. However, freight continued, and the line is still open as far as Leiston to service the Sizewell nuclear power stations.

△ Sent in 1970 by someone staying in Aldeburgh to friends in County Durham, this postcard has a clear holiday message: 'Scorching hot, bungalow perfect, grounds stretch to sea, lovely.'

◁ From 1956, the branch was operated by two-car DMUs, some of which went on to Ipswich. In late June 1961 the train for Saxmundham waits patiently beneath the station train shed, but passengers are few and far between. Two years later the branch was listed for closure, and in 1965 the train shed roof was demolished.

▽ The branch is easily explored as far as Leiston as it is still in use. From Leiston on, much of the route is lost or inaccessible, but keen eyes may spot the platform of Thorpeness station hidden in undergrowth beside a golf course. The station buildings were originally formed of coach bodies. In Aldeburgh, nothing remains.

△ In the early 1950s an old former GER Class F6 tank locomotive, No. 67220, draws its train into Saxmundham station, watched by waiting passengers. The locomotive was cut up in 1955.

MAP 11

⑧ STOKE FERRY

The Downham & Stoke Ferry Railway was a typical independent company supported by local landowners and merchants keen to connect their region to the national network. Its 7-mile branch line from Denver opened in 1882. It was operated by the GER, which took control in 1898. Plans to extend the line were abandoned. Passenger traffic on the line was always light, and the intermediate stations, Ryston and Abbey, were in remote locations. However, agriculture kept the branch alive, particularly after the opening in 1905 of the connecting Wissington Tramway. Built by a local landowner to reclaim and develop land and to improve agriculture, this was, at its peak, an 18-mile network. For many years, the tramway's main line was used to serve the Wissington sugar beet plant, opened in 1924. Meanwhile, on the Stoke Ferry branch, passenger carrying ended in 1930, though general goods traffic continued until 1965. Today, the branch is fairly easy to explore, and stations and other structures survive.

△ This Edwardian card shows an area of land near Stoke Ferry now known as Limehouse Drove. It gives a sense of the remoteness of a region little known, then as now, to tourists.

▷ This photograph of Ryston station, probably dating from the 1920s or 1930s, illustrates the character of the branch. The line runs straight across the flat landscape, and trains are few and far between – allowing plenty of time for gardening. Nevertheless, the buildings were substantial and well designed, with decorative bands of coloured brick.

△ The terminus at Stoke Ferry included a grand station, a goods shed and a stationmaster's house, all built in the same decorative style. Originally the branch was planned to continue further, and this determined the nature of the station. Passenger carrying had ceased years before this photograph was taken, probably in the 1950s, but the sidings are full of goods wagons. Some of the buildings survive.

▷ Despite years of closure, a number of buildings and other structures live on to reveal the history of the Stoke Ferry branch. Here, at Ryston, the station house, platform and, overgrown but just visible beyond, some crossing gates survive in private ownership, offering a rather romantic insight into a lost railway world.

④ LAXFIELD

The Light Railways Act of 1896 helped to bring into being a number of lines that had previously been dismissed on grounds of cost and practicality. A typical example was the Mid-Suffolk Light Railway's scheme for a cheaply built cross-country line to link Halesworth to Haughley, on the GER's main line, with a branch running south to Westerfield, near Ipswich. Work started in 1902, and in 1904 the line opened from Haughley as far as Laxfield. Some further progress was made towards Cratfield, and towards Debenham on the branch line, but it all ground to a halt when the money ran out. Somehow the truncated line staggered on, despite the remoteness of its route. Airfields kept it alive during World War II, and services continued until 1952. Most of the line has since disappeared, but at Brockford & Wetheringsett station a heritage society has made a Mid-Suffolk Light Railway museum and runs trains along a short length of track.

△The Mid-Suffolk Light Railway was built as cheaply as the Act allowed, with minimal engineering and stations made from corrugated iron. This is Worlingworth, a typically basic structure and clearly in the middle of nowhere.

◁At Aspall & Thorndon, another economy-model station, a railwayman keeps his eye on the visiting enthusiasts, whose bikes have been dumped on the platform while photographs are taken. At this point, closure of the branch must have been imminent. Needless to say, none of the branch's original stations survive, and much of the trackbed has vanished into the farmland.

⑤ FRAMLINGHAM

The East Suffolk Railway was one of several local companies keen to bring the benefits of the railway age to East Anglia. One of its creations was the 6-mile branch line from Wickham Market to Framlingham, opened in 1859 with intermediate stations at Marlesford, Hacheston Halt and Parham. Initially successful, the branch seemed to encourage both passenger and goods traffic, particularly as Framlingham soon established itself as the railhead for a large surrounding area. There were excursions and school trains, and business expanded when the GER took control from 1862. This pattern continued until the 1930s, when road competition threatened the survival of the branch – a story that affected branch lines all over Britain. Once British Railways took charge, the writing was on the wall, and in 1952 passenger services were withdrawn. Freight followed in 1965. A notable survivor is Framlingham's grand Italianate station, now in retail use, and the route can still be explored.

△This photograph must have been taken before 1952, when passenger services were withdrawn, as the station is still clearly active, with a train ready to depart for Wickham Market.

◁This card, showing the ruins of Framlingham's 12th-century castle, was posted from the town to Sussex in 1905. At this time, many visitors, keen to see the castle, would have come on the branchline trains.

MAP 11

⑩ HUNSTANTON

The line from King's Lynn to Hunstanton, opened in 1862, was one of the first in Britain to be built primarily for holiday traffic. Hunstanton station, sited right by the beach, was designed for long excursion and holiday trains from many parts of Britain. At its head was the famous Sandringham Hotel, and adjacent were the promenade and pier. In its heyday the station could handle a holiday express every ten minutes. Changing holiday patterns and the rise of the car from the late 1950s changed Hunstanton's fortunes, and there was a rapid decline in the 1960s, resulting in the loss of long-distance services and much of the station. The line, by then literally a branch, closed in 1969.

Huts, Old Hunstanton Beach

◁ This typical seaside holiday card was posted by Harry, enjoying a typical family holiday in 1935: 'We are spending the week down here & the children are having a lovely time on the beach.' No doubt they came by train.

▷ A classic view of Hunstanton, perhaps taken during the 1930s, shows the scale of the station, the long platforms and the many sidings for handling holiday and excursion trains. There was also significant freight traffic at that time.

⑦ SOUTHWOLD

One of England's most famous narrow-gauge lines was the Southwold Railway, whose 9-mile, riverside route from the main line at Halesworth opened in 1879. Dependent on holiday traffic, it did much to make an isolated part of the Suffolk coastline accessible before the days of buses and cars. By the 1920s, competition was killing the Southwold Railway and it closed in 1929, lamented by the many who had enjoyed its eccentricities.

⑨ UPWELL

Opened in 1883, the Wisbech & Upwell Tramway was a roadside branch line built by the GER to serve a remote agricultural region. Passengers were carried until 1927, but freight kept the branch alive until 1966. A famous feature of the line was its distinctive series of steam tram engines, the result of Board of Trade regulations that demanded slow speeds, control from both ends of the locomotive, and the fitting of cowcatchers and skirts over the wheels.

Branchline luggage labels

LNER | B 877
LUGGAGE
From LIVERPOOL STREET
To THAXTED

B. 167 (34G)
SOUTHERN RAILWAY.
Victoria to
SELSEY

London Brighton & South Coast Railway.
South Hayling to
Ryde Pier

London and South Western Ry.
87 | TO
Sidmouth

G.W.R.
Calne

G. E. R.
From _____
TO
STOKE FERRY

G.W.R.
Kingsbridge

HORSMONDEN

SOUTHERN RAILWAY.
(4/31) | (787)
FROM WATERLOO TO
COMBPYNE

London and South Western Ry.
787
FROM WATERLOO TO
BISLEY CAMP

GREAT WESTERN RAILWAY. | (135 a)
TOLLER
TO
SHEFFIELD L.N.E.
No. of Packages | CARRIAGE PAID
Route via _____

344
C.R.
Bodmin Road to
MORETONHAMPSTEAD

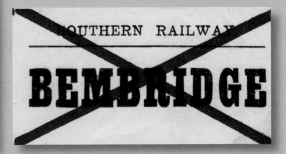
SOUTHERN RAILWAY
BEMBRIDGE

MAP 12

LEICESTERSHIRE, RUTLAND, NOTTINGHAMSHIRE & LINCOLNSHIRE

BRANCH LINES

It is a quiet day at Uppingham station in 1953.

Closed branch lines

Closed passenger lines

Open passenger lines

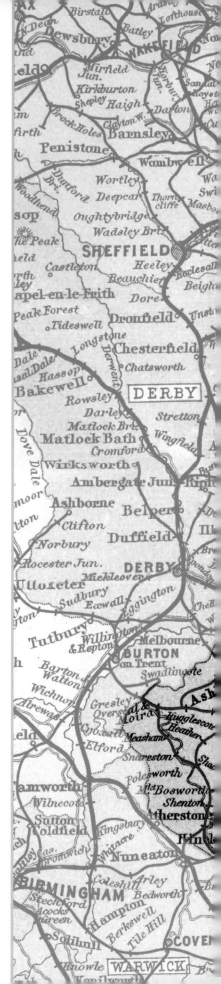

MAP 12

❶UPPINGHAM

Uppingham joined the railway network in 1894, when the LNWR opened its short branch, just over 3 miles long, from Seaton, on the Rugby-to-Stamford line. The LNWR and the Midland Railway were rivals in this part of England, so the building of the branch was territorial but of benefit to the town. The Midland's Kettering-to-Melton Mowbray line crossed over the branch, and the nearest station on that line, Manton, was at one time called Manton for Uppingham. So this part of Rutland was well served by railways, most of which are now closed, including the Uppingham branch, which lost its passenger service in 1960 and its freight traffic four years later. However, school specials, once so important in this area, continued to use the branch until the final closure. Since then, not much has happened to the branch, and most of the route can be explored. Uppingham station, set in the valley well away from the town centre, has disappeared beneath an industrial estate, but elsewhere there is plenty to be seen, including a variety of bridges and a blue-brick viaduct that carried the line over a tributary of the river Welland. Nearby, on the Midland Railway route, is a much more impressive structure, the Welland, or Harringworth, viaduct, whose 82 arches make it the longest in Britain.

△A 1960s card reflects Uppingham's popularity with visitors. The market town's major sights include the 14th-century church and the market square, looking much the same today.

Uppingham, from S.E.

△This Edwardian view, depicting an LNWR train in the platform, and published when the branch was still quite new, shows how distant the station was from the centre of the town.

△The most striking relic of the branch is this viaduct, taking the branch over a stream near Valley Farm. Sturdy, but not without elegance, this structure reveals in its style and materials the late date of the line's construction.

▷In the 1950s, a British Railways autotrain waits in the station, ready to depart for Seaton. The platform is deserted, as was so often the case with branch lines by this time.

❷ SPILSBY

The Spilsby & Firsby Railway was a typical product of regional enterprise and ambition. The 4-mile branch from Firsby, on the Boston-to-Grimsby main line, built by the East Lincolnshire Railway years before, was authorized in 1865. It was a local curate, the Revd Edward Rawnsley, who cut the first sod and, though money was short and construction erratic, the branch opened in 1868. There was one intermediate station, Halton Holgate. The line was operated by the GNR, which took control in 1891. Passenger traffic was always limited, and agriculture was the branch's mainstay. When the LNER took over in 1923, things remained much the same, with six trains each way on weekdays. In September 1939 the branch was closed as a wartime economy measure. Passenger services were never resumed, though freight continued until 1958, when closure was prompted by the state of the bridge carrying the line over the river Deeping. Built over low-lying farmland, the branch had no significant features, so there are few clues as to its route through the landscape, but the station at Halton Holgate, and other surviving structures, are helpful guides.

△ Although much of the trackbed has vanished, some buildings and structures survive, including stations, bridges and the sites of level crossings. This is one near Mill Lane, where the concrete crossing-gate supports still stand, along with a crossing-keeper's cottage and these tumbledown remains of a wooden gangers' hut.

◁ This is Spilsby, and a former GNR Class J6 locomotive shunts the goods from Firsby one week before the line's closure in December 1958. Ironically, the station appears to be busy with freight traffic and parcels, which are piled on the platform trolleys. Today, no trace of all this can be found.

◁ This Edwardian card, issued by a famous railway publisher of that era, shows Spilsby station in 1870, soon after the branch was opened, with a typical train headed by a Sharp Brothers locomotive of 1847.

▷ A busy platform at Spilsby in about 1910: this is an image full of period detail, including advertising posters, some cyclists and a little girl watching the approaching train.

MAP 12

③ HORNCASTLE

The Horncastle & Kirkstead Railway was set up by local merchants and farmers, keen to connect their town to the railway network. In 1854 the company changed its name to the Horncastle Railway, and by September 1855 the 7-mile branch from Kirkstead, or Woodhall Junction as it was later named, was fully open. From the start, the line was busy with freight, and passenger services included a through carriage to London. Unlike most branch lines, the Horncastle Railway was profitable, and remained independent until 1923, when the LNER took over. The GNR, which had operated the line from the start, tried to buy it several times, but the owners always resisted. The branch also did well from the late Victorian growth of Woodhall Spa, whose combination of health-giving waters, comfortable hotels and golf had a wide appeal. During World War II the branch was kept busy by the local RAF bases, but after the war the decline was rapid and the branch closed to passengers in 1954. Freight continued until 1971. Today, part of the route survives as the Spa Trail, a section of the long-distance Viking Way from Oakham to the Humber.

△The Stanch, depicted in this Edwardian card, was built to control the water levels of the river Bain as part of the construction of the Horncastle Canal, which opened in 1802.

▷At Woodhall Spa the branch crossed the town at an angle, as shown in this Edwardian photograph. Today, the station has gone but the crossing point is there, along with the shops.

△Exploring the Horncastle branch is easy, as some of the route is an official footpath and cycleway. It is a pleasant and easy walk across the Lincolnshire landscape, with sculptural route markers indicating the area's Viking history. The rest of the trackbed can be traced but is not always accessible.

△Horncastle station was a handsome building in the Classical style of the 1850s. Behind was the single platform, with its awning, and a large goods yard. Busy sidings reflected the branch's extensive freight traffic, much of which was agricultural. This photograph is from the 1960s. When the line closed in 1971, all the station buildings were gradually demolished and today nothing remains.

❹ WHITTON

The North Lindsey Light Railway opened its branch from Scunthorpe to Winteringham in 1907, and this was extended to Whitton, on the bank of the Humber, three years later. The branch was backed and operated by the Great Central Railway, keen to keep the Lancashire & Yorkshire Railway out of this corner of England. However, it remained independent until 1923, when the LNER absorbed it. Passenger services, always rather erratic, ended in 1925, and freight continued on the Winteringham-to-Whitton section until about 1951. At the southern end, part of the branch is still in use, serving a landfill site at Roxby.

OPEN & PRESERVED LINES
❺ BARTON-ON-HUMBER

The origins of this branch lie in the Great Grimsby & Sheffield Junction Railway's 1848 line to New Holland, which until 1981 was the port for the Humber ferries to Hull. The short branch from New Holland to Barton-on-Humber opened in 1849, and other lines followed. Today, the branch lives on, Barton being the terminus of the Barton Line from Grimsby and Cleethorpes.

△ Woodhall Junction station, for the Horncastle branch (*see* opposite), has been lovingly restored as a private house.

Lost line legacy

MAP 13

SHROPSHIRE, STAFFORDSHIRE, CHESHIRE & DERBYSHIRE

BRANCH LINES

By the 1970s not much remained of Ipstones station, on the Waterhouses branch.

Closed Passenger Lines

Closed Branch Lines

Open Passenger Lines

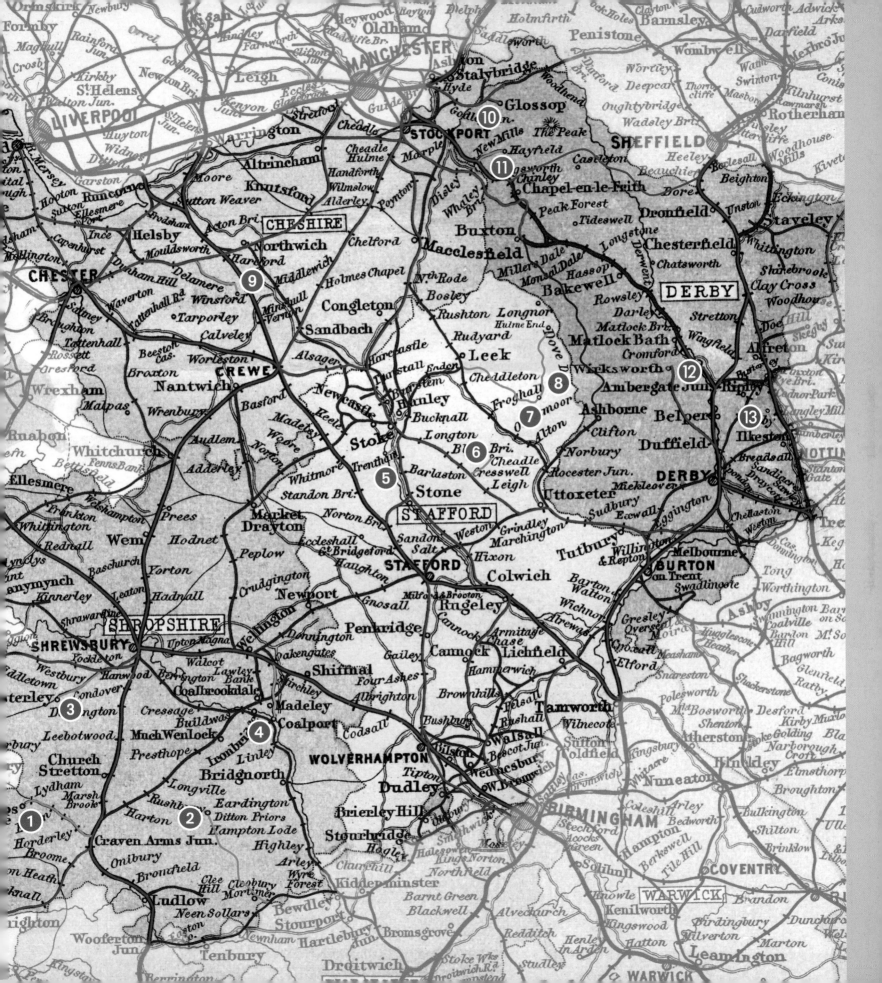

MAP 13

❻ CHEADLE

There had been many abortive schemes to link Cheadle to the railway network before the Cheadle Railway Mineral & Land Company opened the first section of its line in 1892. Finally completed in 1901, the branch was operated by the North Staffordshire Railway, which took control in 1908. Coal mines around Cheadle were the inspiration, and freight traffic was always significant on the branch. Continuous problems with a tunnel led to the route being diverted in 1933. Passenger numbers were never high and by the end, which came in June 1963, services had been reduced to three trains a day. Freight lived on, serving a brickworks and a quarry, the latter closing in 1978. British Rail kept the branch open for engineering purposes until the mid-1980s, and a Pullman special carrying guests to Alton Towers travelled to Cheadle in 1985. The branch was then closed, but the track and infrastructure were left in place pending decisions about a possible reopening or use as a footpath. It is, therefore, easy to explore the remains of the branch, though the site of Cheadle station and the section leading into the town were used for housing in the 1990s.

△This card, posted from Cheadle in 1906 and sent as a thank you for a 'lovely present', shows a view of the town hardly changed today.

▽Steam was replaced by diesel in 1958, but by that date the branch was little used. This 1950s view of Cheadle station already has a sense of decline and decay, and the place is deserted.

◁The entrances to the tunnel that caused so many problems were bricked up in the early 1930s, when the tunnel was taken out of use. This is the southern portal, which, as can be seen, was the site of mining operations during the 1980s.

▷The busy quarry traffic was well away from the town, so after the end of passenger traffic in 1963 Cheadle station and its surrounding buildings were razed to the ground.

❶ BISHOP'S CASTLE

A classic example of misplaced local enthusiasm, the Bishop's Castle Railway was an 1860s scheme to build a line from Craven Arms, on the Shrewsbury & Hereford main line, to Montgomery, on the Oswestry & Newtown's line. Partially opened in 1866, it was soon closed owing to financial problems. It reopened in 1877 but never went further than Bishop's Castle. This section was planned as a branch, and therefore required complicated reversals. For much of its life the line was operated by a receiver, but optimism remained and the hope of reaching Montgomery was never given up. Always short of money, and operating with a hotchpotch of ancient rolling stock, the railway somehow kept going until 1935, maintained partly by the traditional English enthusiasm for eccentricity, and partly by the needs of local farmers and traders. The route followed the valley of the river Onny, and much can still be explored. The eastern section is a footpath.

△Before World War I, the railway gave every impression of being busy and operating normally. This photograph shows plenty of activity and a sense of pride.

◁It is the 1920s, and things have changed dramatically. Bishop's Castle station looks almost derelict, although trains are still running. Here, a locomotive is running round its single carriage, but it is the bus in the foreground that tells the real story: competition is killing the branch.

❸ MINSTERLEY

△A man and two dogs pose for the camera on the otherwise deserted station platform at Minsterley, possibly in the 1920s. The bargeboarded stationmaster's house reveals the branch's mid-Victorian date. Today, nothing of this remains, and the site has been comprehensively redeveloped..

The Minsterley branch was created jointly by the GWR and the LNWR as part of a scheme to build a through route from Shrewsbury to the Welsh coast. It opened in 1861 and for much of its life it was a typical local branch line. It was important in that it was the access route, via Pontesbury, to the narrow-gauge Snailbeach Railway, which opened in 1877 primarily to serve lead mines and quarries. In its final form, Snailbeach closed in 1959, by which time passenger traffic had already ended on the Minsterley branch, although freight – mainly serving the local creamery – continued until 1967. Most of the trackbed of the Minsterley line survives, along with some railway cottages, and there are plans to turn it into a cycleway as part of the Shrewsbury cycle network.

MAP 13

② DITTON PRIORS

The Cleobury Mortimer & Ditton Priors Railway was a creation of the Light Railways Act, and its 12-mile line opened in 1908. It ran from Cleobury Mortimer, on the GWR's Bewdley-to-Woofferton line, and included a surprising number of intermediate stations and local halts. A connection to quarries on Clee Hill supplied some of the freight traffic.

Independent until it was absorbed by the GWR in 1923, the branch continued to operate in a typically local way until the end of passenger services in 1938. During World War II the line came back to life to serve a massive naval armaments depot. In 1957 the Admiralty took control of the line, and continued to use it until 1965. Today, despite the branch being cheaply built, much of the trackbed can be traced, and even platforms can be found.

△By 1961, when GWR railcars were still in use on the main line at Cleobury Mortimer, the branch was under the control of the Admiralty.

◁A GWR train takes on water at Ditton Priors, probably in the 1930s. The station is little more than a wooden shed, but there is an attractive garden on the low platform, a feature of the line. The guard watches, carriage doors are optimistically opened, but there are no passengers to be seen.

④ COALPORT

Another line born out of competition, the LNWR's branch to Coalport East was an attempt to challenge the GWR's dominance of the Severn Valley. Generously engineered and built to double-track standards, the branch south from Wellington opened in 1861, well equipped to handle the extensive business that was never to materialize. Little of the local coal and mineral traffic came onto the branch, while connections with the Severn and the local canals, already in decline when the branch opened, were equally unprofitable. The route brought Madeley and its iron works into the railway network, which was beneficial to the line. When British Railways took over, it maintained passenger services until 1952, although they had long been operated by one- or two-coach trains. Freight continued until 1964, when the branch closed, along with most of the lines around Ironbridge and the Severn Valley. Today, surviving bridges and cuttings give a sense of the line's heavy engineering and its contribution to the region's complex history. Part of the route is now the Silkin Way long-distance footpath.

▽On a summer's day a leisurely platform conversation passes the time at Coalport East, while a small boy watches the waiting train. Grassy tracks and platform, and brickwork in need of attention, hint at the reality of life on a quiet branch line where traffic expectations had always been about hope, not experience.

❺ TRENTHAM GARDENS

A late arrival on the railway map, the short branch to Trentham Gardens was built by the North Staffordshire Railway and opened in 1910. There was a plan to extend the line towards Newcastle-under-Lyme, to form a southern suburban loop, but nothing happened beyond the building of one road bridge on the proposed route. There was never much local traffic, apart from regular excursions to Trentham Gardens. Indeed, the last train on the branch in 1957 was an excursion from Birmingham. The branch's busiest period was during World War II, when the Bank of England's clearing house was relocated to Trentham, and there were many services, including freight traffic. Today, nothing remains to tell the story of the branch.

△ The North Staffordshire Railway issued this postcard soon after the branch had been opened, to encourage passengers to visit and enjoy the nationally famous gardens.

◁ By the 1950s excursion trains were the major traffic on the branch. Here, an excursion has just arrived at the minimal station's long platform, and the passengers are spilling out to enjoy their day at the gardens. The locomotive is a rather grimy former LMS Class 4MT tank, No. 42494, from a large Stanier-designed class.

❾ WINSFORD & OVER

The Winsford branch was planned by the West Cheshire Railway, but by the time it was completed in 1870 it was under the control of the Cheshire Lines Committee. Later, it became part of the Great Central network. The terminus station was named Winsford & Over to distinguish it from the other Winsford station on the LNWR main line. The route, from Cuddington, on the main line from Northwich to Mickle Trafford, had one intermediate station at Whitegate. Though passengers were carried from the start, the main purpose of the branch was to service the local salt industry, and this was to remain the backbone of the line until closure in 1967. However, brine pumping by the salt industry caused many problems, and parts of the line were periodically closed by subsidence. The branch was an early victim of road competition, and buses linking Winsford and Northwich soon offered faster journey times than the train. As a result, passenger services ended in 1931. Five miles of the trackbed now form the Whitegate Way. This bridleway and footpath begins at Whitegate station, which now houses a visitor centre.

▽ The public baths at Winsford, housed in a rather strange timber-framed building, opened in 1887 but burnt down in 1918. This card was sent from Winsford in 1905 by a lady to her grandchildren, wishing them a good holiday.

WINSFORD, PUBLIC BATHS.

◁ The Winsford branch was visited by a number of enthusiasts' specials long after the end of passenger services. Here, in the 1950s, a former Great Central tank locomotive of about 1907 waits at the head of a rather small two-carriage special organized by the RCTS.

MAP 13

⓭ HEANOR

There was a rapid and extensive development of the railway network on the Derbyshire and Nottinghamshire borders from the 1840s, and soon most of the major towns of the region had at least one railway connection, with particularly dense lines around Langley Mill. For various reasons, Heanor was ignored, much to the annoyance of its population. Eventually the Midland Railway built a branch from Ripley to Heanor. This line, completed in 1890 and extended to Langley Mill in 1895, closed to passengers in the late 1920s but remained in use for freight until 1951. Meanwhile the Great Northern, keen to encroach upon traditional Midland Railway territory, opened its own branch to Heanor, from Ilkeston, in 1891. Freight was the primary reason for the building of the branch, with industries along the route including coal and iron, but passenger traffic was also introduced. At first, both the Midland and the Great Northern stations were called simply Heanor, no doubt causing confusion, and subsequently the GN station became unofficially known as Heanor Gate. British Railways finally made a formal distinction, calling them North and South, but by that time passenger traffic was a distant memory. Passenger services on the GN branch ended in 1925 and were then briefly reintroduced in 1939 before final closure at the start of World War II. Freight continued on parts of the branch until the 1960s.

▽Immaculate and well cared for, a former Great Northern Class C12 tank locomotive of 1899, with an Annesley shed plate, sits at the head of a rake of equally tidy carriages in Heanor's GNR station. It is the 1950s and this must be an enthusiasts' special.

❼ WATERHOUSES

The North Staffordshire's branch from Leekbrook Junction to Waterhouses was opened in 1905 as part of the same scheme as the Leek & Manifold (see below). The two railways shared Waterhouses station and were mutually dependent. Tourism was a factor, but the most profitable traffic was milk from Ecton Creamery on the L & M. Passenger services ended in 1935, freight in 1945. The station is now the Manifold Way's cycle hire base.

❽ LEEK & MANIFOLD

Opened in 1904, the Leek & Manifold Light Railway was, for its short life, one of England's premier narrow-gauge lines. Built to a high standard, it catered for the Manifold valley tourist trade and local dairies. The route ran from Hulme End, near Hartington, to Waterhouses, where there was a connection to the North Staffordshire Railway (see above). Under LMS control from 1923, the line suffered from road competition and closed in 1934. The Manifold Way footpath and cycleway now runs along the route.

⓫ HAYFIELD

The Hayfield branch, opened in 1868 from a junction near New Mills Central on the Hope Valley line, enjoyed a long life, thanks in part to the attractions of the Sett valley, along which the line ran. Later, it was given a boost by transporting men and materials required for the construction of the Kinder reservoir. Despite being a predominantly local line, the branch did not close until 1970. The stone station at Hayfield has gone, but in 1973 the trackbed became the Sett Valley Trail, a cycle path and bridleway.

OPEN & PRESERVED LINES

⑫ WIRKSWORTH

The Midland Railway's branch from Duffield to Wirksworth opened in 1867, mainly to serve local stone quarries. Passenger services ended in 1949, though stone traffic kept the line alive until the early 1990s. Since 1996 the branch has gradually been reopened as the Ecclesbourne Valley Railway, and trains now operate between Wirksworth and Duffield. This is a rare example of a heritage railway restoring a complete branch line.

⑩ GLOSSOP

Glossop, one of the busiest stations in Derbyshire, is in fact part of the Manchester Metrolink network. The station was opened in 1847 at the end of a short branch from the Woodhead line, paid for by the Duke of Norfolk, who wanted to bring the railway to his town. A stone lion, emblem of the Norfolk family, crowns the handsome station. When the Woodhead route closed beyond Hadfield in 1981, the surviving section became another branch line from Manchester.

△Until 2012, part of the Cheadle branch (*see also* page 146) still looked like a railway, with the track left in place, albeit broken and overgrown.

Urban branches

↑ The London & South Western Railway opened its Friary terminus at Plymouth in 1891. Closed to passengers in 1958, it was pulled down in 1976.

↑ Opened as Cardiff Docks in 1840, and later called Bute Road by the GWR, this is now Cardiff Bay. Modern trains do not use the old station.

↑ The terminus of a short branch built by the London, Brighton & South Coast Railway in 1869, Brighton Kemptown was demolished after closure in 1971.

↑ Maldon East's grand, Dutch-style station building was opened by the Eastern Counties Railway in 1848 and closed in 1966. It survives as offices.

↑ Neither of Cirencester's two stations is in use today. This is Cirencester Town, opened in 1841 as the terminus of the GWR branch from Kemble.

↑ The North Eastern Railway opened Durham's Elvet station in 1893. Little used, it closed to passengers in 1931, except for annual miners' gala trains.

↑ Ilkeston Town was the terminus of a short Midland Railway branch opened originally in 1847 and rebuilt in 1879. Passenger traffic ended in 1950.

➔ Seen here in 1965, Lanark opened in 1855 as the terminus of a short Caledonian Railway branch. It was rebuilt and electrified in 1979.

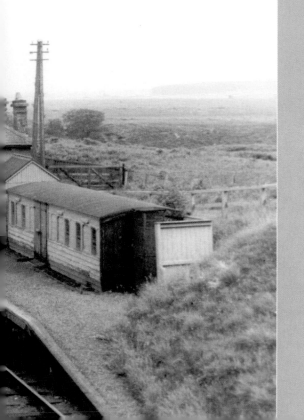

NORTHERN ENGLAND

TOP LEFT: *By 1975 Alston's grand station, having already lost its covered train shed, was looking unkempt and abandoned.*

BOTTOM LEFT: *On a wet spring day in 1963, a DMU and its crew wait for passengers under Richmond's fine train shed.*

TOP RIGHT: *A train from Carlisle enters Silloth station in 1956, when the branch was still busy with summer visitors.*

BOTTOM RIGHT: *Longwitton, on the Rothbury branch, was a typical branchline station, with an old carriage body used as a platform building.*

MAP 14

LANCASHIRE

BRANCH LINES

Knott End station survived for some years after closure in 1950.

Closed branch lines

Closed passenger lines

Open passenger lines

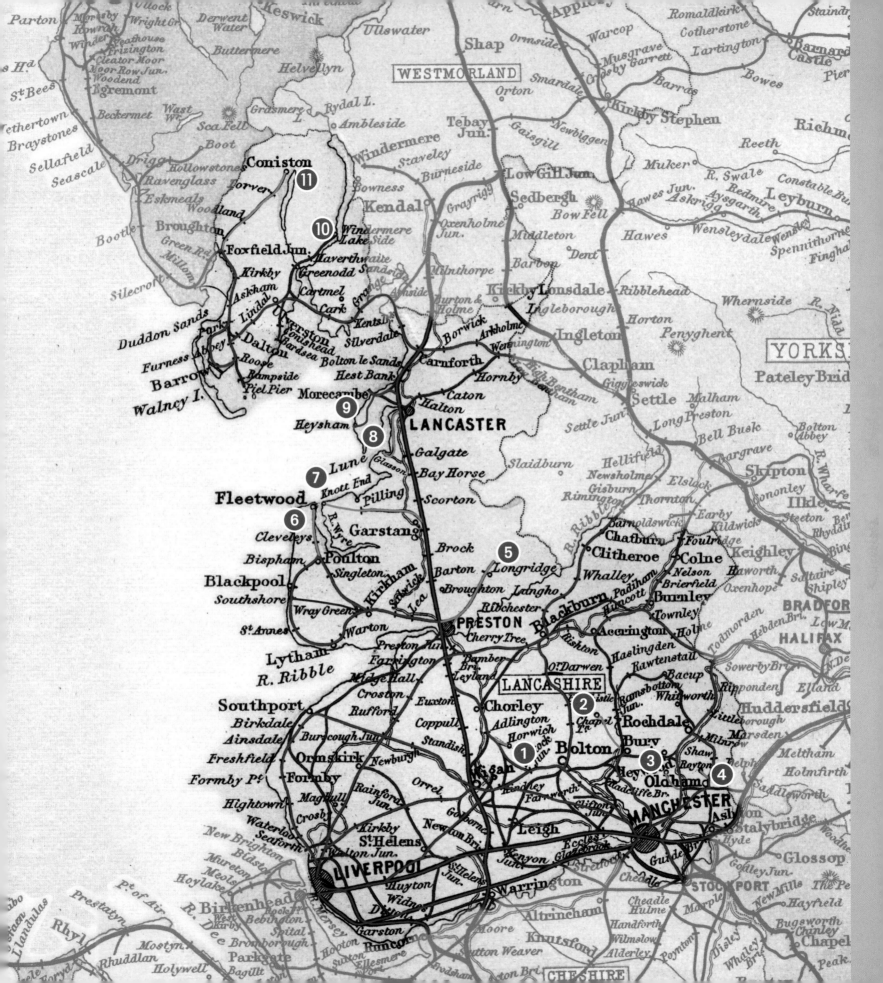

MAP 14

⑪ CONISTON

Apparently independent, the Coniston Railway was in reality closely allied to the much larger Furness Railway so, when its branch to Coniston from Foxfield opened in 1859, it was not long before the Furness was in control. The Lake District was tempting territory for railways, partly because of the region's supposed mineral wealth and partly because of the potential for tourism. The Coniston branch was driven primarily by copper mines in the hills above the terminus, but these proved to be disappointing. Tourism also failed to live up to expectations, mainly because Coniston was quite isolated and did not have easy connections to the rest of the Lake District. However, the branch kept going, passing from Furness to LMS and then to British Railways, which ended passenger services in 1958. Freight continued for another four years. Today, much of the route can be identified in the landscape, but it is not always accessible. Bridges survive, along with stations at Broughton-in-Furness and Woodland, but nothing remains of Coniston's grand terminus.

△Taken soon after closure, this photograph shows Coniston's well-detailed station, along with the engine shed and signal box. Left to decay, all this was eventually demolished.

▽In the 1950s, an LMS Class 2MT locomotive, No. 41217, sits at Coniston with its carriages in the station's fine train shed. The stationmaster and driver chat while the passengers get on board.

△The trackbed sits well with the surrounding landscape. Here, near Torver, a long section of grassy embankment, flanked by traditional stone walls, leads to one of the surviving bridges on the 8-mile route.

◁This 1960s card shows the famous Coniston foxhounds, one of six well-known hunting packs traditionally linked to the Fells. Prior to World War II, it was not uncommon for packs of hounds to travel to distant meets by train.

▷Near Woodland the trackbed is a shallow depression across the high fields, carpeted with wild flowers and offering magnificent views to the hills. It must have been a delightful journey.

② HOLCOMBE BROOK

Though built by the local Bury & Tottington District Railway, the branch from Bury's Bolton Street station to Holcombe Brook was always operated by the Lancashire & Yorkshire Railway, which took control in 1882, six years after the line's opening. The route was steeply graded, with three viaducts and several intermediate stations. Steam railmotors were used from 1905 and then, in 1913, the branch was experimentally electrified with overhead wires. In 1916 it was changed to the three-rail electric system used on the Manchester-to-Bury line. As such, it enjoyed a steady branchline existence until 1951, when the worn-out electrical equipment was abandoned. There was a brief return to steam before passenger services ended in 1952 and freight ten years later. Much of the trackbed lives on as the Kirklees Trail.

△ This 1960s card of Holcombe Brook, a popular postcard view, shows how the village is dominated by Harcles Hill and its famous tower, built in 1852 as a memorial to Sir Robert Peel, who was born in Bury.

◁ This is a classic photograph of one of the Lancashire & Yorkshire Railway's steam railmotors, introduced onto the Holcombe Brook branch from 1905. Crew and station staff pose proudly on the new-looking locomotive, No. 4 of eighteen Hughes-type vehicles built for the railway at Horwich.

③ MIDDLETON

A short branch from Middleton Junction to the centre of Middleton was opened in January 1857. Hitherto, the traditional mill town had been served by Middleton Junction, a station opened in 1842 as Oldham Junction by the Manchester & Leeds Railway on its line to Chadderton and Oldham Werneth. The latter was one of five stations built by various railway companies to serve Oldham. The engineer of the Manchester & Leeds Railway was George Stephenson. The station at Middleton was a conventional two-track terminus with long platforms and matching awnings, surrounded by extensive sidings, mostly for coal traffic and for the local mills. Passenger services continued until September 1964, with freight traffic lasting a year longer.

△ This photograph shows Middleton station, perhaps in the 1920s. Passenger traffic, even then, was limited, but the sidings on either side of the station, filled with open wagons mostly for the coal trade, show that freight was still busy. The station hotel, out of sight here, was at the far end of the platforms.

MAP 14

❼ KNOTT END

▽This card, posted to Manchester in 1907, shows Dolly's Cottage, a popular thatched tearoom. Syd was having 'grand weather'.

The branch to Knott End had a difficult history. It was first planned by the Garstang & Knot End Railway, which took more than five years to build 7 miles of line as far as Pilling from the junction at Garstang, on the Preston-to-Lancaster main line. This opened in 1870, but services were suspended in 1872 owing to financial difficulties. It then had an erratic existence until taken over by a separate company, the Knott End Railway, which completed the line by 1908. More financial problems ensued, but the line was saved by the opening of salt mines at Preesall, near Knott End. By then, Knott End, set on Morecambe Bay, was developing into a small resort, and this helped to keep passenger services running until 1930. There was also a ferry service to Fleetwood. The section above Pilling finally closed in 1950, but some freight traffic remained on the southern section until the mid-1960s. Today, the route can be followed, and the final mile to Knott End is a public footpath. Some crossing-keepers' cottages survive as private houses.

▷This 1930s photograph shows a line of camping coaches on a siding at Knott End. At that time, this type of holiday was quite new and was being promoted by the LMS.

❶ HORWICH

In February 1870 the Lancashire & Yorkshire Railway opened a short double-track branch from Blackrod, on the Manchester-to-Preston line, to Horwich. A site near Horwich was to become the railway's locomotive works. Passenger services continued to Horwich until September 1965, but the branch remained open for the works until they closed in 1983. The modern Horwich Parkway station is, as its name implies, some distance from the town centre.

❺ LONGRIDGE

The Longridge branch started life in 1840 as a horse-drawn quarry line to Preston. Later, there were various plans to incorporate it into ambitious schemes to link the Lancashire coast to Leeds – none of which came to fruition. By 1848 the line from Longridge to Preston had been rebuilt as a conventional branch line. This continued to carry passengers until 1930, though it remained open until 1957 to serve the short line from Grimsargh to Whittingham Hospital.

❹ ROYTON

In 1864 the Lancashire & Yorkshire Railway opened a branch just over a mile long to serve the cotton town of Royton. It was built to double-track standards, though Royton station was a simple structure. It had only one platform, but that was long enough to handle excursion trains. Famously, in February 1961, a DMU ran out of control as it approached the station and went through the buffers onto the street, wrecking several houses. The branch was busy until closure in 1966 but, unusually, freight ended before passenger carrying, in 1964. Houses now stand on the station site.

❻ FLEETWOOD

The railway reached Fleetwood in 1840, the end of a long branch line from Preston. Later, the line to Blackpool effectively made Fleetwood the terminus of a shorter branch from Poulton-le-Fylde, and this remained the case until 1966, when Fleetwood station was closed. The shortened branch continued to operate until 1970, when the closure of the docks ended most traffic, apart from that serving the ICI chemical works at Burnt Naze, which continued until 1999. Today, the branch line to Fleetwood is a candidate for reopening.

⑧ GLASSON DOCK

Glasson Dock opened in 1787 on the estuary of the river Lune, and a branch from the Lancaster Canal was connected to it in about 1825. In 1883 the LNWR's branch line from Lancaster was opened, and this remained in use as a freight line until 1964. Passenger traffic, always limited, had ended in 1930. The trackbed remains as a footpath and cycleway, complete with bridges, including an iron one over the river Conder, and a station.

⑩ LAKESIDE

The Furness Railway, always keen to develop tourist business, opened a branch from Ulverston to Lakeside, at the southern end of Windermere, in 1869. From the start, trains connected with boats on Windermere and the branch was popular until the early 1960s. Closure to passengers came in 1965, and to freight two years later. Plans to reopen the whole branch as a heritage line were unsuccessful, but in 1973 the preserved Lakeside & Haverthwaite Railway was launched on the upper section.

OPEN & PRESERVED LINES

⑨ MORECAMBE & HEYSHAM

The development of Morecambe, initially for freight and later for tourism, started in the 1860s. The LNWR and the Midland Railway were both involved, opening rival routes, and it was not long before long-distance trains were serving the town. In 1904 the Midland opened Heysham Harbour, with its own branch connection from Morecambe. Nowadays, one branch from Lancaster serves both Morecambe and Heysham.

△ Sections of the Coniston branch (*see also* page 158) seem really lost, with the trackbed overgrown and hidden in woods.

Branchline stations

⬆ Horderley, on the Bishop's Castle Railway in Shropshire, represented the branchline station at its most basic. It opened in the 1860s.

⬆ Stainland & Holywell Green station, in Yorkshire, was opened in 1875, a typical example of a well-built and substantial branchline terminus.

⬆ Another basic station was Waddesdon Road, on the Brill Tramway in Buckinghamshire. A siding served the Rothschild's great house nearby.

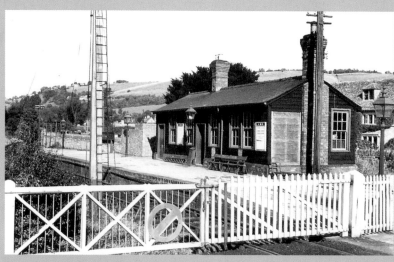

⬆ Woodchester, on the Nailsworth branch, Gloucestershire, opened in 1867. Though simple, the station building was well proportioned and decorative.

⬆ Richmond, in Yorkshire, boasted one of Britain's grandest branchline termini. Opened in 1847 and designed by GT Andrews, it survives as a leisure centre.

At Reedness Junction station, Yorkshire, in the early 1970s, a shed stands on the trackbed of the Fockerby branch where it diverged off the line to Haxey.

Lossiemouth, Elginshire (now Moray), was a handsome branchline terminus, built in the 1850s from local stone in a classical style.

The Fort Augustus branch, Inverness-shire, was built in a grand manner. This is Gairlochy, a local halt, looking more like a mainline station.

MAP 15

YORKSHIRE

BRANCH LINES

Closed branch lines

Closed passenger lines

Open passenger lines

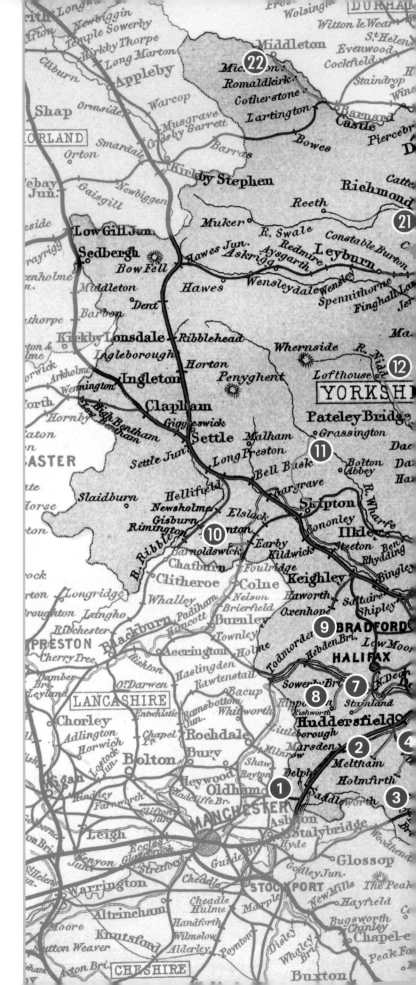

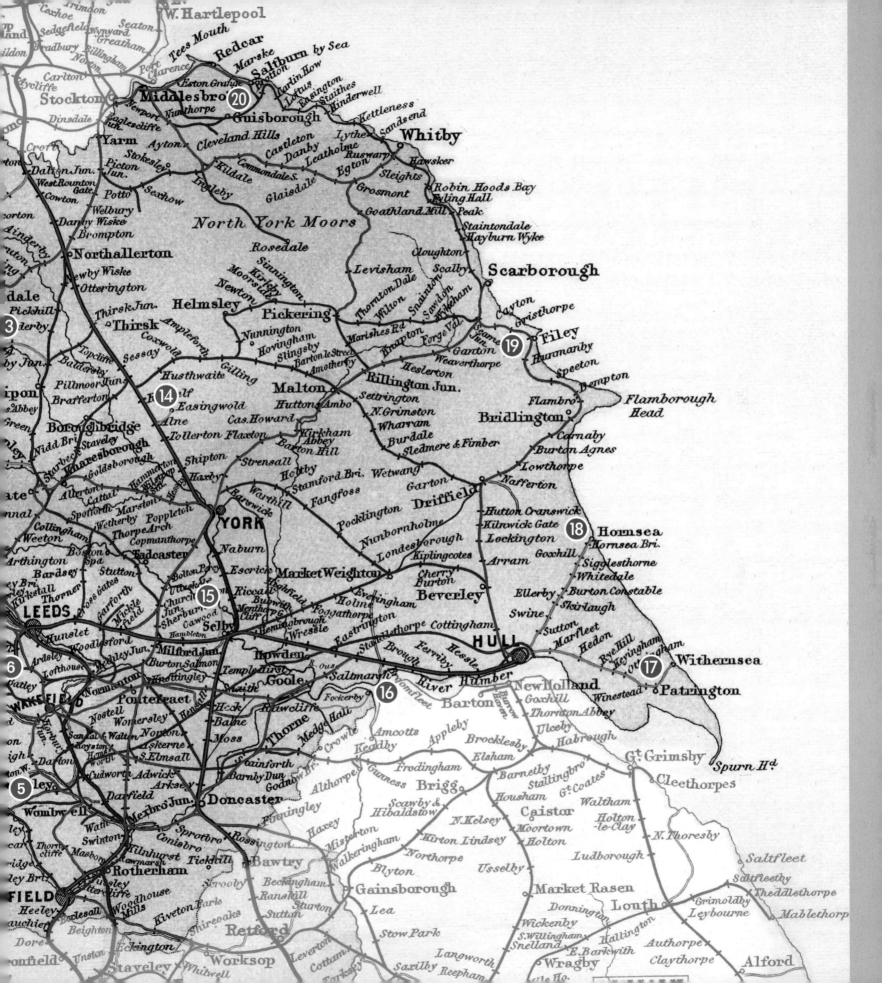

MAP 15

⑪ GRASSINGTON

A sequence of railway schemes from the 1840s to the 1880s nearly brought trains to Grassington, mainly as part of grand plans to link Liverpool and Manchester with Newcastle. The lure of mineral traffic was also an important factor. In the event, nothing happened until 1897, when the Yorkshire Dales Railway started to build a line from Embsay Junction, near Skipton, to Darlington. In 1902 this was opened as far as Grassington, but it never went any further, so this Yorkshire Dales market town became the terminus of a rural branch. The Midland Railway was the operator, but the branch remained independently owned until 1923. Passenger traffic ended in 1930, just before the rise in popularity of both the Yorkshire Dales and country walking. Had the branch survived a few more years, it might have been a different story. Freight lived on until 1969, and then the branch was cut back to Swinden, where a large quarry still keeps the remainder of the line open. The section southwards from here to Skipton is therefore easy to explore, but much of the route of the closed part can also be traced thanks to surviving cuttings and bridges.

△ This fancy card was sent from Manchester to Oldham in 1912, confirming the day for a forthcoming visit. At this time, cards were often used simply to communicate information, and the image may have had no relevance to the message.

▷ In 1962 Grassington & Threshfield, to use its full title, had not seen regular passengers for over 30 years, yet everything was still in place at the station, if a bit overgrown. Here, an old LMS Class 4F runs round the long excursion special it has brought in.

△ Only a small boy and a railwayman wait to greet the excursion special drawing slowly into Grassington station. The Midland Railway's iron trespass notice adds period interest.

◁ Looking south, Swinden quarry and the active railway can be seen in the distance. In the centre, the trackbed of the closed section of the line crosses the marshy land on a low embankment, now the province of geese and sheep. The route can be followed northwards from here, but Grassington station has gone.

⑫ PATELEY BRIDGE

In 1862 the North Eastern Railway opened a 14-mile branch from Ripley Junction, on the Harrogate-to-Ripon line, to Pateley Bridge. The route followed the valley of the river Nidd and there were five intermediate stations. Later, in 1907, the Nidd Valley Light Railway added an extra 6 miles, to Lofthouse-in-Nidderdale. This further extension was owned and operated by Bradford Corporation, to carry men and materials to build and maintain reservoirs at Scar House and Angram. This upper section, famously wild and remote, closed in 1936, but trains continued to carry passengers to and from Pateley Bridge until 1951. Freight traffic ceased in 1964. When it was opened, the branch made a hitherto little-known part of the Dales accessible and, while the main aim was the carriage of minerals and agricultural produce, the possibilities of tourism were soon realized. Indeed, the NER, and later the LNER, actively promoted excursions to a region known as Little Switzerland. Today, most of the very attractive route along the Nidd valley can be followed, and much of the trackbed survives, though it is not always accessible, as do bridges and some stations.

▽This 1960s postcard gives a sense of the landscape of the Nidd valley, and the setting of Pateley Bridge. The railway ran along the valley across the centre of the card.

▷The trackbed of the Nidd Valley Light Railway follows a spectacular route above Pateley Bridge, and much of it can be followed through the glorious landscape. Here, the line ran right beside Gowthwaite reservoir.

△Stone-built Pateley Bridge station still stands, complete with stepped gables and side wings. Now, with no obvious railway connection, it is a private house, as is Hampsthwaite's station.

▷In April 1950 a train waits at Pateley Bridge station, ready to set off for Harrogate. A year later passenger services ceased on the branch. The line used to continue up the Nidd valley, to the left of the photograph.

MAP 15

⑭ EASINGWOLD

The story of the Easingwold Railway is, as so often with small companies, the achievement of local enterprise. In the 1880s this quiet market town, with fewer than 2,000 inhabitants, decided it wanted a railway and set about getting one. The money was quickly raised, and the short branch to link the town to the North Eastern Railway's main line at Alne opened in 1891. It was, from the start, determinedly independent. The railway owned its own locomotives, two tank engines, and its own rolling stock, and maintained this independence throughout its life. It never became part of the NER, the LNER or even British Railways. Like most small branch lines, the Easingwold Railway survived largely by looking after the local freight traffic, and this kept it going until December 1957, passenger carrying having ended in 1948. Today, there is no station at Alne and much of the lightly engineered branch has gone back into the fields. However, the low embankment that carried the line as it approached Easingwold is still to be seen, along with the former station hotel.

◁ By the late 1950s the railway was in a poor state, with overgrown and uneven track and broken windows in the engine shed. Here, shortly before the line's closure, the resident locomotive, an old NER Class J72 from about 1900, waits for its day's duties. This locomotive hauled the final train on 27 December 1957.

△This closure notice for the Easingwold Railway was photographed at Alne station on 21 December 1957, a week before the closure took place.

△Posted in July 1908, this card depicts the centre of Easingwold, with plenty of detail. It was sent to Driffield from Loftus by two girls who had returned from holiday: 'It is wretched here now and we have started hay making.'

◁Nothing remains of Easingwold station which, judging by photographs, was an unremarkable timber building. Much more impressive is this former station hotel, dated 1892, whose style and use of detail reflect the sense of pride aroused in the town by the opening of the railway. The adjacent buildings are former railway offices. The station was situated to the right of the hotel, where the trees now are.

㉑ RICHMOND

By the time the branch to Richmond from Eryholme opened in 1846, it had had three owners, but by 1857 it had settled into the expanding North Eastern Railway network. The branch was built generously, with some fine buildings. Most notable is Richmond's Gothic-style station, perhaps Britain's best branchline terminus, designed by GT Andrews, architect of York station. The opening of the line to Catterick Camp greatly increased traffic and helped to keep it busy until the 1960s. Passenger services on the branch ceased in 1969, freight as far as Catterick Bridge a year later. Much of the 9-mile route can be followed and explored. Stations and other structures survive, including, on the Catterick Camp line, the bridge over the Swale.

△The scale and quality of Richmond's station can be seen in this photograph from about 1900. It is now a cultural centre and café.

◁The architectural and historical nature of Richmond is shown in this card, posted in June 1905 from the town to Massachusetts, USA.

△The stations and railway buildings on the Richmond branch were well designed and decorative, and some of the intermediate stations live on as private houses. This is a surviving platform and the trackbed at Scorton. The station house is to the left. Much of the trackbed survives in the open landscape.

▷By 1968 Richmond station, and the line itself, were in a poor state, but services continued to operate for another year. Here, a DMU waits to depart for Darlington.

MAP 15

㉒ MIDDLETON-IN-TEESDALE

Stone quarries were the driving force for the Tees Valley Railway, whose branch from Barnard Castle to Middleton-in-Teesdale opened in 1868. It was operated from the start by the North Eastern Railway, which took control in 1882. There were three intermediate stations along the 8-mile line. The route along the Tees valley was dramatic and made accessible a wild and remote region, so when the stone traffic began to diminish, tourism and the new enthusiasm for walking helped to keep the branch alive. Passenger services continued until 1964, and freight ended a few months later. Today, much of the route is an official footpath, the Tees Valley Way, a walk through an exciting landscape made more interesting by surviving railway structures. These include bridges, the Lune viaduct and stations that are now private houses. There is car parking at Mickleton station.

△▽The Tees Valley Way is enlivened by structures built in chunky limestone. The highlight is the five-arch viaduct that carried the line high above the Lune valley.

△This 1960s multiview card shows some of the sights of Middleton-in-Teesdale and the surrounding area, notably the waterfall, that helped to keep the railway alive.

△By 1963 the branch was listed for closure, prompting visits by enthusiasts' specials such as this North Eastern Railtour organized by the RCTS (Railway Correspondence & Travel Society) and the SLS (Stephenson Locomotive Society). The locomotive, an LMS Class 4MT, is running round its train.

△This 1930s photograph shows Middleton in its Dales setting. It also illustrates the importance of the stone trade, with wagons from the GWR, SR and LMS waiting to be loaded from a narrow-gauge quarry line.

② MELTHAM

Built by the Lancashire & Yorkshire Railway, the short branch from Lockwood to Meltham opened fully in 1869, with passenger services following nearly a year after the start of freight traffic. The line was heavily engineered and required three tunnels in as many miles. Freight was always important, for local needs as well as for the Meltham brickworks and, later, the David Brown tractor factory. Passenger services were essentially local, though there was some tourist traffic to visit sights such as Folly Dolly Falls, which could be reached from a special halt on the branch. Passenger services ended in 1949, but freight continued until 1965. Part of the route is now a footpath, but Meltham station has gone.

△In this 1910 photograph Meltham station looks very tidy, if rather empty, with the two people present ignoring the train. Posters encourage travel to exciting places.

▷This early 20th-century postcard, bought at the time as a souvenir and not used, gives a good view of Folly Dolly Falls. This was a popular tourist spot, made easily accessible by the railway.

◁Meltham station survived for some years, though in a derelict state. Surprisingly, when this photograph was taken the station clock was still hanging on the wall.

⑩ BARNOLDSWICK

One of Britain's shorter branches was opened in 1871 from Earby, on the Skipton-to-Colne line, to Barnoldswick. The line, under 2 miles long, was built by the independent Barnoldswick Railway but was operated by the Midland Railway, which took over in 1899. A planned extension to Gisburn, near Hellifield, would have made it a through route, but this never happened. At its peak, the branch had 24 services a day, with trains running almost as a shuttle, but by the 1950s this was greatly reduced and in the end there were only a couple each day, timed to take children to and from school in Skipton. Passenger services came to an end in September 1965, and freight, which had mostly been coal and other local traffic, followed a few months later. Diesel railcars were tried out on the branch, but steam remained until the end. Barnoldswick, the only station on the branch, and its goods yard have since disappeared under a supermarket, but the stationmaster's house survives. There never was a signal box.

▷Posted in 1910 from Barnoldswick, this card shows town views, including the station. Sent by Peter to his mother, he says he is very well but 'weather awful, hay time'.

▷Excursions were popular on the branch and this photograph from about 1910 shows the platform at Barnoldswick packed with people, mostly family groups with plenty of small children, all in their Sunday best, watching the arrival of their train.

MAP 15

❸ HOLMFIRTH

Another short branch built by the Lancashire & Yorkshire Railway was the line to Holmfirth, which ran from Brockholes, on the Huddersfield-to-Penistone main line. The branch opened early, in 1850, with one intermediate station at Thongsbridge. The main engineering challenge was the Mytholmbridge viaduct, originally constructed from timber trestles but replaced in 1867 by a thirteen-arch stone structure. Traffic was largely local, though the town's regular floods brought visitors curious to see the devastation. Coal and products from local woollen mills were the backbone of the freight business. Passenger services ended in 1959, freight in 1964. Much has gone since then, including the viaduct, which was demolished in 1976. Part of Holmfirth station survives.

△Holmfirth has long been famous as the home of Bamforth postcards, particularly its comic cards from the Edwardian era. This typical example has a matching message on the back from the same era: 'It is not very often you see a woman going to get the horn, what say you kid?'

◁An early 20th-century view of Holmfirth station reveals the railway's, and the town's, dramatic setting. The buildings are substantial, and well built from local stone. As usual, everyone is watching the photographer and posing – except the horse. Today, nothing remains but the Gothic-style station house at the end of the platform, whose architecture reflects the branch's early construction date.

❹ KIRKBURTON

In the 1860s there were many battles between rival railway companies over the highly profitable coal trade. The Kirkburton branch started as a scheme by the LNWR to build a line to access the coal mines around Barnsley, an area dominated by the Lancashire & Yorkshire Railway. Work started at Deighton, near Huddersfield, in 1865, on a heavily engineered route that included the substantial Rowley viaduct. However, it all ground to a halt at Kirkburton, and the result was an unplanned branch line with three intermediate stations. For much of its life, the branch was primarily a freight line, and passenger services finished early, in 1930. Freight traffic continued for another 35 years. Today, plenty survives, including the viaduct and a number of stone-built bridges along the route.

△The design of Kirkburton's simple timber station, seen here in about 1910, shows it was not planned as a terminus station, and the line was originally meant to continue beyond the buffers. A porter poses with a couple of suitcases on his trolley but there are no passengers, a not uncommon situation on a branch that was dominated by freight traffic.

▽Kirkburton's church dates back to the 11th century. This card, posted from the vicarage to Redditch in 1916, is all about Ada, the writer, and her need for a little grey hat to wear when carrying in the coal buckets.

⑤ CLAYTON WEST

A rare example of a branch line brought back to life, the Clayton West branch was built by the Lancashire & Yorkshire Railway from Shepley Junction on the Huddersfield-to-Sheffield main line, and opened in 1879. It was always single track but, like many other Yorkshire branches, it was built for double-track operation, resulting in generous stone bridges and other structures. The branch enjoyed a long and uneventful life, its main claim to fame being that it outlasted most other branch lines, not only in Yorkshire, but throughout Britain, with closure not coming until 1983. Collieries along the route had helped to keep it open. The track was then lifted, only to be replaced from 1991 by the Kirklees Light Railway, which has opened a 15in gauge, miniature heritage line along the length of the former branch, with stations either rebuilt or added.

▽Trains on the Clayton West branch ran through to Huddersfield and other destinations, via the Penistone line. Here is a typical branch train on the main line in the 1950s, headed by a familiar workhorse, an old LMS Class 4MT.

◁The Clayton West branch closed on 27 January 1983, and on that day people gathered at stations along the route to watch the last trains, operated by the then ubiquitous DMUs. The bridge at the intermediate station of Skelmanthorpe shows the scale to which the branch was built, planned as it was for double-track running.

⑯ FOCKERBY

One of Britain's many minor, rather obscure companies that was engendered by the passing of the Light Railways Act was the Axholme Joint Light Railway, formed in 1902 from two other small companies in the Goole area. The NER and the Lancashire & Yorkshire were involved, as the Axholme and its components offered links between the networks of those large companies. One of the lines completed by the Axholme was the short branch to Fockerby from Reedness Junction. This opened in August 1903, with two intermediate stations, Eastoft and Luddington. It was a very basic railway, with simple buildings and limited facilities. Passenger services ended almost 30 years after the opening of the branch, in 1933, while freight traffic continued until 1965.

◁This is Reedness Junction station, looking towards Goole. The Fockerby branch diverted to the right, just beyond the old lower quadrant signal. It is the early 1970s, shortly before the track was lifted.

▷A group of railway enthusiasts, touring the remote corners of the network in their Bedford Dormobile in the 1950s, visited Fockerby, where some freight traffic, presumably coal, was still just about active.

MAP 15

⑰ WITHERNSEA

In June 1854 the Hull & Holderness Railway opened its branch line to Withernsea. Over 17 miles long and with a large number of intermediate stations, the branch initially started from Hull's Victoria Docks station and continued thus until 1864. In 1860 the NER took over the running of the branch, and assumed full control two years later. Although the town's population in 1851 was just 109, the railway built its own hotel at Withernsea. In fact, tourism quickly developed and became a mainstay of the branch until passenger services ended in 1964. Freight traffic continued on the Hull section of the line until the early 1970s. Most of the trackbed survives, with parts used as a footpath. Withernsea station has gone, but all the intermediate stations live on as private homes.

▽In this 1950s view, Withernsea station seems a rather bleak spot. There are flowerbeds, but that part of the platform has been cut off by some benches, on which a mother and her children sit, looking lonely. The train for Hull waits, headed by a Class L1 locomotive.

◁As this 1960s multiview card suggests, Withernsea was a popular resort over a long period. The convalescent home, among the sights depicted, was once the railway hotel.

⑱ HORNSEA

The branches that served Hornsea and Withernsea followed similar stories. The Hull & Hornsea Railway branch was the second, opening in 1864, and in due course it was absorbed by the NER. The 13-mile line had a number of intermediate stations, and traffic developed as tourism expanded. The branch started from Hull's Wilmington Street station and originally ran to Hornsea Bridge, outside the town. However, it was later extended right to the beach, and the cost of doing this caused years of financial problems. Following the usual decline in the late 1950s, which the introduction of DMUs did not halt, the branch was closed to passengers on 19 October 1964, the same day the Withernsea branch closed. Freight continued to Hornsea Bridge for just over six months. Much of the route survives as part of the Trans Pennine Trail, and a number of intermediate stations are now private houses, some still with platforms. The most important survival is Hornsea station and house, now converted into flats. This handsome classical structure, with its grand portico and elegant arcaded windows, was designed by Rawlins Gould.

HORNSEA POTTERY

◁The Hornsea Pottery, founded in 1949, brought many visitors to the town. This 1960s card shows the tableware, and hairstyles, of that era. The pottery's golden age was probably the 1950s and 1960s, when visitors came by train.

▽As well as fine buildings, Hornsea station boasted a train shed, open on one side. Here, in August 1949, a holiday relief train from Hull has arrived at the excursion platform, headed by a former NER tank. The train shed has since gone.

① DELPH

The Delph branch, known as the Delph Donkey, was opened by the LNWR in 1849. It was usually served by trains from Oldham, which left the main line at Delph Junction, near Dobcross. Freight was important, and the line was used for holiday specials for local factory workers. Passenger services ended in 1955, freight in 1963.

⑥ BIRSTALL

Opened in 1852 by the LNWR, the Batley-to-Birstall branch was, after plans to continue the line to Bradford had been abandoned, primarily a freight line. Passengers were carried, particularly after the opening of Carlinghow station in 1872, but this ended in 1916. Freight continued until 1962. Trackbed and bridges remain.

⑦ STAINLAND

The short Stainland branch, another Lancashire & Yorkshire line, was opened in 1875 primarily to serve the local textile mills. The junction station was Greetland, on the Calder Valley line, but services usually operated through to Halifax. Although there were sixteen trains a day, competition from trams caused a decline, and passenger services ended in 1929. Freight continued until 1959.

⑧ RISHWORTH

The Lancashire & Yorkshire Railway's branch from Sowerby Bridge to Rishworth was opened in stages from 1878 to 1881. A planned extension to Littleborough, on the Calder Valley line, was abandoned. The branch was steeply graded and the route included one tunnel and three intermediate stations. Passenger services ended in 1929, freight in 1958. Footpaths follow parts of the route.

⑬ MASHAM

After various false starts, the NER opened a branch from Melmerby, on the Harrogate-to-Northallerton line, to Masham in 1875. Little used from the start, the branch had one intermediate station on its 8-mile route. When the LNER took over, it soon closed it to passengers, in 1931, but freight continued until 1963.

⑮ CAWOOD

Authorized in 1896, the Cawood, Wistow & Selby Light Railway completed its short branch in 1898. The route ran across level farmland, and the company had one locomotive and its own station outside Selby. In 1900 the NER took control, introducing through running to Selby, and railcars. Passenger services ended in 1929, freight in 1960. Some of the trackbed remains.

⑲ FILEY HOLIDAY CAMP

In May 1947 a short branch line was opened by the LNER to serve Butlin's Filey holiday camp. It had four long, island platforms designed to handle holiday specials from all over the country. Traffic declined as more holidaymakers arrived by car, and the branch closed in July 1977. All the platforms survive.

OPEN & PRESERVED LINES

⑨ KEIGHLEY & WORTH VALLEY

Backed by local support and finance, the Keighley & Worth Valley Railway opened its branch to Oxenhope in 1867. The Midland Railway operated it, taking control in 1881. As well as the freight generated by local mills, the branch also attracted visitors interested in the Brontës. After the usual period of decline, the branch closed in 1962, only to be taken over and reopened in 1968 as a heritage railway. The railway is one of only two complete branches in Britain run as heritage lines.

⑳ SALTBURN

Saltburn-by-the-Sea is a typical Victorian resort consciously created by the railways. Now the terminus of a modern line from Darlington and Middlesbrough, but always at the end of its own short branch, Saltburn has a splendid 1862 station, fronted by a fine brick porte cochère designed in a classical style by William Peachey. Adjacent, and connected to the station, is the former Zetland Hotel, developed at the same time.

Modern branches — as they were

↑On a wet day in the 1950s a train formed of two GWR railcars arrives in Windsor & Eton Central, in Berkshire, from Slough.

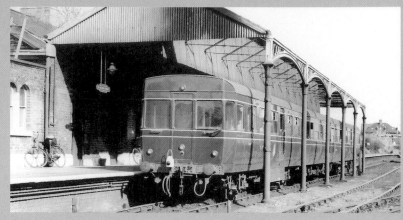

↑St Albans Abbey, Hertfordshire, is now a very minimal station, hardly worthy of the name. It was once much grander, as this 1950s photograph shows.

↑Until its recent rebuilding, Henley-on-Thames, Oxfordshire, seen here in the 1960s, was a classic branchline terminus with a substantial train shed.

↑In 1975 a single-car DMU runs along the short branch to Stourbridge Town, Worcestershire. Today, it is operated by Parry People Movers.

↑A single passenger leaves a Central Line tube train at Blake Hall, Essex, in 1981. The Epping-to-Ongar line, closed in 1994, is now a heritage railway.

↑A three-carriage DMU waits at Southminster, Essex, in September 1969. The branch is now part of Liverpool Street's electrified suburban network.

↑In 1976 a DMU waits at Braintree, Essex, a domestic-style station typical of the Great Eastern Railway. Since then, the line has been electrified.

MAP 16

CUMBERLAND, WESTMORLAND & COUNTY DURHAM

BRANCH LINES

❶ **Windermere**
Westmorland (page 182)

❷ **Ravenglass & Eskdale**
Cumberland (page 182)

❸ **Silloth**
Cumberland (page 180)

❹ **Port Carlisle**
Cumberland (page 182)

❺ **Brampton Town**
Cumberland (page 182)

❻ **Alston**
Cumberland (page 181)
See also **Map 17** (pages 184–5)

❼ **Wearhead**
County Durham (page 181)

❽ **Coxhoe**
County Durham (page 182)

❾ **Marsden**
County Durham (page 182)

This 1950s view shows Rothbury's tidy terminus with its turntable and engine shed.

Closed branch lines

Closed passenger lines

Open passenger lines

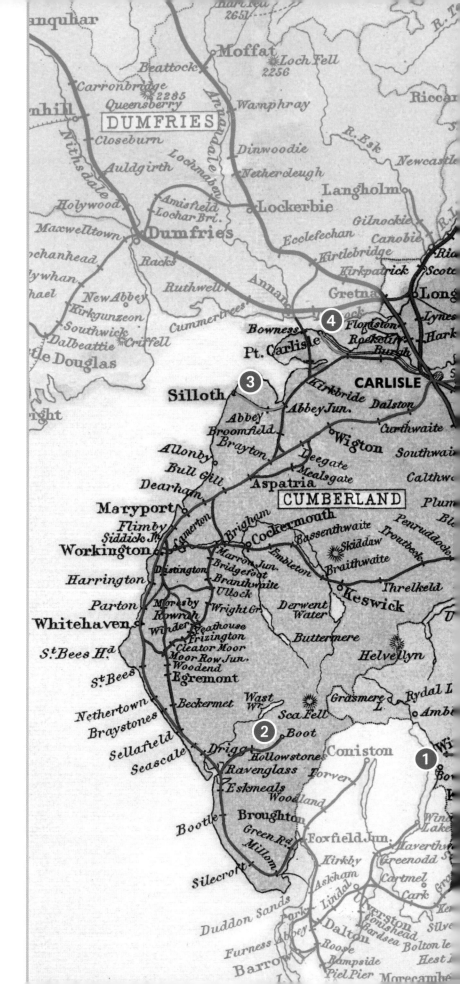

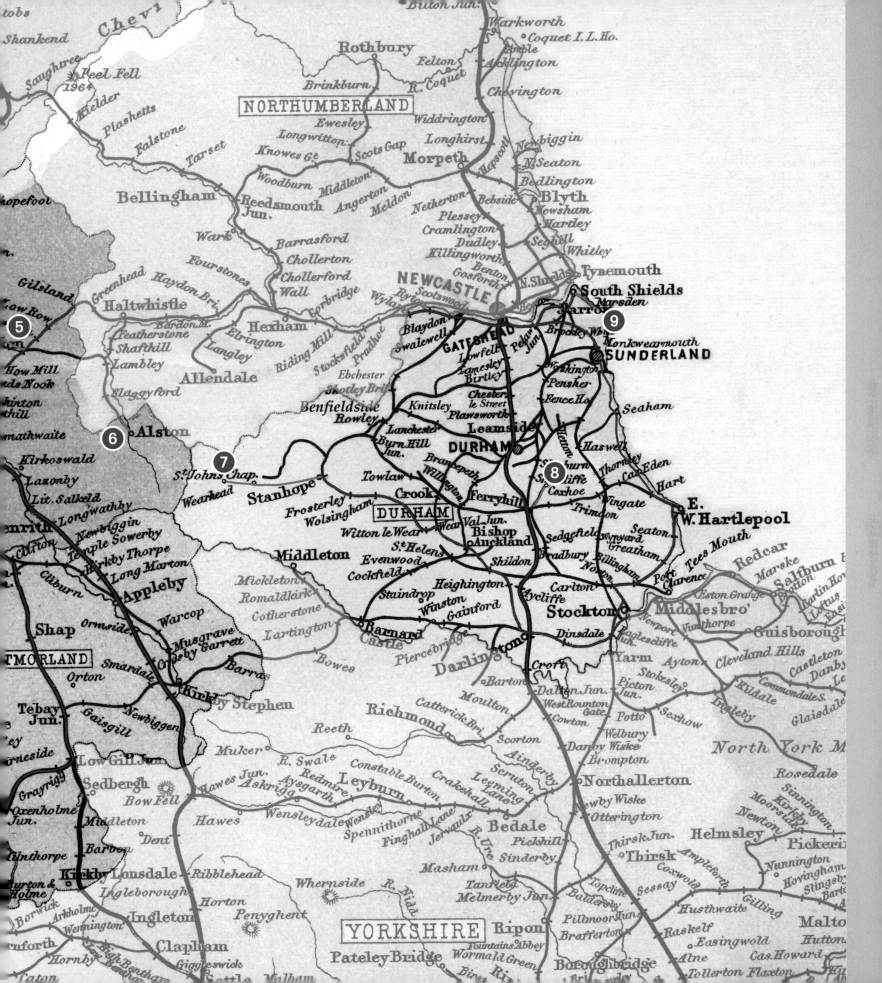

MAP 16

❸ SILLOTH

In 1854 the Port Carlisle Dock & Railway completed its line from Carlisle to the Solway Firth, building the railway along a route originally planned for a canal. Two years later the company opened its branch to Silloth. Later developments included a line south towards Aspatria and another northwards to cross the Firth to Annan on a spectacular 2-mile viaduct. This effectively put Silloth at the end of a much shorter branch, from Abbey Town. The Silloth branch was built with high expectations, based on the harbour, but these were not fulfilled and in due course the North British Railway took control. Business improved, from the docks and local industries and, especially, from tourists drawn to the town, the Solway landscape, its beaches and its golf courses. This pattern continued until the 1950s, when declining passenger numbers led British Railways to introduce diesel railcars in November 1954, the first time these had been used on a branch line. In 1964 the branch and much of the local network closed. Now, there is little evidence of its existence.

▽ Posted from Silloth in July 1931, this card gives a good sense of the town and its attractive grid of streets. The sender, writing to her daughter in Whitehaven, was 'having a nice time with Jack & May & Dad'.

▽ Today, very little is left of Silloth station, though others along the route survive as private houses. Near the docks, an unusual reminder of the railway's presence is the remains of a fence made from weathered sleepers.

△ Before it closed, the Silloth branch was visited by a number of enthusiasts' specials. This, the Solway Ranger Railtour organized by the RCTS in June 1964, was headed by a famous preserved locomotive, the Great North of Scotland's Class F of 1920, No. 49, 'Gordon Highlander'.

▷ The Silloth branch was lightly engineered, and much of its route across the low-lying landscape has disappeared, making it hard to explore today. Here, a farmer's accommodation bridge survives, isolated in the fields with nothing to be seen to right or left, many years after the trackbed was ploughed up.

⑥ ALSTON

The Newcastle & Carlisle Railway, with its eye on lead and coal mines in the area, planned to build a branch from Haltwhistle to Nenthead, south of Alston, in the 1840s. In the event the branch, which went only as far as Alston, did not open until 1852, largely owing to the demanding nature of the terrain and the expensive engineering involved. Famous for its bridges and the grand Lambley viaduct, the branch also had impressive stations, designed by Benjamin Green. Scheduled for closure in the 1960s, the branch managed to live on until 1976, mainly because during bad winters the railway was often the only means of access to Alston, there being no all-weather road until that date. The poor state of Lambley viaduct (now fully restored) was also a factor in the decision to close the line. In 1983 the South Tynedale Railway reopened the section from Alston to Lintley Halt as a narrow-gauge heritage railway. This has since been extended, and there are plans to take the line to Slaggyford.

△In the 1960s, an old LNER Class J39 locomotive, No. 64812, a Gresley design from the 1920s, rests at Alston, having hauled a heavy enthusiasts' special up the branch. The engine shed and covered train shed were demolished in the 1960s, but the fine station building remains.

◁This Edwardian card, bought as a souvenir and never used, shows the striking elegance of Lambley viaduct and the rugged nature of the landscape the railway had to cross.

⑦ WEARHEAD

The story of the branch from Bishop Auckland to Wearhead is complicated, the line having been built in stages by several companies between 1847 and 1895. The Wear Valley Railway, the Frosterley & Stanhope Railway and the NER were involved. Minerals were the inspiration, and passenger services were always second to freight traffic, though they survived until 1965 on the southern section. The northern section, from Eastgate to Wearhead, was abandoned, but freight continued to run over the rest of the branch until 1993, serving a cement works near Eastgate. When this section finally closed, the track and infrastructure remained in place, and plans were introduced to reopen the branch as a heritage line, the Weardale Railway. After a difficult start, trains are now running again on the 18-mile section from Eastgate to Bishop Auckland, where a connection with the national network has been re-established, allowing charter specials and other excursion trains to run directly through to the branch. While primarily a heritage line, the Weardale Railway is keen to bring regular passenger services back to the branch and is also working with modern freight operators to use the line for coal and stone traffic.

△Tourism was always important, as the branch served relatively inaccessible regions. This Edwardian card reflects that, showing views of Stanhope, a popular place on the route.

△In the early 1950s, a train pulls into Wearhead station on what seems a quiet summer day, the end of the line for passengers from Darlington and Bishop Auckland. Passenger services to Wearhead ended in 1953, and since then much of the line west of Eastgate has disappeared. Sections can be explored, however, and the main buildings of Wearhead station survive as a private house, complete with the station clock.

MAP 16

④ PORT CARLISLE

The line to Port Carlisle from Carlisle opened in 1854 to serve the harbour, following the route of a former canal. Two years later, the line to Silloth opened, rendering Port Carlisle obsolete. From 1856 to 1914 the remaining short section to Port Carlisle was operated by a horse-drawn tram. This was replaced by a steam railmotor, but services were limited and the branch closed in 1932. Today, the route can be followed and embankments survive, along with a section by the sea that leads to the derelict Port Carlisle harbour.

⑤ BRAMPTON TOWN

This branch started in 1775 as the Earl of Carlisle's waggonway, and from the 1830s until 1881 a horse-drawn passenger service operated between Brampton (later called Brampton Town) and the Newcastle & Carlisle's Brampton Junction station, a mile out of the town. In 1913 the NER took over, updated the line and ran regular passenger services until 1923. Most of the route is a public footpath. Brampton Junction is now called Brampton (Cumbria).

⑧ COXHOE

The Clarence Railway was set up in 1828 to compete with the Stockton & Darlington. This was the earliest example of competition between railway companies. By 1834 the railway had reached Ferryhill, but plans to extend the line to Sherburn ended at Coxhoe, resulting in a short branch line. In 1851 the Clarence's network was taken over by the West Hartlepool Harbour & Railway and in 1865 it became part of the NER. Passengers were carried on the Coxhoe branch, but the main traffic was coal, stone and pottery products.

⑨ MARSDEN

The branch from South Shields to Marsden was built in 1879 to serve Whitburn colliery and local stone quarries, and the first station was just for the miners. In 1926 Marsden station was built and a full passenger service started. This was run by the Harton Coal Company, which had taken over the Whitburn interests. While the carriage of miners remained the primary concern, passenger services, by then under the Coal Board, ran until 1953.

OPEN & PRESERVED LINES

① WINDERMERE

The first branch line to penetrate the Lake District was opened by the Kendal & Windermere Railway in 1847. After some difficulties, the branch was taken over by the Lancaster & Carlisle Railway in 1858, before becoming part of the LNWR in 1879. By that time, the railway had turned Windermere into a popular resort, with through trains from London and other cities. Since then, passenger services have continued to operate between Oxenholme, on the main line, and Windermere. This makes it one of the oldest original and traditional branch lines still in use.

② RAVENGLASS & ESKDALE

Opened in 1875 as a 3ft gauge line, the original Ravenglass & Eskdale Railway was built to serve haematite mines near Boot. Passengers were carried from 1876. The railway closed in 1913 after financial problems. Rebuilt as a 15in gauge miniature line by Bassett-Lowke and others, the railway reopened from 1917, carrying passengers as well as granite from local quarries. During the 1920s the line became popular with visitors. Sold in 1960, the railway faced an uncertain future until a preservation society took control, and now the Ravenglass & Eskdale is a major heritage railway.

Branchline freight

HAY or STRAW
LONDON & NORTH EASTERN RAILWAY.

Zt. 5/10 50,000 10/33 — O. 6027

Date

From

TO _____ Section _____ Coy.

VIA

Sender _____ No. of Trusses _____
Consignee _____
Owner and No. of Wagon _____ Total Sheets _____
Whether carriage "Paid" or "to Pay"

URGENT
FOR IMMEDIATE DELIVERY
Via G.W. Ry.

(4796)

20,000—N.B./4—1939 (S) S.

L.N.E.R.
O. 6029
____ 19

From

POTATOES

TO _____

_____ RLY. _____ SECN.

VIA _____

Owner and No. of Wagon

3

Sheets in or on Wagon

No. of bags _____

Whether carriage " Paid " or " To Pay "

Consignee _____

GREAT WESTERN RAILWAY.
(1135)

EGGS
WITH CARE

400 Pads, 100 lvs.—N.B. 4 41—1937-8. (8) S.

L.N.E.R.
O. 6322

SHUNT
WITH
CARE

LONDON & NORTH EASTERN RAILWAY.

Zt. 6082—180,000—9/36.

LIVE STOCK LABEL P. 3053

LIVE STOCK

GREAT WESTERN RAILWAY.
(5041 k)

MILK
FROM

TO
BOW (L.M.S.)
VIA KENSINGTON

Date _____ No. of Tank _____ Train _____

6,000 BM. 884 4/47.

BRITISH TRANSPORT COMMISSION
BRITISH RAILWAYS

B.R. 21239

GREEN PEAS

LIMESTONE
TO
Melting Shop

MIDLAND RAILWAY. G F 161
189
CATTLE.

From

To _____ Railway,

Route

Owner and No. of Truck }

Consignee

Charges to Pay £ s. d.
Charges Paid £ s. d.

E.R.O. 33899

TRAFFIC IS WAITING FOR THESE WAGONS
UNLOAD IMMEDIATELY PLEASE

BRITISH TRANSPORT COMMISSION
BRITISH RAILWAYS

USE BLOCK LETTERS

B.R. 21225/14
____ 19____

From

SUGAR BEET

To NETHERFIELD & COLWICK
(Nottingham Colwick Estates Ltd., Rly. Sidings)
G.N. Section

Via _____

Letter Wagon | Number | **2** | Contract No.

Sender's Name _____

Consignee **BRITISH SUGAR CORPORATION**

MAP 17

NORTHUMBERLAND

BRANCH LINES

After closure, Darras Hall station had various lives before being demolished.

Closed branch lines

Closed passenger lines

Open passenger lines

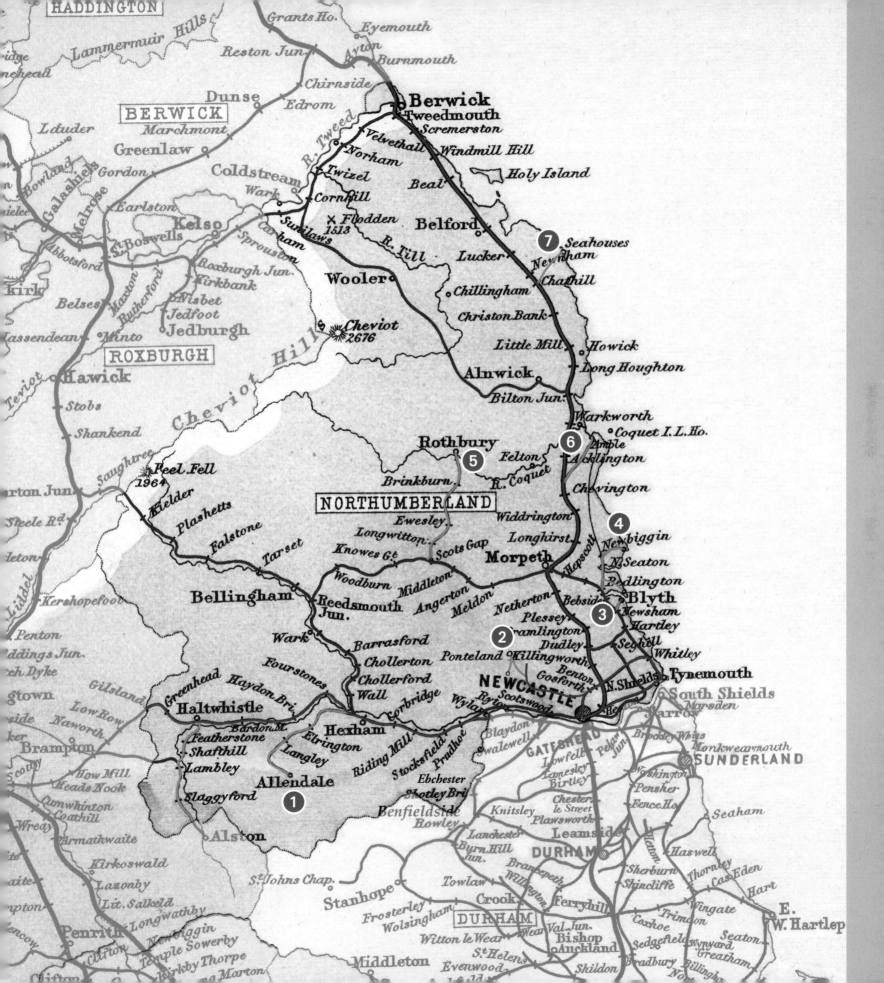

MAP 17

① ALLENDALE

In 1869 the Hexham & Allendale Railway opened its 12-mile branch line. It was expensive and difficult to build, climbing 700ft through tough terrain from Border Counties Junction, near Hexham, on the Newcastle-to-Carlisle main line. The line was constructed to carry lead ore, with the intention of going beyond Allendale to Allenheads, where the mines were. In fact, the branch stopped a mile short of Allendale, near Catton. Until 1898 the terminus station was known as Catton Road. There were three intermediate stations. The lead traffic was below expectations, so the Hexham & Allendale sold out to the NER in 1876. From then on, an adequate passenger service was maintained and revenues were helped by local freight, mostly agricultural. However, by the late 1920s bus competition was increasing, ticket sales from the small communities served by the railway were falling, and the LNER, having taken over in 1923, realized closure was the only option. Passenger traffic ended in 1930, but freight kept the branch open until 1950. Considering how long it has been closed, the Allendale branch is in a remarkable state of repair. Most of the route can be traced, though it is not always accessible, and the trackbed is often visible in the open landscape. Embankments, cuttings and bridges generously built from local stone, and several stations that are now private houses, can be seen. Allendale station is in a caravan park.

△Posted in March 1905, this card commemorates the Allendale wolf, which escaped from a private zoo in December 1904 and caused mayhem to local sheep before being killed by a Midland Railway express.

▷Reminiscent of sections of Hadrian's Wall, these stone abutments supported an iron bridge over a steep track on the approach to Catton. The route across the fields alternates between embankment and cutting.

△This 1930s photograph shows Allendale station after passenger traffic had ended. Apart from the LNER lorry on the platform, there is not much evidence of freight activity either.

△Stations were sold off after closure and, as this card indicates, by the early 1950s Staward had become a holiday cottage.

△All the stations on the line survive, with their platforms. They are built to a pattern, but this one, Elrington, is end-on to the track, looking along the embankment that took the line across the fields. This big station was built to serve a small cluster of houses and farms, typical of the branch's remote route.

➎ ROTHBURY

The Northumberland Central Railway was authorized in 1863 to build a line from Scotsgap, on the Wansbeck Railway, to Ford on the Berwick-to-Kelso line, with a short branch to Cornhill. In 1870 it was opened as far as Rothbury but went no further, creating in the process a long rural branch. Two years later, this was taken over by the NER. Eventually the railway did benefit Rothbury, turning the remote market town into a minor resort offering golf, fishing and other facilities, including a large and impressive railway hotel. As ever, local freight traffic helped to keep the branch alive. A dramatic event in the history of the branch was the derailment of a train near Longwitton in July 1875, resulting in three deaths and 25 people injured, a rare event for a rural railway. The branch survived the LNER era, though suffering increasingly from road competition. British Railways, faced with irreversible decline, closed it to passengers in 1952. Freight lasted another eleven years, and there were occasional visits from enthusiasts' specials. Much of the trackbed can still be found, as well as bridges and stations, and the branch's often dramatic route across the landscape can be enjoyed.

△Among the individual relics of the railway are some fence posts that have been made from old rails banded together.

△This Edwardian card depicts Cragside, the famous house designed by R Norman Shaw for Lord Armstrong from 1863. Visitors would certainly have travelled by train to Rothbury.

△Much of the Rothbury branch can be traced, with embankments and cuttings still marking the branch line's route across the hills and fields of the open landscape. There are also bridges and other structures including, rather surprisingly, these remains of the platform at Fontburn Halt, the smallest station on the line.

◁ Most railway closures of the 1950s went almost unnoticed, but the Rothbury branch was an exception. The last train from Rothbury on 13 September 1952 was marked by special signs, wreaths on the locomotive and a cheerful-looking group posing on the buffer beam, under the watchful eye of the stationmaster. 'Good Luck' seems a strange farewell comment.

MAP 17

❷ PONTELAND & DARRAS HALL

By the late 1890s Newcastle was spreading northwestwards into an area where there were no passenger railways. To rectify this, the NER promoted a light railway to run from South Gosforth, on the Newcastle-to-Whitley Bay line, towards Ponteland. This opened in 1905, with plans to electrify the branch in line with other Newcastle suburban routes. This did not happen, but in 1913 an extension opened to serve Darras Hall, which was then being planned as a garden suburb development. A further extension served Belsay colliery. In the event, none of the hopes for the branch were realized. Darras Hall grew very slowly and supplied few passengers, Belsay colliery was shortlived, and traffic on the Ponteland line was disappointing and suffered early from road competition. As a result, the LNER withdrew passenger services in 1929. Freight continued on parts of the branch until the 1980s. In 1981 a section was rebuilt and reopened as part of the Newcastle Metro network, with an extension from the Ponteland branch to serve Newcastle airport. The line was then electrified, fulfilling the plans made 50 years before. Today, the route of the Darras Hall line is a footpath. Darras Hall station, an unusually decorative timber building in the Arts & Crafts manner, spent a few years as a church before being demolished in 1993.

△On this early 20th-century card Ponteland is depicted as a country village, but by then it was becoming more suburban.

▷The last passenger train to reach Ponteland was the North Eastern Railtour of September 1963, organized by the RCTS and the SLS. Here, the enthusiasts crowd the single platform, probably making the station busier than it had ever been during its 24 years of normal passenger service.

❹ NEWBIGGIN-BY-THE-SEA

In the late 1840s a number of established waggonways and colliery lines north of Newcastle came together to form the Blyth & Tyne Railway. The main line linked Newcastle and Morpeth via Monkseaton, Hartley, Newsham and Bedlington. Others were planned, including one to Warkworth harbour. Never completed, this ended up as a branch to Newbiggin-by-the-Sea, opened in 1872. There was a huge wooden viaduct, later rebuilt in steel, and a station for excursion trains. In 1874 the network became part of the NER. Passenger traffic ended in 1964. Most of the line from Bedlington is still open for freight.

△This card is a reminder that before the railway came Newbiggin was a little fishing village. By 1951 its population was over 10,000.

❸ BLYTH

Blyth's first station, opened in 1847, was replaced by a much bigger one in 1867. By then the branch had become an important part of the Blyth & Tyne network. Coal and dock lines were at North Blyth, across the estuary. Traffic ended on the branch in 1968.

◁In August 1964, three months before the branch closed, a DMU sits in the empty platform at Newbiggin. The station, unusually decorative for the Blyth & Tyne Railway, was demolished in the 1970s.

⑥ AMBLE

In 1849 the York, Newcastle & Berwick Railway opened its branch from the East Coast main line to Amble and Warkworth Harbour. It was built as a coal line linking local collieries to the harbour, and there was no passenger traffic until 1879. Even then, coal remained the core of the line, with 750,000 tons being carried each year in the 1920s. Unusually, the railway played little part in the development of Amble as a resort, and passenger services ended in 1930. At that point the branch reverted to its primary function, the carriage of coal, and this continued until 1969, when the last coal shipment left the harbour, prompting the closure of the branch.

▷ By the 1960s, when this card was issued and passenger trains on the branch were long forgotten, Amble was changing from an industrial town into a resort, making the most of the local beaches and Warkworth's history.

△This typical view of the Amble branch shows an old Class J27 goods locomotive, No. 65852, making a lot of smoke as it hauls a train of empty coal wagons away from Amble. The date is May 1952, and the branch had been exclusively a coal line for over twenty years.

⑦ SEAHOUSES

The North Sunderland Railway was a small independent company set up in 1892 to build a branch from Chathill, on the East Coast main line, to Seahouses, where a new harbour had opened. It took a while to raise finance, and the 4-mile branch did not open until 1898. A planned extension towards Bamburgh and an intermediate station at Fleetham never materialized. Seahouses was a busy fishing port, and tourists were beginning to discover the Northumberland coast, so the company hoped – in vain, as it turned out – that this would support the railway.

Nevertheless, the railway managed to keep going until 1939, when the LNER, its major creditor, took over the running. After World War II the company remained independent, never becoming part of British Railways, and the owners closed it in 1951. No trace of Seahouses station remains.

△This 1960s card shows the attractive harbour at Seahouses. Boat trips to the Farne Islands and good beaches added to the town's appeal.

◁Shortly before closure in 1951, a tired-looking former NER Class Y9 locomotive, No. 68089, dating from the 1880s, and a couple of ancient carriages wait at Seahouses's basic station. British Railways never owned the branch, but operated it for the owners. After closure, everything was demolished and the site was cleared for a car park.

Steam railmotors

↑ The autotrain, a linked carriage and locomotive designed to be driven from either end, was a common branchline sight. This is a GWR set in 1947.

↑ This 1910 postcard shows a London, Brighton & South Coast autotrain, or railmotor, featuring a Class A1 Terrier tank locomotive.

↑ This wintry scene shows a GWR-built, two-carriage autotrain set in use near Yeovil Town in 1964. The locomotive is Class 1400, No. 1442.

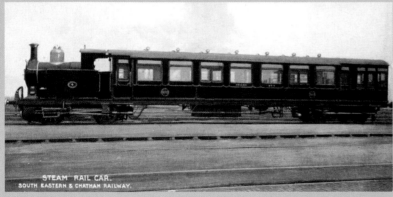

↑ Another 1910 postcard, this features a South Eastern & Chatham Railway railmotor, in this case built as a unit with the locomotive fully attached.

↑ Designed for branchline use, the GWR motor carriage, or railmotor, had the steam engine built into the carriage. The card is from the Edwardian era.

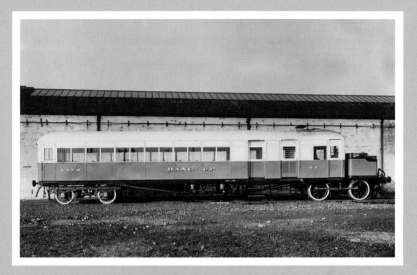

↑The LNER used three types of railmotors, including one inherited from the GNR. This is 'Bang Up', one of eleven built by Clayton from 1927.

↑The most successful LNER type was the Sentinel, with 80 in service from 1924. This is 'Flower of Yarrow', sitting in Carlisle some time in the 1920s.

←In the 1920s the Nidd Valley Light Railway acquired a couple of former GWR railmotors, one of which is seen here at the Lofthouse terminus.

SCOTLAND

TOP LEFT: *In September 1960 the local freight for Whithorn pauses at Whauphill station's overgrown platform.*

BOTTOM LEFT: *At Ballinluig station in 1961, the branchline train for Aberfeldy waits in the bay platform.*

TOP RIGHT: *A train is ready to depart from Macduff's splendidly sited seaside station in the summer of 1949.*

BOTTOM RIGHT: *In 1936 a mixed passenger and freight train, typical of the Strathpeffer branch, waits beneath the station's elaborate canopy.*

MAP 18

PEEBLESSHIRE, SELKIRKSHIRE, ROXBURGHSHIRE, BERWICKSHIRE, EDINBURGHSHIRE & HADDINGTONSHIRE

BRANCH LINES

Enthusiasts and spectators enjoy the visit of the last day special to Lauder in 1958.

Closed branch lines

Closed passenger lines

Open passenger lines

Line under constuction

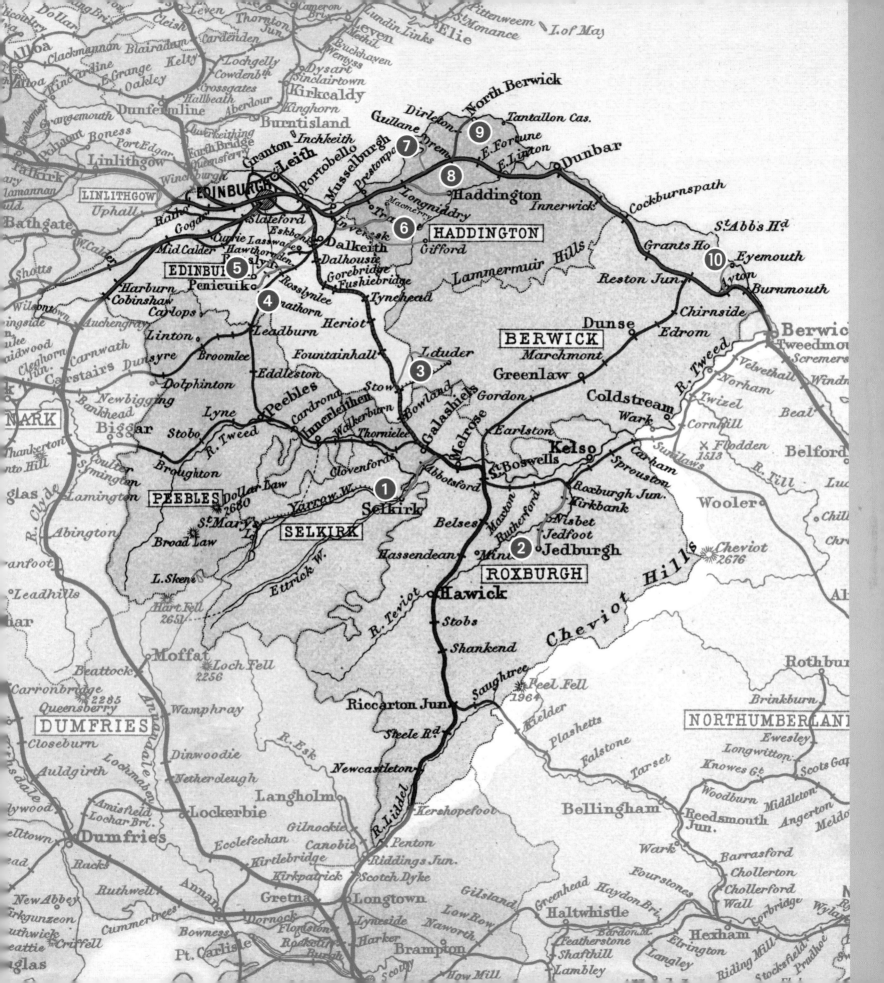

MAP 18

❶ SELKIRK

In 1856 the Selkirk & Galashiels Railway opened its 6-mile branch from the Waverley main line, a local venture backed by Selkirk tweed manufacturers. There were two intermediate stations, Abbotsford Ferry (where a chain ferry operated across the river Tweed to Sir Walter Scott's house) and Lindean. Sir Walter's family had a private waiting room at Abbotsford Ferry station. The North British Railway operated the branch and took control from 1859. Although Selkirk's mills benefited from the railway, passenger traffic was always limited and remained so through the LNER era, albeit helped to some extent by specials and excursions. Abbotsford Ferry station closed in 1931, and all passenger services except for occasional excursions ended in 1951. Freight traffic carried on until 1964, mostly for the mills and local businesses. Today, much of the route survives and parts of it can be walked. A short section, including most of Lindean station, has vanished beneath the A7. Selkirk station was demolished in 1971, leaving an empty site alongside Ettrick Water, surrounded by cloth mills.

△ A 1930s multiview card depicts some of Selkirk's highlights, though leaping salmon were probably not an everyday sight.

▽ The route of the Selkirk branch can be traced, though it is not always accessible. Here, a surviving bridge crosses the trackbed as it runs beside the Tweed. Abbotsford Ferry station was nearby, with views of Sir Walter Scott's house.

◁ Lindean was one of two intermediate stations. Set on a curve, the station had a wooden waiting room, seen here in this 1930s photograph, and a stationmaster's house, behind the photographer.

▷ On a sunny day in about 1950 an old Class J36 locomotive dating from the late Victorian era, and an equally ancient carriage, wait at Selkirk while the crew and the stationmaster pose for the camera on the deserted platform.

❷ JEDBURGH

Until the 1960s the Scottish Borders area was well served by railways. A typical line ran from Tweedmouth to St Boswells via Coldstream and Roxburgh, and it was from the latter that the independent Jedburgh Railway built its branch. Opened in 1856, the line, with three intermediate stations, wandered along the valleys of the Teviot and Jed Water. This was a North British Railway region, and it was that company that worked the branch from the start and took control in 1860. Local freight and tourism kept the branch reasonably busy, aided by increasing interest in Borders history and culture, and in due course the line passed into British Railways' care. In August 1948 it was badly damaged by flooding and immediately closed to passengers. Limited repairs enabled freight traffic to carry on, and the branch was not finally closed until 1964. Much of the route can be seen and explored, and part of it now forms the Borders Abbeys Way. Station houses and platforms survive.

▽ Despite being closed to passengers in 1948, the branch did see occasional enthusiasts' specials. This is the Scottish Rambler of May 1963, headed by a Class B1, No. 61324 – something larger than Jedburgh was used to, and being enjoyed by the signalmen in their box. After closure, the station was demolished and the area was given over to an industrial estate.

△ The platform at Jedfoot station is visible from the road and is on the Borders Abbeys Way. Other platforms remain at Kirkbank and Nisbet, in private hands.

▷ The branch followed river valleys through woods and farmland. Here, a level farm track marks the route across the fields. Elsewhere, embankments make it a more obvious feature in the landscape.

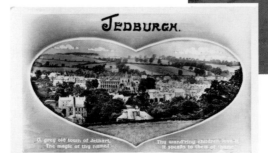

JEDBURGH.

O, grey old town of Jethart,
the magic of thy name!

Thy wand'ring children love it
it speaks to them of 'hame'

◁ The writer of this card, sent to Dornoch in April 1932, says he is 'having a rare old time' and Jedburgh 'is a lovely place, very friendly surroundings, a lovely change from the City'.

MAP 18

❼ GULLANE

The opening of the branch to North Berwick in the 1850s drew attention to the qualities of the coastline, and tourism soon became an important factor. The Aberlady, Gullane & North Berwick Railway was launched in 1893 with the aim of bringing more visitors to the region by linking a series of coastal villages with North Berwick. In 1898 the line was completed from Longniddry as far as Gullane but went no further, becoming instead a branch catering for local needs. However, it initially proved quite popular, with nearly 15,000 passengers using Aberlady station in 1900. Golf was also helpful, and a private halt was built for a local golf club. The North British Railway took it over in 1900. In the 1920s traffic declined rapidly, partly because of a competitive bus service, and in 1932 the LNER ended passenger traffic on the branch. Freight continued until 1964. In World War II, during visits by the king to Edinburgh, the royal train would shelter in the branch overnight. Today, sections can be traced but much of the branch has been lost. Houses have been built on the site of Gullane station, but at Aberlady the station platform survives.

△Like many Scottish branches, Gullane had its fair share of enthusiasts' specials. In June 1960, members of an SLS (Stephenson Locomotive Society) tour explore Gullane's station while the former NBR Class J35 0-6-0 locomotive of about 1908 prepares for the next leg.

◁By about 1960 Gullane station was overgrown, run down and looking like many branchline termini all over Britain at that time. A bit of local freight and the coal yard were keeping the branch alive, but it was all soon to end. Houses now cover the site, and nothing remains.

△An Edwardian card of the smithy at Gullane hints at the rural nature of this part of Scotland at the time. Local agriculture was important for the branch, particularly after the end of passenger services in 1932.

◁The most impressive survivor on the Gullane branch is the curving platform of Aberlady station, now part of a caravan park. Beyond the end of the platform, the trackbed virtually disappears, having been ploughed back into the fields. This was frequently the fate of long stretches of rural branch lines that were built without enduring engineering features such as embankments and cuttings.

⑧ HADDINGTON

When the North British Railway was planning its section of the main Edinburgh-to-London line, the route was to pass through Haddington. In the event, the route missed the town for reasons of cost, so the NBR, aware of Haddington's importance, built a branch line, just under 5 miles long. This opened in 1846, well engineered and constructed to a high standard with generous cuttings, embankments and bridges. Offering easy journeys to Edinburgh via Longniddry, later the junction for the Gullane branch as well, the line was popular through the 19th century and remained so until the 1920s. In 1948 flooding damaged parts of the branch. British Railways, by then in charge, carried out repairs, but used the floods as a reason for ending passenger services a year later. Freight continued until 1968. Today, most of the route survives as a footpath and cycle track, giving ample opportunity to enjoy the sweeping curves, cuttings and embankments, and the fine sea views. There are handsome stone bridges, reflecting in their design the branch's early date, along with parts of both Haddington and Coatyburn stations.

△This card, bought in the early 1900s but kept as a souvenir, highlights Haddington's character and the history that attracted visitors.

▽The branch was built to double-track standards, but was only ever single track. Bridges, now spanning the footpath along the trackbed, are therefore generous and elegant.

◁The Haddington branch was probably at its peak in the Edwardian era. Dressed for an outing, perhaps a day in Edinburgh, the waiting passengers enjoy the sun before boarding their train, with its well-polished NBR engine.

▷Approaching the former junction at Longniddry, the trackbed leaves the trees for a low embankment raised above the fields, with fine views towards the sea beyond the East Coast main line and Redhouse Castle.

MAP 18

⑩ EYEMOUTH

Another company driven by local concerns was the Eyemouth Railway, authorized in 1884 to build a 3-mile branch to Burnmouth, on the East Coast main line. At that time tourism was growing in the region, and Eyemouth wanted to make the most of its setting, beaches and picturesque harbour, which were also seen as a source of trade for the branch. Building took a long time, and the line was not opened until April 1891. The NBR worked the branch and took control in 1900. From then on, the story was the same as for other branch lines in the area – several decades of relative popularity followed by a rapid decline from the 1920s. The floods of 1948 caused extensive damage, closing the line for a year, but full repairs were undertaken by British Railways, and passenger services then continued until 1962, when the branch was closed to all traffic. Today, it is quite hard to follow the route, as sections have disappeared or are inaccessible. Eyemouth station has gone, but a bridge outside the town still carries the main road. The piers that carried the Eye Water viaduct are the most significant relics from the branch.

▽The appeal of Eyemouth to tourists developed with the railway, and the features that attracted visitors in the Edwardian era were the same as in the 1950s, as this card indicates.

△The line's most dramatic and expensive feature was the Eye Water viaduct, a sequence of iron trusses carried on high brick piers. The ironwork has gone but the piers survive, along with the approach embankment.

△When this photograph was taken, perhaps in about 1960, the Eyemouth branch was nearing its end and the single carriage would have been amply sufficient for the short journey to the junction at Burnmouth, especially on a miserable, wet day. The locomotive, one of the ubiquitous Class J39s, No. 64917, a 1936 Gresley design, has, like the station, seen better days. Nothing of the station survives.

△The branch closed in February 1962. Here, a year or so later, the track has gone but the station still stands, along with the loading gauge. The lorry is probably loading sleepers.

❸ LAUDER

There were a number of schemes to connect Lauder to the railway network but nothing happened until 1901, when the Lauder Light Railway opened its branch from Fountainhall Junction. The 10-mile route, via Oxton, was meandering, indirect and heavily graded, and there were many complaints about the lack of facilities at Lauder station. The NBR operated the branch, but it remained independent until absorbed by the LNER. Passenger traffic ended in 1932. During World War II a strategic food store was built beside Lauder station, and this kept it alive into the 1950s and ensured 1948 flood damage was repaired. Final closure came in 1958.

▷This is Lauder in 1936, four years after the end of passenger services. Everything is still in place, and the station's basic nature is apparent. Later, the platform was shortened, and eventually all was demolished.

◁Lauder has several buildings that date back to medieval times, including the corn mill and bridge depicted in this Edwardian card. The growing appreciation of history and architecture in the early 1900s encouraged the branch line's backers.

❻ MACMERRY & GIFFORD

Two linked branches, to Macmerry and Gifford, ran from Inveresk, on the East Coast main line. The first, to Macmerry, was built by the North British Railway mainly to serve local collieries and an iron works. It opened in 1870 but passenger services did not start until two years later, when the five stations along the line had been completed. The second branch, built by the independent Gifford & Garvald Light Railway, opened in 1901 but was operated by the NBR. This double-track branch, with three intermediate stations, left the Macmerry line at Ormiston. Both lines were primarily freight, so passenger facilities were quite limited. In 1923 the branches passed into the control of the LNER, which did not take long to begin to close them. First to go were passenger services on the Macmerry branch north of Ormiston in 1925, followed by passenger services to Gifford in 1933. Freight lasted much longer, with a series of closures between 1960 and 1965, though a short section serving Dalkeith colliery lasted until 1980. Predictably, there were visits by enthusiasts' specials. Today, a section of the Gifford branch is an official footpath.

▽By the 1950s, there was not much to see at Macmerry other than an overgrown platform and a set of buffers. Passenger services had ended in 1925 on a branch where freight was always more important.

◁In September 1958, an enthusiasts' special organized by the SLS (Stephenson Locomotive Society) visited Macmerry and Gifford. Here, members of the group are watching the locomotive, an unusual Class C16, No. 67492, a 1915 Reid design for the NBR, run round its train at Macmerry.

MAP 18

④ PENICUIK

The Penicuik Railway, a small independent company, opened its 4-mile branch from Hawthornden, on the main line of the Peebles Railway, in 1872. Four years later both railways came under the control of the NBR. The route along the North Esk valley was heavily engineered, with seven river crossings, a big viaduct and two tunnels. Freight traffic included ironstone and gunpowder, but the main support came from paper mills along the valley. Passenger services ended in 1951, freight in 1967. The route is now part of the National Cycle Network.

OPEN & PRESERVED LINES

⑨ NORTH BERWICK

The North British Railway's branch from Drem Junction to North Berwick opened in 1850. A lack of immediate support nearly closed the line, but by the end of the century, thanks to commuter and holiday traffic, it was well established. The line was electrified in 1991, and services now operate from both Edinburgh and Glasgow, making it more of a mainline terminal than a traditional branch.

⑤ ROSLIN & GLENCORSE

The Edinburgh, Loanhead & Roslin Railway opened its branch from Millerhill, on the Waverley line, to Roslin in 1874. Three years later it was extended to Glencorse. Coal was the inspiration and remained important throughout the branch's life. Initially the branch was successful, with passenger services helped by a nearby military camp, but the decline was rapid after World War I and passenger carrying ended in 1933, apart from excursions and specials. Freight was another matter, thanks to the many collieries along the route, particularly in the Loanhead area, and these, notably Bilston Glen, kept the northern section open until 1989. Today, a cycleway and footpath follow part of the trackbed southwards from Loanhead, crossing the Bilston Glen viaduct.

△A narrow path flanked by hedges marks the trackbed of the Gullane branch as it nears the end of the line (*see also* page 198).

Branchline luggage labels

G.W.R.

PORTHCAWL

57† 5,000 | 3 | 11.

TO

CONISTON

From the Furness Railway.

NORTH EASTERN RAILWAY.

From YORK.

STANHOPE

NORTH EASTERN RAILWAY. *FROM FARM*

RICHMOND.

G.W.R.

Blenheim

AND

Woodstock

(A. 474)

THE HIGHLAND RAILWAY.

L U G G A G E.

From _____

TO EMBO

L. & N. W. RY.

Llangefni

G. E. R.

From _____

TO

ONGAR

(46/556) London Midland and Scottish Railway Company

'CALEDONIAN SECTION'

BLAIRGOWRIE

FROM

DUNBLANE

G. E. R.

Eye

Taff Vale Railway

LLWYNYPIA

TO

Newcastle Emlyn

Via Treherbert

G.E.R.

IPSWICH

From

TO

SP

HORNCASTLE

via G.N. & G.E. Joint Line
and Spalding.

NEWSPAPER LABEL

1D. LABEL

Wick and Lybster Railway.

No. 2236

Carried at Owner's risk, and to be
called for by Consignee at the
Station to which it is addressed.

MAP 19

WIGTOWNSHIRE, KIRKCUDBRIGHTSHIRE & DUMFRIESSHIRE

BRANCH LINES

This is Wigtown, on the Whithorn branch, shortly after final closure in 1964.

Closed branch lines

Closed passenger lines

Open passenger lines

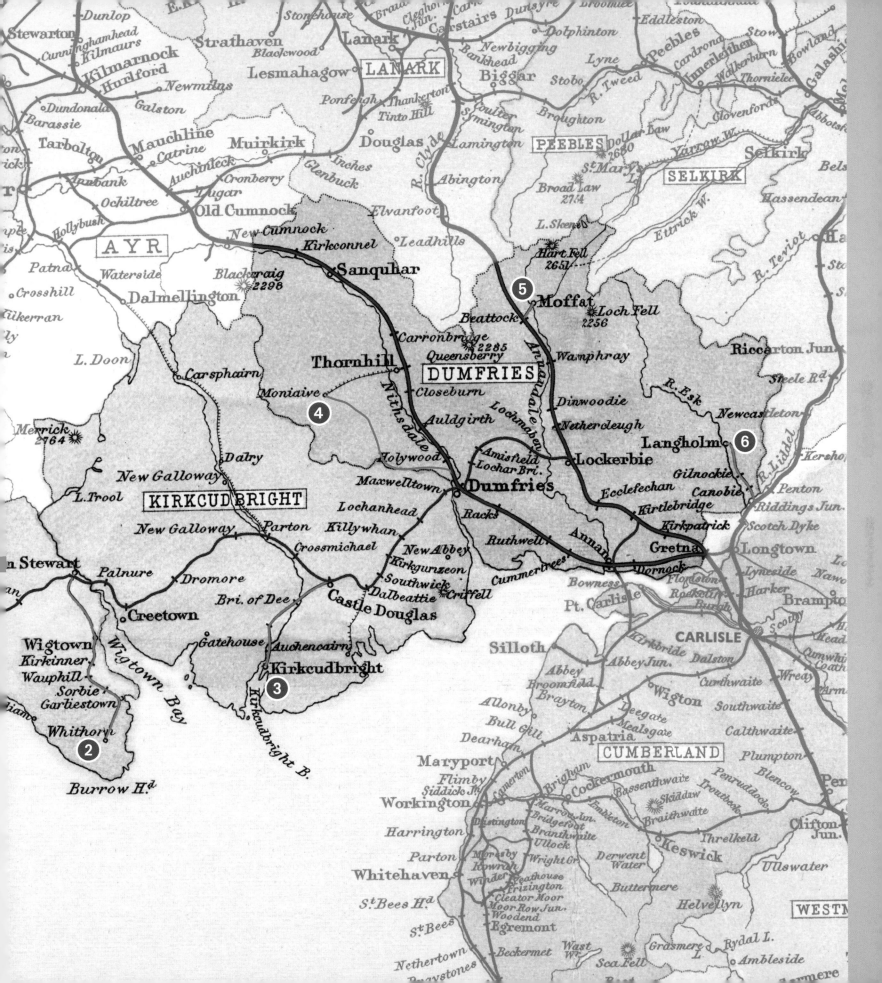

MAP 19

❷ WHITHORN

The southwest of Scotland once enjoyed a good railway network, assembled over some years by a number of independent companies. One of these was the Wigtownshire Railway, authorized in 1872 to build a 19-mile branch from Newton Stewart to Whithorn, with a short branch to Garliestown. It was all open by 1877 and settled down to a quiet, rural existence catering for local needs, mostly agricultural. Annual receipts were about £7,000, but the branch kept going until the 1880s, when financial problems led to a merger with the nearby Portpatrick Railway, which was also in a parlous position. The new company had four important backers, the LNWR, the Midland, the Caledonian and the Glasgow & South Western, all with vested interests in keeping the lines open. The two Scottish companies ran it all until the formation of the LMS in 1923. Passenger services ran until 1950, when they were quickly killed off by British Railways, but freight continued until 1964. Much of this remote and rural branch line can still be explored.

△Whithorn Priory is one of the earliest sites of Christianity in Scotland and has been a place of pilgrimage for centuries. This 1930s card shows early crosses preserved in the priory museum.

▽In the early 1960s local freight trains were still plodding their way along the Whithorn branch. This example, photographed in August 1960, was headed by an old Class 2F, a Caledonian Railway design dating back to the 1880s.

▽The Wigtownshire Railway's line ran through a delightful landscape, making modern explorations of the route well worthwhile. There is plenty to see, including bridges and other structures. Here, the trackbed, now a farmer's access lane, curves away from Kirkinner, with the estuary and the peaks of Knockeans and Cairnholy in the background.

❸ KIRKCUDBRIGHT

A small company fired by local ambitions, the Kirkcudbrightshire Railway completed its 10-mile branch from Castle Douglas in 1864. A year later the Glasgow & South Western took control and ran it until it all became part of the LMS. During the heyday of the branch, at the end of the 19th century, there were through trains to London, taking up to twelve hours for the 371-mile journey. Fish traffic was important then, as was tourism. The appeal of Kirkcudbright and the region became well known in the 1880s, particularly to a group of artists from Glasgow who established a colony here, and that still exists. By the 1950s the branch was in terminal decline, and it all came to an end in 1965, along with most of the railways of Southwest Scotland. Today, most of the branch can be traced through the landscape as far as the outskirts of Kirkcudbright, at which point the route vanishes under modern roads and houses. The station building, however, survives. Inland, there are bridges, well built from local stone, and stations converted into private houses.

△This card, posted in July 1961, shows the colourful appeal of Kirkcudbright. A family on holiday were having a 'very nice time' despite the weather. Their son had arrived by train.

△In July 1960 the train for Castle Douglas is getting ready to depart. The locomotive is a Stanier-designed Class 3MT, No. 40152, a familiar branchline workhorse. At this point, there was still plenty of freight traffic on the branch, though passengers, as ever, were thin on the ground.

△One of the major features on the branch was the viaduct at Tongland, which carried the line across the Dee. Today, though the iron girder sections went immediately after closure, the stone piers and the approach arches still stand, a kind of memorial to the branch.

▷Kirkcudbright station is a handsome building, as befitted the town, and a reflection of the local optimism and ambition that brought the branch into being. It is seen here in British Railways days, probably not long before closure, but still looking elegant and well cared for. Today, it is home to a beauty salon. The rest of the site is covered with modern housing.

MAP 19

❺ MOFFAT

The Caledonian Railway's main line northwards, opened in 1848, passed through Beattock, much to the annoyance of Moffat, a well-established and famous spa town 2 miles to the east. Eventually local interests and finance, which had been behind the setting up of a hydropathic resort in the town in 1878, brought into being the Moffat Railway, whose short branch from Beattock opened in 1883. Taken over by the Caledonian in 1889, the branch was initially very popular and attracted many summer visitors to the town and its spas. For a while, there was a through train from Glasgow. After World War II, the branch's fortunes declined rapidly, and closure to passengers came in 1954 under British Railways, with freight following ten years later. Today, the site of Moffat's station is a children's playground and industrial complex, but the route can be followed outside the town.

△ The approach to Moffat was along a low embankment, seen here looking very manicured beside the children's playground. The station was beyond the conifers.

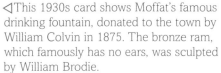

◁ This 1930s card shows Moffat's famous drinking fountain, donated to the town by William Colvin in 1875. The bronze ram, which famously has no ears, was sculpted by William Brodie.

▽ Beyond the town the trackbed quickly becomes apparent as a low and overgrown embankment crossing the fields of this important sheep-farming area. Bridges survive, and at Beattock a short siding marks where the branch started.

▽ This is Moffat station, looking quite tidy but nearly deserted in August 1931. At this point an old former LNWR steam railmotor was in use on the branch, shuttling to and from the main line at Beattock. Freight wagons fill the sidings.

❹ MONIAIVE

There were various plans to build a railway towards Moniaive but nothing happened until 1905 when, inspired by the Light Railways Act, the Cairn Valley Light Railway opened its 17-mile branch from just north of Dumfries. The line meandered along the river valley, with six intermediate stations serving small places. It was controlled from the start by the Glasgow & South Western Railway. At the time of the opening, Moniaive had about 500 inhabitants, so the branch was never likely to be much of a success. This proved to be the case, and passenger services ended in 1943, freight four years later. The railway was used during World War II by Norwegian troops, whose base was close by.

▷In about 1910 railway staff pose at Moniaive, in a cheerful and apparently busy scene with shunting going on in the background. All that is missing is passengers. The timber station and the goods shed still stand, over 60 years after closure.

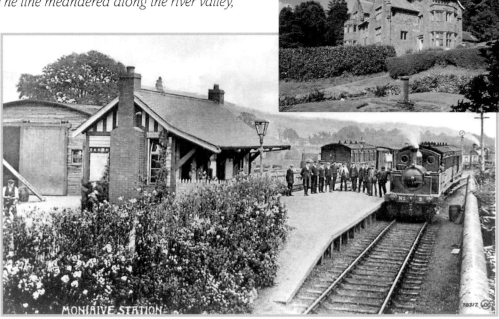
MONIAIVE STATION

▽This card shows Glenluiart, a famous Arts & Crafts house at Moniaive, built for the Monteith family in 1898 and now under restoration.

▽The station at Langholm was a substantial structure incorporating a single-track engine shed and a water tower. Both are still visible in this 1961 photograph, though the engine shed had been abandoned for years and was by then roofless. Here, in October that year, the lunchtime train for Riddings Junction is departing, headed by an Ivatt-designed Class 4MT, No. 43139. Nothing remains today.

❻ LANGHOLM

Battles between railway companies resulted in the building of the Waverley route from Edinburgh to Carlisle. The Border Union Railway, in league with the North British, built part of the line, plus a 7-mile branch from Riddings Junction along Eskdale to Langholm, which opened in 1864. Successful for some decades, notably with freight, the branch, unlike many in Scotland, had a long life, aided by the army in both world wars. Passenger traffic lasted until 1964, the line being a typical Beeching closure, and freight to 1967.

MEETING OF THE WATERS LANGHOLM

△A 1930s card, bought but not posted, shows the typical landscape of the Langholm region and the Esk valley.

❶ PORTPATRICK

By opening branches to Stranraer and Portpatrick in 1862, the Portpatrick Railway forged a link between London and Belfast. Overshadowed by Stranraer, the Portpatrick branch closed in 1950.

Dock & harbour branches

↑In March 1962 a former Southern Railway locomotive hauls a mixed freight along the Southampton Docks branch, in Hampshire.

↑At Seaham harbour, County Durham, in the 1950s, No.18, a famous 0-4-0 dock locomotive built in 1863, shunts traditional chaldron coal wagons.

↑An ancient double signal was still in use in 1955 on the dockyard branch from Portsmouth & Southsea, Hampshire, by the Edinburgh Road crossing.

↑A former Southern Railway Class R1, No. 31147, is ready to take its train away from Whitstable harbour, Kent, in October 1957.

↑ In 1948, a Class Z4, No. 68190, originally built in 1915 for the Great North of Scotland Railway, waits on the quayside at Aberdeen harbour.

↑ The railway reached Portsoy, Banffshire (now Aberdeenshire), in 1859, and a branch was built to the harbour. Closed in the 1960s, it is now a footpath.

↑ An 0-4-0 shunter, GWR SHT Class, No. 1144, built by Hawthorn Leslie in 1909, rests between duties at Swansea docks, South Wales, in the 1950s.

↑ Banff Harbour station, seen here soon before closure in the 1960s, was the end of the branch line from Tillynaught (now Aberdeenshire).

MAP 20

AYRSHIRE, RENFREWSHIRE, DUMBARTONSHIRE, LANARKSHIRE & LINLITHGOWSHIRE

BRANCH LINES

Locomotive Class 2P No. 40572 waits at the head of its train at Dalmellington in 1955.

Closed branch lines

Closed passenger lines

Open passenger lines

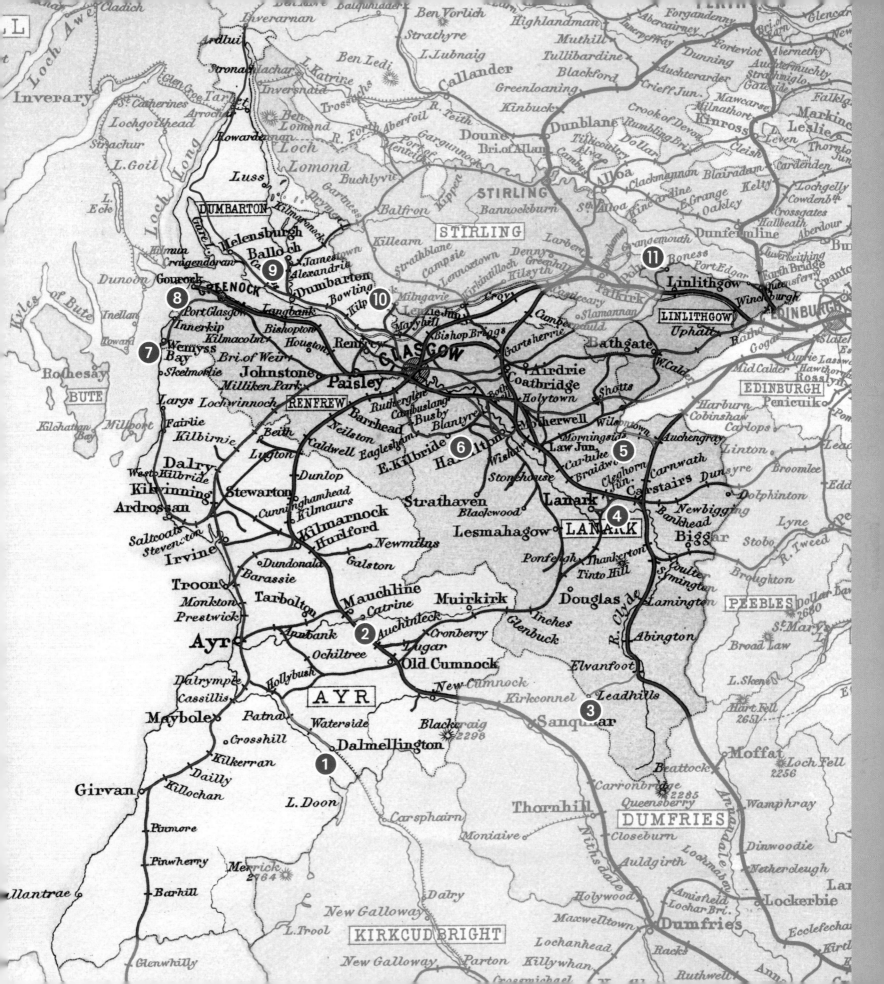

MAP 20

The Road to Loch Doon, Dalmellington

❶ DALMELLINGTON

In the 1840s a grand scheme to build a line to connect Ayr with Castle Douglas ended up as a branch line, along the Doon valley, to Dalmellington. It was opened by the Ayr & Dalmellington Railway in 1856. There were intermediate stations and junctions with later lines, along with private connections with coal mines, one of which was via an inclined plane. A major feature was the sixteen-arch Burnton viaduct, a notably elegant design by John Miller. A few years later the Glasgow & South Western took control and tried in vain to close the branch in 1900. After that, always busy with coal and iron works traffic, it thrived. Passenger services ended in 1964 but, as much of the branch is still used by the local coal industry for various opencast sites, there is now a campaign to reopen the branch to passengers.

△ In July 1943 Jean Neilson, writing this card to a friend in Lanarkshire, said she was on holiday in the Doon valley and 'having a very nice time. Weather has been quite good.'

▷ In August 1955 a scheduled service waits for passengers, ready to leave Dalmellington for Ayr via Holehouse Junction. The rather grubby locomotive is a 4-4-0 Class 2P, No. 40572, one of a large group built for the LMS from the late 1920s.

❸ WANLOCKHEAD

The Leadhills & Wanlockhead Light Railway was built in extreme physical conditions and at great cost, as though to prove that no challenge was too great for a railway engineer. The short branch from Elvanfoot, completed in 1902, included the highest standard-gauge summit in Britain, at 1,498ft. Also notable was the eight-arch Rispin Cleugh viaduct, built of concrete – then a new building material – and faced with terracotta bricks for aesthetic reasons. Lead mines, gold mines and tourism inspired the building of the branch, but all were a disappointment to the Caledonian Railway, which had backed the line's construction and operated it. Local support from the scattered hill villages also failed to live up to expectations and, after the branch had in due course passed to the LMS, passenger services ended in 1938. Freight continued for a while, then the whole venture was abandoned. Much later, in the 1980s, Rispin Cleugh viaduct was blown up, having begun to shed its facing bricks. Since then a smaller viaduct at Elvan Water has also been demolished. A 2ft gauge heritage line runs on part of the line, based at Leadhills.

▽ The branch was run by the Caledonian Railway until 1923, when it was absorbed into the LMS. Here, in 1931, an LMS 0-4-4 Class 2P tank locomotive, then only a few years old, waits at Wanlockhead station. The station nameboard is battered, but the sign above proclaims '1413 feet above sea level'.

❷ CATRINE

The Glasgow & South Western Railway opened a branch from Brackenhill Junction, south of Mauchline, to Catrine in 1903, presumably inspired by the local cotton industry, which had been started in the late 18th century using water power. At the start, the branch was operated by a Manson autotrain. Closed briefly in 1917, the branch was reopened and passenger services were then maintained until 1943. Freight, for the cotton and bleaching mills and for local needs, continued until 1964. Some of the trackbed survives, along with bridges and other structures.

❺ WILSONTOWN

The origins of the Wilsontown branch lie in the Wilsontown, Morningside & Coltness Railway, a line opened in 1845 to serve local collieries and iron works. In 1876 a new branch was opened by the Caledonian Railway, from Auchengray to Haywood and the Wilsontown iron works, and later extended to serve a colliery at Kingshill. Passenger services continued until September 1951 but freight, mostly coal, survived until 1964.

OPEN & PRESERVED LINES

❼ WEMYSS BAY
❽ GOUROCK
❾ BALLOCH

A number of branch lines operate in this part of Scotland today. Some, though built as branches, have always been served by through trains from Glasgow and other mainline termini. These include Wemyss Bay, opened in 1865 to serve Clyde steamers and electrified in 1967; Gourock, opened by the Caledonian Railway in 1889 to serve a new steamer terminal, now the headquarters of Caledonian MacBrayne; and Balloch, originally built to serve steamers from the pier station but now operating as a commuter line, the station having been moved into the town centre when the pier closed in 1986.

❹ LANARK
❻ EAST KILBRIDE
❿ MILNGAVIE

Other branches in use today in this region have been rebuilt or developed from earlier railways, for example Lanark, which opened in 1855 as a true branch from the Caledonian Railway's main line, and later became a modern suburban commuter line. Another example is East Kilbride, first opened in 1868 and then extended. In the 1960s the whole branch was threatened with closure but survived, having been cut back to East Kilbride, now a minimal station at the end of a branch. Milngavie, opened in 1863 as part of the Glasgow & Milngavie Junction Railway, was built with a substantial station, now much reduced. Again, commuter traffic keeps the branch alive.

⓫ BO'NESS

The modern Bo'ness & Kinneil heritage line can be traced back to the Slamannan Railway of the 1840s, whose line to Bo'ness opened in 1851 primarily for freight and to serve the harbour. Passenger carrying ceased in 1956 and the line closed in the 1960s. The heritage railway used some of the harbour branch, but most of its route has been built from scratch.

↑ In 1973 Barry Island is looking a bit worn. Since Barry Pier station closed, it is the only stop on the Barry Island branch of the Vale of Glamorgan line.

↑ A classic branchline terminus was Windermere, in Cumberland, seen here in the early 1960s. Today's more minimal station is still well used.

↑ Overlooked by mountains of slate, a train for Llandudno Junction waits to depart from Blaenau Ffestiniog North, in North Wales, in the 1960s.

↑In the 1950s Barton-on-Humber, Lincolnshire, had seen better days, though there was still some freight traffic. Now it is a minimal branchline terminus.

↑The North Berwick branch, Haddingtonshire (East Lothian), was still steam hauled in the 1950s. The crew pass the time of day while the train waits.

↑In Yorkshire, Saltburn's classical station, having been replaced by a basic passenger shelter, now houses shops. Much of this 1970s view is a supermarket.

↑Balloch Pier, Dumbartonshire, seen here in the 1960s, when it was the line's original terminus, closed in 1986. The resort is now served by a new station.

MAP 21

STIRLINGSHIRE, CLACKMANNANSHIRE, KINROSS-SHIRE, FIFE, PERTHSHIRE & FORFARSHIRE

BRANCH LINES

Closed branch lines

Closed passenger lines

Open passenger lines

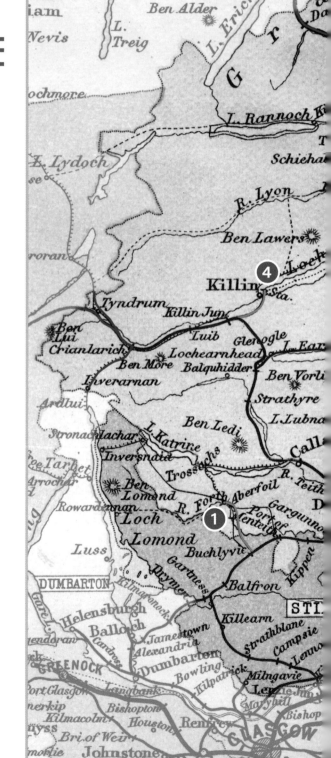

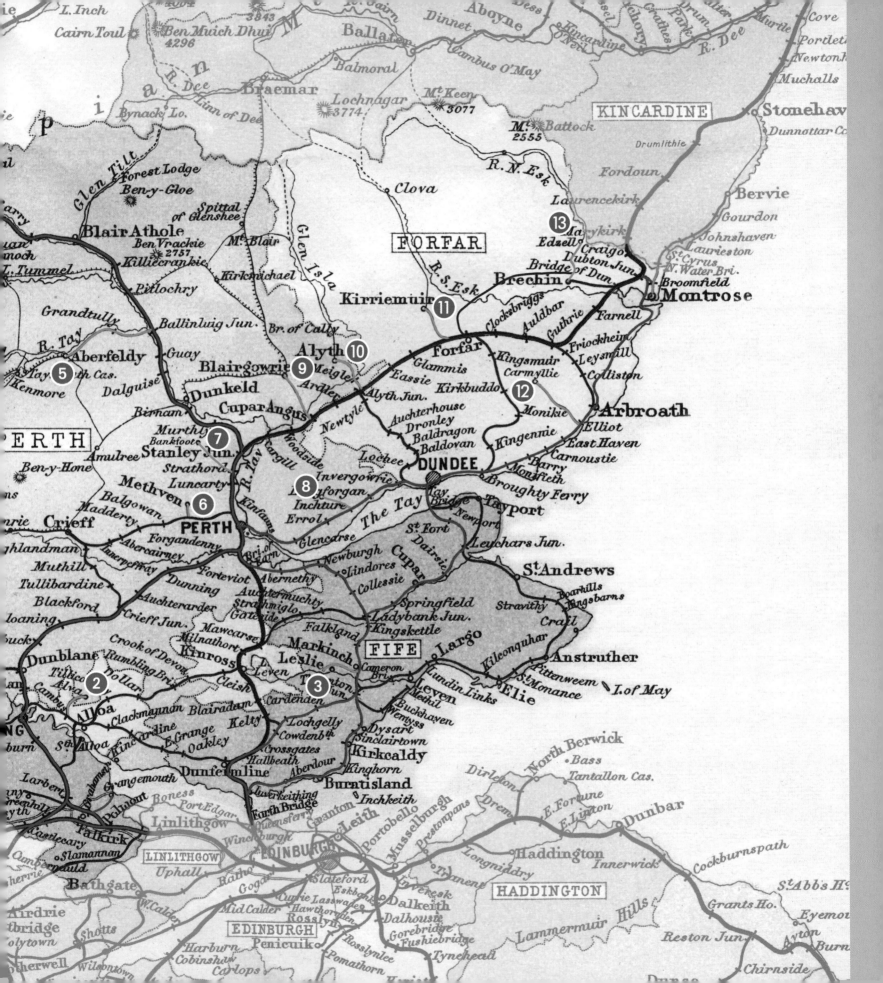

MAP 21

① ABERFOYLE

The railway came to Aberfoyle in three stages. First, there was the Edinburgh & Glasgow Railway's Campsie branch from Lenzie, on their main line, opened in 1848. Next came the Blane Valley Railway, extending the branch by 8 miles to Killearn, in 1867. Finally, the Strathendrick & Aberfoyle Railway completed the last section in 1882. In 1891 the NBR took control. Tourism and local freight were the mainstays of the branch, and all went well until the 1920s, when competition from bus companies became severe. The branch closed in sections, in reverse order to construction: first, in 1951, the section to Aberfoyle; next, the Blane Valley section, in 1959; then the original Campsie section, which lost its freight traffic in 1966. Today, there is plenty to see, and one stretch is now the Strathkelvin Railway Path.

△This Edwardian postcard, portraying a rather romantic view of Highland cottage life, is typical of cards produced to encourage tourism.

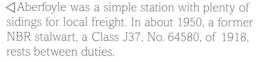

◁Aberfoyle was a simple station with plenty of sidings for local freight. In about 1950, a former NBR stalwart, a Class J37, No. 64580, of 1918, rests between duties.

▽ Much of the route can be explored, and stations and other structures survive. Here, on the approach to Aberfoyle, the trackbed curves across farmland towards the hills (seen dominating the station in the photograph to the left).

▷Before the branch closed, there were visits from enthusiasts' specials. In May 1958 a railtour organized by the SLS (Stephenson Locomotive Society) reached Dumgoyne (formerly Killearn) which, as the Aberfoyle section had already closed, was then the end of the line. Enthusiasts have turned up by car in considerable numbers to greet the train, which is headed by an old NBR Class J36, No. 65315, from the late Victorian era.

❹ KILLIN

By 1880 the Callander & Oban Railway had made a remote but beautiful part of Scotland accessible, and tourism, as well as local trade, inspired the building of the 5-mile branch to Killin and Loch Tay, with the terminus at the loch's steamer pier. The independent Killin Railway was responsible, and the branch opened in 1886. It was operated by the Caledonian Railway. The line made a significant contribution to the local community and lived through the LMS era and well into the time of British Railways, although passenger carrying to the Loch Tay terminus had come to an end when the steamer was withdrawn in 1939. Passenger and freight services continued to Killin until 1965. Today, almost the entire route along the trackbed can be walked, from Killin Junction, deep in the forest, to the shores of Loch Tay. Killin station has gone, along with much of the route through the town, but at the site of the junction, the platform remains.

△The typical Edwardian view of Highland scenery is depicted on this card of Killin and Loch Tay, 'the most charming of the lochs'.

▷After leaving Killin Junction, the main line continued towards Callander while the branch dropped down towards Killin and Loch Tay. Today, both survive as footpaths, bringing to life what must have been delightful journeys.

△In August 1961 the single-carriage branch train waits at Killin Junction, hoping that passengers will appear from the mainline train. The locomotive, built by the LMS in 1925, shares its ancestry with the station lamps that someone is trying to mend.

▷In July 1931 a few passengers, perhaps at the end of their holidays, are ready to take the branchline train on Killin station, where there was a fine array of advertising. A smart lady, perhaps the photographer's companion, watches him anxiously as he has crossed the track, leaving his camera bag on the platform slope.

MAP 21

⑤ ABERFELDY

The branch to Aberfeldy started as an ambitious scheme by the Inverness & Perth Junction Railway to drive a main line through this part of Scotland. In the event, only a 10-mile branch to Aberfeldy from Ballinluig was built. By the time it opened, in 1865, its builders had become part of the Highland Railway. The branch was successful for many years, thanks to developing tourism in the region. Attractions included golf, fishing and whisky distilleries, as well as glorious landscape, notably around Loch Tay. However, by the early 1960s road competition was taking traffic away, and the branch closed in 1965, along with much of Scotland's rural network. Long stretches of the trackbed, never far from the Tay, are there to be explored. Near Ballinluig the original Tay bridge, with its iron battlements, carries a minor road. Aberfeldy still has a station hotel, but no station.

△In July 1968 Brian, Janice and their daughter Eleanor were on holiday in Aberfeldy and sent this multiview card to a friend in Kirkcaldy. They wrote: 'It's buckets of rain but we're enjoying ourselves.'

▷On a sunny August day in 1961, the branchline train to Ballinluig waits at Aberfeldy. Passengers are assembling, and there is a pile of parcels to be loaded. An old former Caledonian Class 2P tank locomotive, No. 55217, one of the branch's regulars, is on duty.

▽Some sections have been lost, but there is plenty still to explore. The trackbed is often apparent through woods and across the fields, particularly on the low embankment that carries it towards Aberfeldy. Here, it is a path through the trees, with lovely views of the Tay.

△This shows a single-carriage train pausing at Grandtully, one of the two intermediate stations. The locomotive is the same one as above, but looking a bit grubbier on this May day in 1960. The station and its gardens are in good order.

⑨ BLAIRGOWRIE

The Scottish Midland Junction Railway, set up in 1845 to link Perth and Forfar, was one of a number of independent Scottish companies working in the 1840s to tie up some of the loose ends in the emerging network in this area of Scotland. In 1866, after various mergers, it all became part of the Caledonian Railway, but in the meantime, in 1855, the SMJR had opened a branch to Blairgowrie from Coupar Angus. The linen mills in Blairgowrie were the incentive, but later the major freight on the branch was soft fruit for the town's jam-making industry. That did not help the passenger service, which was withdrawn in 1955, though freight carried on for another ten years. Today, some of the route can be traced in the fields.

◁ A famous Blairgowrie landmark is the Meikleour beech hedge, planted in 1746 and, at 100ft high, the world's tallest. In this 1930s card, it dwarfs the flock of sheep. The road is now the busy A93.

▽ Blairgowrie's station and the related buildings, including the engine shed, lived on for some years after closure. The train shed had various chapters of casual use before it was demolished. A supermarket stands on the site.

△ The enthusiasts' railtours of the early 1960s often had the pick of a number of interesting locomotives, survivors from an earlier era soon to be withdrawn and cut up. Here, in May 1962, it is a former Caledonian Class 3P, No. 54465, dating from 1916, heading a special visiting the branch. This is Blairgowrie, with its covered train shed and sidings still busy with fruit vans.

▷ Blairgowrie station was set well below the town. Trains setting off for Coupar Angus crossed the fields towards the river Isla, where there was a bridge supported on iron caissons. Much of the trackbed through the fields has gone, but here the route, curving away from Blairgowrie towards the Isla, is clearly marked by a line of trees. The iron bridge supports still stand in the river. The 18th-century road bridge can be seen on the right of the photograph.

MAP 21

⑩ ALYTH

The independent Alyth Railway opened its 5-mile branch from Alyth Junction, on the Scottish North Eastern's main line, in 1861. Local interests, notably the textile mills, which employed 350 people, and the brewery, backed the branch, and were its mainstay for some decades. The Caledonian Railway took over in 1874. There were three intermediate stations, including a halt for a golf club. Alyth enjoys a long history dating back to Pictish times, and has early royal connections, but this, it seems, was not enough to generate significant tourist interest. Passenger services, never busy, were withdrawn by British Railways in 1951. Freight continued until 1965. Today, parts of the route can be traced, and surviving elements to look out for include several bridges, as well as the abutments of a bridge that carried the line over the Dean Water near Meigle.

△This card, sent in 1908, shows Alyth's mills and the dominant spire of the 1839 church. The message is about the family: 'John is boy at the Big House and Hugh is mill-boy at Redheugh.'

▷ The site of Alyth station has disappeared beneath houses and industry, but the trackbed soon becomes apparent as a private road heading out across the fields. It is closed to vehicles, but is the start of a section that is accessible to walkers and cyclists.

▽In June 1960 a week-long tour of Scottish branches and minor lines was organized by the RCTS (Railway Correspondence and Travel Society) and the SLS (Stephenson Locomotive Society). Here, the Scottish Railtour train, headed by a former Caledonian Class 2F, No. 57441, from 1896, has paused at Alyth Junction on its way to or from the branch.

△Alyth station, of which there is no trace today, was one of several local termini that had a covered train shed and an adjacent engine shed. Here, the train shed was short, so it would have sheltered only the locomotive, leaving the passengers out in the open on the platform. In this photograph, probably from the 1920s, the whole place is deserted.

② ALVA

The Alva Railway opened its 4-mile branch to Cambus, on the Stirling & Dunfermline Railway, in 1861. Later, it became part of the North British network. The branch did not fulfil its expectations, despite being given a late boost by the opening in 1952 of Glenorchil colliery, which was served by its own branch line. Sadly, the colliery was also a disappointment and closed in 1962. Meanwhile, passenger services ended in 1954. Parts of the route can be traced, including the colliery branch.

▽In May 1963 the branch was visited by an enthusiasts' railtour, headed by an 1880s veteran, former North British Class J36, No. 65323. As ever, the members of the tour are wandering about all over the place. The station house survives in private hands.

△This Edwardian card gives a rather vague impression of Alva, but shows the magnificent setting.

△Although passenger carrying ended early, in 1932, the little stone-built terminus station at Leslie lived on, along with the engine shed and other structures. As this photograph shows, the layout was always cramped, complicating the handling of freight. Here, in the 1950s, the daily freight has arrived.

③ LESLIE

Another independent and locally supported company, the Leslie Railway, completed its branch from Markinch in 1861. There was also a line to Auchmuty, built to serve paper mills. Worked from the start by the Edinburgh, Perth & Dundee Railway, it became part of the North British in 1872. Passenger traffic, never significant, ended in 1932, but the branch remained busy with freight until 1967. In the 1950s the new town of Glenrothes was built all around the branch but ignored it, a reflection of the attitudes of the time. Today, it remains one of the few new towns without a station, the nearest being Markinch and Glenrothes with Thornton, both well away from the town. The entire route is now a cycleway, part of a large local network, and bridges and other railway features survive along the route.

MAP 21

❻ METHVEN

The complex history of this branch starts with the opening in 1858 of the Perth, Almond Valley & Methven Railway's line from Dunkeld Bridge to Methven. Later, in 1866, another line was built westwards to Crieff, from a point south of Methven, which then became known as Methven Junction. Thus, the remaining mile and a half from the new junction to Methven became a branch line. In due course it was all taken over by the Caledonian Railway. Passenger traffic, always limited on the Methven branch, ended in 1937, and on the main line through Methven Junction it ended in 1951. The latter was helped in World War II by the presence nearby of RAF Methven. The main line and the Methven branch both remained open for freight into the 1960s, allowing for visits by enthusiasts' specials and railtours. Today, not much remains. The site of Methven station is now an industrial estate.

▽The June 1960 joint RCTS and SLS Scottish Railtour visited many branchline sites, and used a variety of old locomotives. Here, a very smart Class 3P, No. 54485, a Caledonian design from 1920, runs round its train at Methven Junction while the tour members gossip with railway staff.

❼ BANKFOOT

One of the lines inspired by the passing of the Light Railways Act, the Bankfoot branch was built from Strathord Junction, on the Caledonian Railway's Perth-to-Forfar line, by the independent Bankfoot Railway. Opened in 1906, it was taken over by the Caledonian three years later. Unlike branches built by small companies in the late Victorian era, when optimism and ambition were powerful, and the desire for local railways was understandable, remote lines like this seem to have had little to justify them. Like many others, it offered the village a connection to the outside world, but passenger traffic was never significant. It was ended by the LNER in 1931 and, as usual, it was freight that kept the branch alive, in this case until final closure in September 1964.

△The stationmaster, with his dog, and other staff pose for the camera on Bankfoot's platform in about 1910. The single-carriage train waits, but it is the large freight shed and crowded sidings that indicate what really mattered.

▷In May 1962 a small former Caledonian Class 3F tank locomotive, No. 56347, dating from 1912, hauls a heavy enthusiasts' special into Bankfoot station. The train is crowded, and plenty of people have turned out to watch what was clearly an important event for the village.

⑪ KIRRIEMUIR

The incentive for the branch line to Kirriemuir, which opened in 1861, came from the town's textile industry, which in the 1850s employed 2,000 people in the making of linen and jute. Later, the town became famous as the birthplace of JM Barrie, who wrote a sequence of stories based on the town, which he fictionalized as Thrums. This had little impact on the branch, however. It was controlled by the Caledonian Railway until 1923, and its passenger service, always limited, was ended by British Railways in 1952. Freight continued until 1965. Today, the route can be explored, with much of it on a footpath. Bridges still stand, and the site of Kirriemuir station has a platform preserved in a public park, but all other buildings have been replaced by new houses.

◁ Published in about 1907, this card shows children posing by the Gairie Burn in the Den, Kirriemuir's main public park.

▽ Kirriemuir was one of the stations on the itinerary of the RCTS and SLS Scottish Railtour of June 1960.

⑫ CARMYLLIE

The Carmyllie branch started out in about 1854 as a private line built by Lord Dalhousie to transport slate and stone from his quarries to the Dundee & Arbroath Railway's main line at Elliot Junction. Later, it was taken over by the Scottish North Eastern Railway, and in due course by the Caledonian, which reclassified it as a light railway in 1898 and opened it to passengers two years later. There were four intermediate stations, but these generated little passenger traffic, so the LNER ended passenger services in 1929. Freight continued until the 1960s, helped by a Metal Box factory on the branch near Elliot and the usual farm traffic. Today, little remains to be seen of this branch, and most of the trackbed has either been lost or is part of a nature reserve. Some railway cottages remain near the site of Carmyllie station.

▽ The famous battle between a locomotive and a traction engine, in the film The Titfield Thunderbolt, was recreated in 1960 for a railtour visiting the Carmyllie branch. This time, there were neither winners nor losers, and the much younger LMS-designed Class 2MT, No. 46463, of 1950 was able to continue the tour.

△ Carmyllie station, seen here in the 1960s, was a basic, timber structure, typical of a light railway, with one of the shortest platforms in Scotland. Not surprisingly, nothing remains.

MAP 21

▽ This card records a visit to Edzell Castle made by Queen Mary in about 1921. The ruined 16th-century castle, with its famous walled garden, had earlier been visited by Queen Victoria and Prince Albert.

H.M. THE QUEEN AT EDZELL CASTLE

▷ In 1962 Edzell still had a platform, though the station buildings had been cleared, along with the goods shed and other railway structures. The branch was open for freight, but the grassy tracks suggest that not very much was going on at Edzell by that time.

⑬ EDZELL

The Brechin & Edzell District Railway opened its 5-mile branch in 1896, connecting the town with the Caledonian's Forfar-to-Montrose line, as well as to Brechin. There was one intermediate station, notable for using three different names at various times – Inchbare, Dunlappie and Stracathro. It was hoped that tourism, notably visitors to Edzell Castle, and golf would sustain the branch. However, these hopes were never fulfilled, and passenger services came to an end in 1931, apart from a brief reopening in 1938. Freight finished in 1964, having been helped to some extent by RAF Edzell, a World War I airfield reactivated in 1940. Some of the route has been built over, so not much remains to be seen.

⑧ INCHTURE VILLAGE

Inchture was a station on the Dundee & Perth Railway, opened in 1847. However, it was over a mile away from Inchture village, prompting the building of a horse-drawn tramway to connect the village to the main line. This opened in 1848 and at its peak there were six services each way on weekdays. It was operated by the Caledonian Railway, and services of some kind continued until 1917, when the tramway was closed. Some buildings survive at the Inchture Village terminus. Inchture station closed in 1956, but the line is still in use.

Rules & regulations

G.W.R.

NOTICE.

Passengers joining

Rail Motor Cars

and Trains

at Stations

must obtain

TICKETS

AT THE BOOKING OFFICE.

JAMES MILNE,

Paddington, October, 1931.   General Manager.

LADIES ONLY

BR 29102

CALEDONIAN RAILWAY.

RULES AND REGULATIONS

FOR THE GUIDANCE OF THE

OFFICERS AND MEN

IN THE SERVICE OF THE

CALEDONIAN RAILWAY COMPANY.

From 1st OCTOBER, 1906.

GLASGOW:

McCorquodale & Co. Limited, Printers, 96 Maxwell Street.

1906.

WARNING
PLEASE MIND YOUR HEAD
WHEN LEAVING YOUR SEAT

BRITISH RAILWAYS · SOUTHERN REGION   BR 21782

RESERVED

SEAT BACK TO ENGINE

PENALTY under Bye-Law 18 for UNAUTHORISED
REMOVAL of this LABEL—£5.

1

NO SMOKING

LMS   ERO 34076/12

G

EXPLOSIVES

PLACE AS FAR
AS PRACTICABLE
FROM ENGINE,
BRAKE-VAN AND
VEHICLES
LABELLED
"INFLAMMABLE"

DATE _____ 19 ___ TRAIN _____

FROM Chorley (Euxton R.O.F.)

TO KINETON

SIDING _____ Coy. S & M Jt

VIA RUGBY & Blisworth

Owner & No. of Wagon 318425

C.A.D.

Consignee _____

2

SHUNT WITH GREAT CARE.

LOAD and UNLOAD
OUTSIDE
GOODS SHEDS

This label to be used for **GUNPOWDER** and all other **EXPLOSIVES**

MAP 22

ARGYLL

Mingary
Salen
Corran
L. Leven
Kinlochmore
Strontian
L. Rai

L. Sunart

Croag
Tobermory
Morvern
Ballachulish Glencoe
L. Lydoch
2

Ben Le

Salen
Loch Aline
Appin
Kingshouse

Ulva

MULL
Inveroran
Killin

Ben
More
Craignure
Connel
Ferry
Ben Cruachan
3689
Loch Awe Sta.
Tyndrum
Killin Jun.

Iona
Oban
Taynuilt
L. Awe
Dalmally
Ben
Lui
Crianlarich
Luib
Glen

Port Sonachan
Cladich
Ben More
Balquhidder

ARGYLL
Inverarnan

Easdale
Loch Awe
Ardlui
Ben Ledi

Luing
Kilmelfort
Stronachlachar
L. Katrine
Invernaid

Colonsay
Glen Croe
Tarbet
Trossachs

INVERARY
St. Catherines
Arrochar
Ben
Lomond

Ford
Lochgoilhead
Rowardennan
R. Forth
Aberf

Strachur

Crinan
L. Goil
L.
Ecte
Luss
Loch
Lomond
Buchlyvie

Crinan Canal
Lochgilp
head
Loch Long
DUMBARTON
Gartness

Ardrishaig
Kilmun
Craigendoran
Helensburgh
Balloch

JURA
Dunoon
Gourock
GREENOCK
Dumbarton
Bowling

Paps of
Jura
Kyles of Bute
Innellan
Toward
Port Glasgow
Langbank

Colonsay
Tarbert
Rothesay
Innerkip
Bishopton
Houston
Renfrew

Port Askaig
BUTE
Wemyss
Bay
Kilmacolm
Bri. of Weir
Johnstone

BRANCH LINES

Bridgend
Kilchattan
Bay
Millport
Paisley

Bowmore
ISLAY
● **Campbeltown**
Argyll (page 231)

Port Ellen
Gigha
Loch Ranza
Kilwin
Ardrossa

● **Ballachulish**
Argyll (page 231)

Goat Fell
Corrie
Saltcoat
Steven
Newm

CANTYRE
Brodick
ARRAN
Troon
Barassie

Closed branch lines
Lamlash
Monkton
Prestwick
Tarbolton
Mauchlin

Closed passenger lines
Lag
Ayr
Annbank
Catrine

Open passenger lines
Machrihanish
Campbeltown
1
Ochiltree
Auch

Dalrymple
Hollybush

❷ BALLACHULISH

The remote and scenic Ballachulish branch was built by the Callander & Oban Railway and ran from Connel Ferry, on its main line, northwards along the coast. It opened in 1903 to serve the slate mines near Ballachulish. It also served the Ballachulish ferry, which until 1927 was the only access to Loch Leven. The building of the line was demanding, with two major steel bridges, at Connel Ferry and Creagan. The former is still the longest single-span cantilever bridge in Britain after the Forth Bridge. The route made accessible a number of isolated communities and, by the time it opened, the branch was able to benefit from the rise of tourism in western Scotland, which helped to keep it open for a long time. Closure by British Railways came in 1966, relatively late for Scottish branch lines. Today, the route is easily explored and much survives, including bridges and stations, some now in private use. Connel Ferry bridge carries a road, and a cycleway follows much of the route along the coast.

△Most of the stations along the branch survive in one form or another, sometimes just as a platform. This highly original example is Creagan, carefully preserved as a private house, complete with railway wagon.

▷The Ballachulish ferry, linking Argyll and Inverness across Loch Leven, operated from at least the 18th century until 1975, when a bridge replaced it. Always busy in the tourist season, it featured on many cards, like this 1950s one.

▽From 1909 Connel Ferry bridge was shared by rail and road. At first, vehicles were transported across on rail wagons, but from 1913 they could be driven across, when trains were not using it. This rule remained until the closure of the branch in 1966. This photograph is from May 1962. Today, it is just a road bridge.

△With its route mostly along the coast, the Ballachulish branch offered magnificent views across Loch Linnhe. In many places these can still be enjoyed. This is near Creagan, where the line was raised above the bay and the loch before it curved inland towards Creagan bridge (which has now been replaced by a modern road bridge).

❶ CAMPBELTOWN

Built initially to transport coal across Kintyre, the narrow-gauge Campbeltown & Machrihanish Light Railway opened to passengers in 1908. Remote and isolated, the line closed in 1932.

MAP 23

INVERNESS-SHIRE

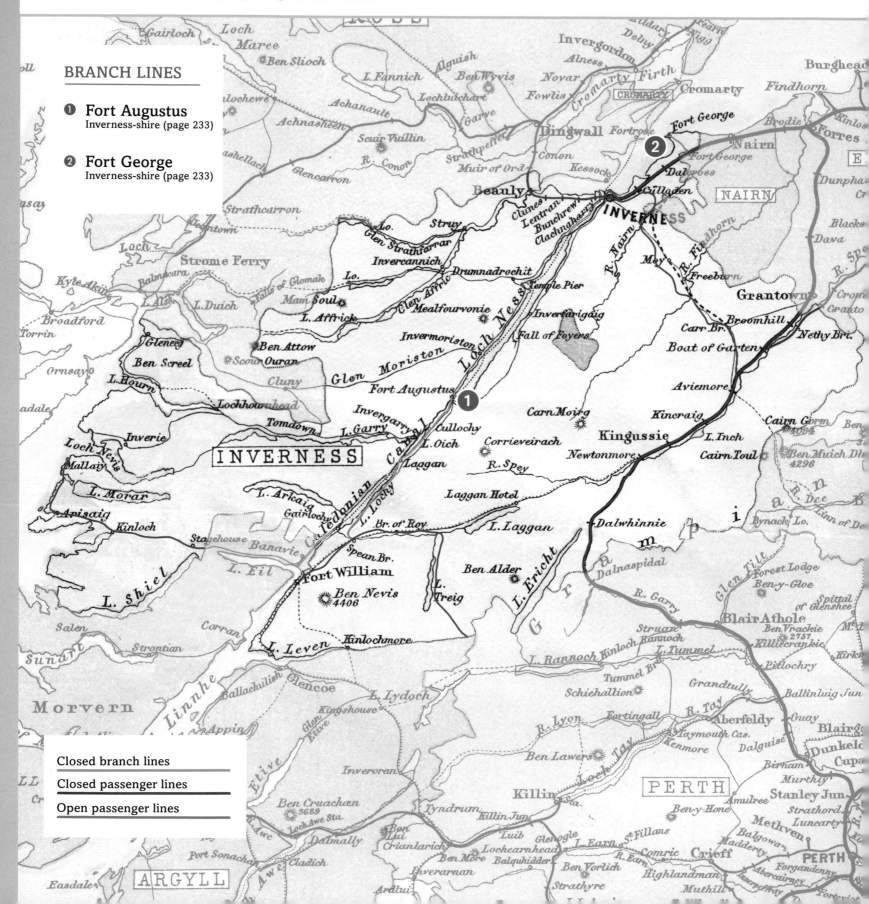

Closed branch lines
Closed passenger lines
Open passenger lines

❶ FORT AUGUSTUS

A line with a complicated history, the branch to Fort Augustus was built by the independent Invergarry & Fort Augustus Railway, but the West Highland, the Highland and the North British were all involved in running it. The original plan was to build a line to Inverness, but building stopped short at Fort Augustus. The resulting branch opened in 1903, running northwards along the Great Glen from Spean Bridge. This closed in 1911, but reopened in 1913, when it was finally taken over by the NBR, and remained in passenger service until 1933. Freight, which had always been more important, continued until 1947. The branch, with its long, remote route, was expensive to build and always underused. Today, much of the route survives, though it is not always accessible. Bridges and cuttings testify to the high cost of construction.

△The train for Spean Bridge is being prepared, and a few passengers are watching and waiting. It is probably the late 1920s or early 1930s, and the branch does not have much of a future. On what looks like a misty day, the views will not be memorable. Fort Augustus station was generously and expensively built, like the whole of the branch, which had been unnecessarily constructed to double-track mainline standards.

▷The branch followed the route of the Caledonian Canal. This early 20th-century postcard shows that, by the time the railway opened, the canal was popular with tourists. The branch line did not have the same appeal.

❷ FORT GEORGE

When the Inverness & Nairn Railway opened in 1855, the route included a station called Fort George, sited to the south of the peninsula on which stood the huge fort, built after the 1745 rebellion and covering 42 acres. However, there was no direct rail link to the fort until July 1899, when the Highland Railway, by then in control, built a short branch to Ardesier, near Fort George, from the main line, primarily to serve the military base. The terminus became Fort George and, when the branch opened, the junction station, hitherto called Fort George, was renamed Gollanfield. Passenger services, always limited, survived on the branch until 1943, while freight continued until 1958. The short branch was lightly built, without any significant engineering, yet much of the route can be traced today, and the station house and goods shed at the Fort George terminus still stand. The junction station building at Gollanfield, long closed, is now a private house.

▽A typical branchline train waits to depart from Fort George in March 1928. It was the military base, which is still in use today, that supplied the branch with most of its passenger traffic, for the railway had closed before the fort became a significant visitor attraction. The locomotive is an LMS Class 3F Jinty, No. 16416, then only a couple of years old.

MAP 24

NAIRNSHIRE, ELGINSHIRE, BANFFSHIRE, ABERDEENSHIRE & KINCARDINESHIRE

BRANCH LINES

Prior to departing from St Combs, the driver attends to his Class J91 locomotive.

Closed branch lines

Closed passenger lines

Open passenger lines

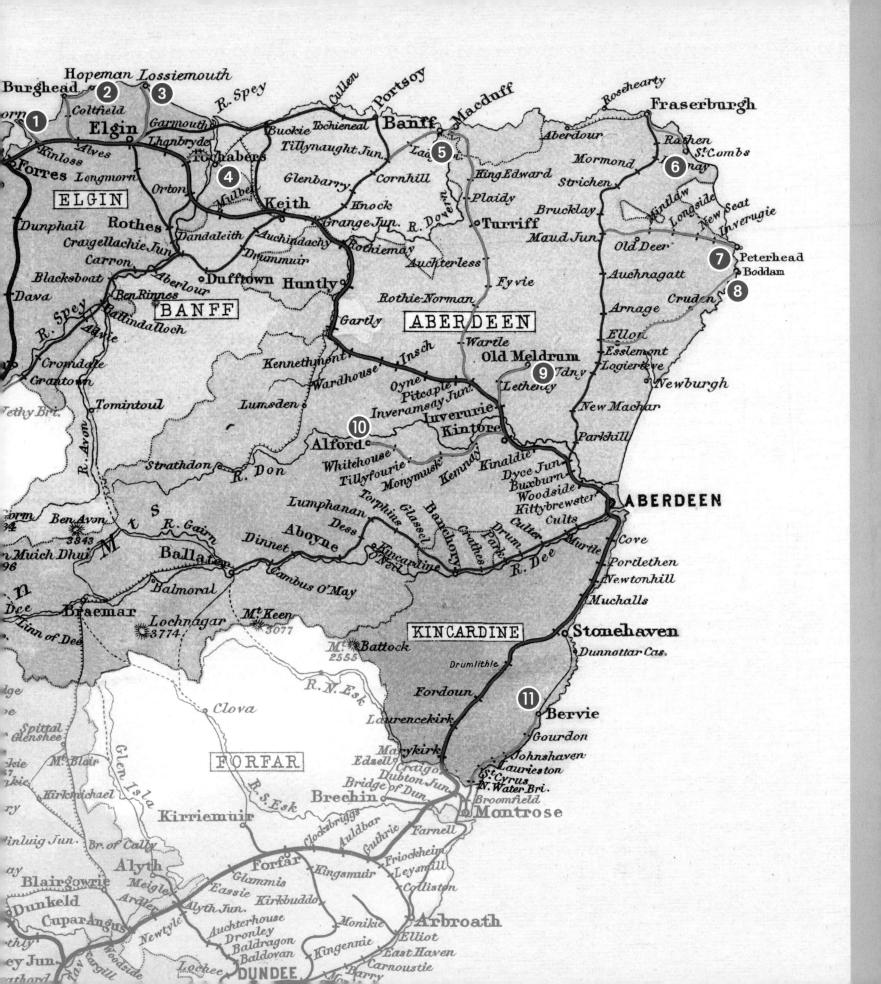

MAP 24

❸ LOSSIEMOUTH

A typically ambitious company of the 1840s, the Morayshire Railway planned a significant network in Northeast Scotland. It started in a small way, opening the line from Elgin to Lossiemouth in 1852. Other lines followed, making connections with adjacent railways, such as the Inverness & Aberdeen Junction and the Strathspey. The line to Lossiemouth ended up as a branch, run by the Morayshire until 1881, when the Great North of Scotland took over. Fishing and the harbour supplied freight, and RAF Lossiemouth, opened in 1939, helped to keep the branch alive until the end of passenger services in 1964. Freight followed two years later. Much of the route is a footpath, but the Elgin end is lost.

△This 1930s multiview card highlights most of the features of Lossiemouth that would have drawn visitors to the town at that time, including golf, the beach and the harbour.

▽A surprising survival at Lossiemouth is some of the track from the line that served the harbour. This was a long siding from the station, which was beyond the line of houses on the right of the photograph.

◁Lossiemouth had a generous station, with handsome stone buildings that reflected the style of the 1850s. The large one on the left was the station hotel, and the single-storey station was beyond it. Now, a platform survives but all else has gone, and the site is a park.

❻ ST COMBS

In 1865 the quaintly named and short-lived Formartine & Buchan Railway completed its main line from Dyce, near Aberdeen, to Fraserburgh, with branches to Boddam and Peterhead. Soon the Great North of Scotland Railway took charge, and, quite a bit later, sponsored the independent Fraserburgh & St Combs Light Railway, whose branch to St Combs opened in 1903. The route is along the coast from Fraserburgh to the small town and port at St Combs, passing a few remote villages on the way. There was little freight traffic apart from local supplies, and the area, though attractive, had limited tourist appeal. It is, therefore, hard to understand why the railway was built, and even harder to understand how it managed to survive so long. Closure did not come until May 1965. At the start, the GNSR tried a steam railmotor on the branch, but it was not successful and the line was then conventionally operated until British Railways introduced DMUs near the end. Today, most of the route can be explored. Buildings remain to mark the site of Fraserburgh station, also closed in 1965. The trackbed is often visible in the low coastal landscape, and part of it is a metalled road. St Combs station has gone.

△North of Cairnbulg the trackbed can be identified as an overgrown grassy path whose flat route along the coast is defined by fence posts. Fraserburgh can be seen on the horizon.

△A two-carriage DMU from Fraserburgh has just arrived at the end of the line, St Combs, surprisingly with some passengers. As it is 1964, soon before closure, they may be enthusiasts keen to capture the branch before it goes.

△From Inverallochy Golf Club a narrow road sets off towards St Combs, following the gentle undulations of the coast. This is the trackbed, here looking back towards Inverallochy. Near St Combs it becomes a grassy track, curving towards the station site, which is now housing.

▷The stations on the St Combs branch were minimal, to say the least. This is Cairnbulg, probably in the 1960s – just a couple of sheds, a nameboard and the remains of a platform garden. The church spire is in Inverallochy. Today, the site of the station can be located in the helpfully named Station Road, but there is not much of interest to be found.

MAP 24

⓫ INVERBERVIE

The main line between Montrose and Aberdeen followed an inland route, so a number of coastal communities, notably the Royal Burgh of Bervie (called Inverbervie from 1926), campaigned for an alternative route, along the coast. This was partially achieved by the locally supported Montrose & Bervie Railway, whose 13-mile line opened in 1865 as far as Bervie. It then went no further and ended up as an uneconomic branch line. To make things worse, there was a long battle between the Caledonian and the North British about operating the line, and for a while they ran competing trains. In the end, the NBR took control. Traffic was always disappointing, and by the late 1930s there were only three trains a day. Closure to passengers came in 1951 and to freight in 1966. The major feature of the branch, the eleven-arch North Water viaduct, still stands. Most of the route also survives.

△This postcard of Bervie's Castle Hotel was sent in 1906 to Aberdeen, from Forfar. The writer, who would certainly have travelled by train, says: 'Had a good time here.'

◁A common lost branchline experience is to find a bridge crossing nothing. This is a classic example. The handsome bridge is the only reminder of the line's route, the actual trackbed having been ploughed out, leaving no trace.

▽In 1962 an enthusiasts' railtour, headed as usual by an elderly locomotive, approaches the North Water viaduct over the North Esk near Montrose, the major engineering feature on the branch. Today, it carries a cycle track, which continues along part of the trackbed.

◁In the late 1950s or early 1960s a mixed freight makes its way along the coast, with a fine view of Inverbervie in the background. This classic branchline scene was then still to be enjoyed all over Scotland. For much of the route, the line followed the coast. Long sections of the trackbed have survived, along with a number of bridges and stations.

❷ HOPEMAN

At the end of 1862 the Inverness & Aberdeen Junction Railway opened a branch from Alves, on its main line, to Burghead Harbour. The line was mainly for freight traffic, but there were intermediate stations. In 1892, harbour traffic having diminished, the branch was extended from Burghead to Hopeman, with the hope of attracting more tourist business. Also important were the maltings along the route, at Burghead and Roseisle, a major source of raw materials for the whisky trade and destined to keep part of the branch open into the 1980s. Indeed, the section from Alves to Roseisle is still technically open, having been mothballed rather than closed. Meanwhile, passenger services throughout the branch had ended much earlier, in 1931. Most of the buildings have now gone, but the route is easy to explore: at first, the overgrown track from Alves to Roseisle can be followed, then the trackbed to Burghead. From Burghead to Hopeman there is less to see.

▽The extension to Hopeman, completed in 1892, was still recent when this photograph was taken. The buildings look new, but the train is a mixture of ancient rolling stock. A lot of men seem to be jumping on and off, presumably involved in shunting operations, while the few passengers wait patiently on the platform.

❹ FOCHABERS TOWN

Quite a number of small towns that were missed by the railways as they built their main lines were subsequently linked to the network by branch lines. Typical was the Highland Railway's short branch from Orbliston Junction, originally called Fochabers, to Fochabers Town, opened in 1893. There was one intermediate station, Balnacoul Halt. Passenger services were ended by the LNER in 1931, but freight lived on for another 35 years, thanks in part to the Baxter food factory in Fochabers. Today, much of the route across the fields can be explored, and the terminus station at Fochabers is a private house.

△The favourite viewpoint overlooking Fochabers has long been the Peeps, depicted on this card posted to Middlesex in 1905. The message is conventional: 'Arrived here yesterday after a good journey.'

◁The branch ran across level farmland, with no major engineering features. This 1962 scene, taken near Balnacoul Halt, shows a Scottish Rambler Railtour visiting the Fochabers Town branch. The locomotive is the famous Highland Railway Jones Goods 4-6-0, No. 103, of 1894. Set aside for preservation by the LMS in 1934, the locomotive was used on a number of enthusiasts' specials in the early 1960s. It is now in the Riverside Museum, Glasgow.

MAP 24

⑤ BANFF & MACDUFF

Banff was served by two branches, which did not connect. First, there was the Banff, Macduff & Turriff Junction Railway, backed by the Great North of Scotland, whose line from Inveramsay, on the GNoSR's main line, finally reached Banff in 1860. In 1872 this was extended the short distance to Macduff, on the other side of the river Deveron, by a separate company. This branch was long and meandering, with nine intermediate stations, but for those travelling from Aberdeen and the south it was a better option than the much shorter branch, from Tillynaught to Banff. This line was completed in 1859 by the Banff, Portsoy & Strathisla Railway, later the Banffshire Railway, and was better for travel from Inverness and the southwest. Although in the end both branches were controlled by the Great North of Scotland, the result was that Banff had more than one station, at various times called Banff, Banff & Macduff and Banff Bridge. There was also a short-lived Banff Harbour branch. In due course, it all passed to the LNER, which maintained services until the British Railways era. Then the closures started: first, passenger services in 1951 on the long route from Inveramsay, then on the shorter branch in 1964. Freight ended between 1961 and 1966 on the former, 1968 on the latter. Today, plenty remains to be explored on both branches.

▷The 1872 terminus station at Macduff was a simple stone train shed, long enough for one carriage and on a high site with a view of the sea. There was still plenty of freight activity in June 1960 when the famous RCTS and SLS Scottish Railtour visited Macduff, with the preserved GNSR locomotive 'Gordon Highlander' in charge of the five-carriage train.

⑦ PETERHEAD

The 13-mile branch to Peterhead, which opened in 1862 as part of the network planned by the Formartine & Buchan Railway, ran from Maud Junction, on the F & B's main Dyce-to-Fraserburgh line. It included a number of intermediate stations, several being very minor or restricted halts. There was also a line serving Peterhead harbour, with a separate docks station. Fish was the primary freight over a long period. Controlled at first by the Great North of Scotland Railway, the Peterhead branch passed to the LNER and then to British Railways, which ended passenger services in 1965. Freight ended in 1970, but continued on the main line until 1979. Today, Maud Junction station survives in good condition, and the route of the Peterhead branch can be followed through the open landscape on part of the Formartine & Buchan Way. Peterhead station has gone.

▽After the Peterhead branch closed to passengers in 1965, there were a number of visits by enthusiasts' specials and railtours. Here, in 1970, a group of local children pose on the overgrown platform beside the Class 26 diesel in charge of the Peterhead Farewell special. The fine station and train shed have been demolished.

△Peterhead Academy, depicted on this 1960s card, is one of Scotland's largest schools, with a history going back to the late 19th century.

⑧ BODDAM

The Great North of Scotland Railway opened its branch to Boddam from Ellon, on the Dyce-to-Fraserburgh main line, in 1897, partly to serve local granite quarries, already linked to Boddam's harbour by a narrow-gauge line, and partly in the hope of developing a significant tourist business based on the coastline and local golf links. A magnificent and extravagant hotel was opened at nearby Cruden Bay, which the railway saw as a potential resort. The hotel and its golf links featured on colourful LNER posters. An electric tramway, built in 1899 to connect Boddam station to the hotel, transported both passengers and freight. Sadly, it was all in vain, and the branch lost its passenger services in 1932 and closed completely in 1945. Little remains of all those hopes and dreams, apart from a goods shed at Hatton. The Cruden Bay hotel was demolished in the 1940s.

△The terminus at Boddam was bleak, remote and rather inconveniently placed for the town or harbour.

◁This shows Cruden Bay station at about the time passenger services ended. The little station is on the left, with a tramcar in front. Elaborate poles carried the wires for the hotel tramway, whose baggage car sits in splendid isolation.

① FINDHORN

The Findhorn Railway was set up in 1859 to build a 3-mile branch to the town and port from Kinloss, on the Inverness & Aberdeen Junction Railway's main line. It opened in 1860, was soon in financial difficulties, was taken over in 1862 and then, having become part of the Highland Railway, was closed in 1869. This was one of Scotland's earliest railway closures. The track was lifted in 1873, and today there is little to be seen, partly because RAF Kinloss was built over much of the route in 1938.

⑩ ALFORD

The Alford Valley Railway opened its 16-mile branch in 1859, linking the town with the Great North of Scotland's main line at Kintore. In 1866 the GNSR took control. Initially successful, the branch did much to put Alford on the map. There were four intermediate stations on the branch, and local quarries supplied plenty of freight traffic. In the 1920s and 1930s road competition caused a predictable decline, leading to the end of passenger services in 1950. Freight lasted until 1966.

⑨ OLD MELDRUM

The nominally independent Inverurie & Old Meldrum Junction Railway opened its branch in 1856, linking the Great North of Scotland's main line to Old Meldrum. Later, in 1866, the GNSR took control. As so frequently happened, local hopes proved to be over-optimistic, and the branch was never successful. Passenger services ended in 1931. Freight continued until 1965, serving agriculture and the local distillery. The last freight train on the line carried a 666-gallon consignment of whisky.

Industrial branch lines

↑ An enthusiasts' special, hauled by former Southern Railway Class O1, No. 31258, visits Tilmanstone Colliery, in Kent, in May 1959.

↑ In the 1960s an industrial locomotive hauls empty coal wagons along the line serving Derwenthaugh Coke Works, County Durham. It opened in 1928.

↑ A typical National Coal Board 0-4-0 locomotive poses with its crew at Preston Grange Colliery, Prestonpans, Haddingtonshire (East Lothian), in 1954.

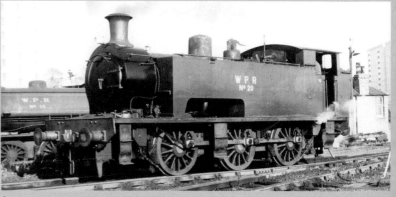

↑ In 1967 a Class J27, No. 65882, hauls empty coal wagons towards Silksworth Colliery, near Sunderland, in use between 1869 and 1971.

↑ The Wemyss Private Railway was built from 1899 to link collieries in the Fife coalfield to the port at Methil. This is a WPR Andrew Barclay of 1939.

↑ In September 1973 the Central Electricity Generating Board was still using steam power at Northampton power station, with modern branding.

↑ The Gas Light & Coke Company had a fleet of industrial locomotives. This example was photographed in 1948 at Kensal Green gasworks, in London.

↑ Andrew Barclay fireless locomotives remained in use at collieries and other industrial sites well into the 1970s.

↑ A mixed freight, hauled by former NER Class J27, No. 65860, shunts at Scotsgap station, the junction for the Rothbury branch, in Northumberland.

↑ Seen in 1955, this is the terminus of the Forcett Railway, in County Durham, a private freight line serving local limestone quarries from 1866 to the 1960s.

↑ An old 1908 Class B4 dock shunter, an Adams design for the LSWR, hauls the afternoon freight along the Turnchapel branch, near Plymouth, in the 1950s.

↑This 1930s image shows a mixed freight on the Wisbech & Upwell branch, in Norfolk, hauled along the roadside line by a typical LNER tram engine.

↑A Beattie Well Tank, No. 30585, takes a train of empty clay wagons through Dunmere Woods en route to Wenford Bridge, Cornwall, in June 1958.

↑In 1959 a GWR 5700 Class pannier tank, No. 8799, takes water at Easton before hauling a stone train along the Portland branch to Weymouth, Dorset.

↑Two former GWR locomotives, No. 4505 and No. 8773, work together on a china clay train from Drinnick Mill to St Blazey, Cornwall, in August 1956.

↑In 1961 'George Jennings', the 0-4-0 locomotive owned by South Western Pottery, hauls a wagon along its private branch from Parkstone, Dorset.

MAP 25

ROSS & CROMARTY, SUTHERLAND & CAITHNESS

BRANCH LINES

A special in June 1960 was the last train on the Fortrose branch, seen here at Avoch.

Closed branch lines

Closed passenger lines

Open passenger lines

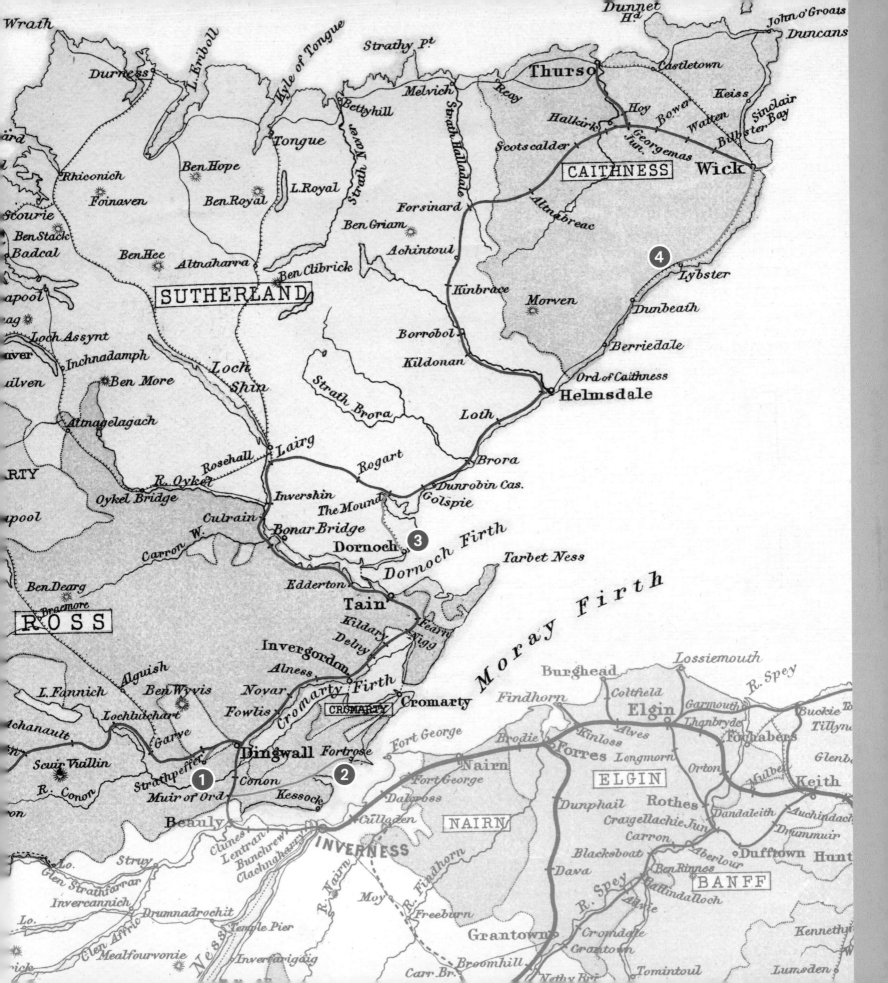

MAP 25

❶ STRATHPEFFER

A famous spa since the late 18th century, Strathpeffer was quick to attract the attention of railway companies. The Dingwall & Skye Railway opened a station called Strathpeffer, later renamed Achterneed, on its main line, but it was more than a mile from the town. In 1885, the Highland Railway did better, with its short branch from near Dingwall directly to the town. For the next 40 or so years this was very successful. There were through coaches from London and elsewhere, and tennis, golf, dancing and walking all contributed to the town's appeal, along with the Highland Railway's own spa hotel. By the 1930s, however, taking the waters was no longer fashionable, and the branch suffered a rapid decline. Passenger services ended in 1946, and freight five years later. Today, the station remains, a reminder of better times.

△In the 1950s, when this card was issued, Strathpeffer was still a popular holiday destination, and the big hotels were busy. However, the 1930s habit of motor touring in Scotland was well established by then, and everyone was coming by car.

△By the 1930s the great days of the Strathpeffer line had passed and, instead of grand expresses, the spa town's elegant station was hosting this mixed train, so typical of a minor branch line. A single, old carriage and a collection of battered freight wagons are about to clank their way to Dingwall.

◁Strathpeffer station, designed by Murdoch Paterson in 1885, has survived, along with the long glazed platform canopy. It now houses a museum, café and craft galleries.

❸ DORNOCH

Dornoch has a long history, based both on its cathedral and on the town's role in the development of golf. It was the latter that inspired the independent Dornoch Light Railway to open a branch from The Mound, on the Highland Railway's main line to Wick and Thurso, in 1902. This leisure-based line, designed to appeal primarily to tourists and holidaymakers, was supported by a large railway hotel, opened in 1904. Though operated by the Highland, the branch retained its independence until 1923. The route, skirting Loch Fleet and visiting remote villages, was attractive, with fine views out towards Dornoch Firth. Towards the end of its life, the branch was popular with enthusiasts because of its ancient locomotives and its mixed freight and passenger trains. The end came in June 1960. Today, much of the lightly built trackbed can be traced, and there is a section of footpath and cycleway. The Mound has disappeared, but Dornoch station remains.

△This 1970s card was sent to the West Midlands by a couple on holiday: 'Dornoch hotel lovely, food excellent, had a round of golf.'

▷On a summer's day in 1955, a typical branchline train prepares to leave Dornoch. Two freight wagons at the rear are being loaded, and the single carriage awaits its passengers. A lady appears to be admiring, from a distance, the rare locomotive, a former Highland Railway Class 1P, No. 55053. The Dornoch branch was the last habitat of this otherwise extinct class.

△It is the mid-1960s and Dornoch station is boarded up and rather the worse for wear. The railway has now gone, but there is still plenty to be seen, including the large timber goods shed.

▷Dornoch station now has a new lease of life as a take-away. Elsewhere along the route other former stations, platforms and crossing cottages can be found in the remote landscape.

MAP 25

❹ LYBSTER

Britain's most northerly branch line was the product of the Light Railways Act. Opened in 1903, the 13-mile Wick & Lybster Light Railway was funded by local supporters, the Highland Railway, which operated it, and a Treasury grant of £25,000. The inspiration came from fishing, agriculture and the need to bring remote communities into the 20th century. The branch was never busy, with three trains a day, but it fulfilled its function in its own quiet way. The LMS took over in 1923, and ran it for another twenty years. Traffic ended in 1944, but the branch was not closed until 1951. Despite being cheaply built, much of the trackbed remains in the landscape, so exploring the route is quite easy. All the stations survive, either as private houses or, in the case of Lybster, as a golf clubhouse. Thrumster station, now in a small park, has been restored, and has a length of relaid track.

△This 1950s card, bought as a souvenir from a hotel in Lybster, features a wide range of local tourist sights, including the harbour. The fishing industry declined soon after the branch opened.

◁In May 1928 a train waits to depart from Lybster's empty platform. The locomotive, LMS 15013, formerly HR 101, a regular on the branch, was one of two that were built in 1892 for service in Uruguay but were never delivered. Instead, the Highland Railway bought them.

▽Sections of the trackbed remain and can be followed in the open landscape. In some places, exposed ballast gives a sense of much more recent closure. Here, near Thrumster, sheep have taken over the slightly raised trackbed as it curves towards Wick.

△In the 1950s, after the branch closed, Occumster station, a typically basic, timber building, became a post office for a while. It is now a private house, as is Ulbster.

❷ FORTROSE

The Highland Railway's Fortrose branch, also known informally as the Black Isle Railway, opened in 1894. The line was planned to go from Muir of Ord, on the Inverness-to-Dingwall main line, to Rosemarkie, but in the event it stopped short at Fortrose. There were four intermediate stations. Traffic was largely local and agricultural, although Fortrose's golf course, harbour and historic cathedral ruins were expected to attract visitors to the town. Tourism had also been behind the line's planned terminus at Rosemarkie, where fine beaches and one of Scotland's largest collections of Pictish stones seemed to justify the building of a railway. However, these expectations were unfulfilled, so the railway enjoyed a quiet life serving the villages along the route until October 1951, when British Railways ended passenger services. Freight continued until 1960, by which time road transport had taken much of the traffic. Today, stretches of the trackbed can be explored, and Redcastle station survives as a private house, along with some railway cottages and bridges.

△Fortrose was built as a through station rather than a terminus, becoming the latter by default. Here, on 8 June 1960, five days before the branch's final closure, a local freight waits to depart, in the care of a Class 3F, No. 57594. Meanwhile, a platform discussion takes place.

◁This 1930s card shows the fine position of Fortrose on the Black Isle peninsula. The cathedral ruins are on the extreme right, and the station, looking very tidy, can be seen in the foreground.

FORTROSE FROM THE NORTH

△Against a magnificent background, the Dornoch branch (*see also* page 249) remains as a low embankment cutting across the fields.

INDEX

Index entries in **bold** are featured branch lines. Page numbers in **_bold italic_** refer to map pages; page numbers in **bold** refer to main descriptions.

AUTHOR'S ACKNOWLEDGEMENTS

Branch lines have always had a particular appeal. When Britain's railway network was at its peak, around the time of World War I, they were to be found all over the country, making their quiet but vital contribution to the local economy and the social life of the communities they served. Today, proper branch lines are rare, but the few that survive still offer the traveller something special.

It seemed an interesting idea to link branch lines to maps of Britain that showed the railway network when it was truly comprehensive, and this became the basis for this book.

It has been a challenge for me, finding the maps, the old photographs and the postcards, and travelling Britain from the West Country to the Highlands to explore lost branch lines and take modern photographs. However, making sense of all this presented a far greater challenge to my editor, Sue Gordon, and designer, Dawn Terrey. They have coped magnificently with what we all agree has been a very difficult book, and we are still good friends. My wife Chrissie has not only worked her usual magic with hundreds of old photographs and documents but created the maps as well, working from imperfect originals more than a century old. She also came with me

on several of the photographic trips, and all this has been accomplished without too much domestic stress.

The great network of railway enthusiasts has been enthusiastic and supportive, as ever, making memorable and enjoyable my many visits to railway fairs in search of elusive items. Special thanks are due to Janet and Godfrey Croughton, Tony Harden and Barry Jones, while Alan Young, Nick Catford and Paul Wright have made available images from the Disused Stations website. Once again, Richard and Judi Furness have been generous in supplying images from their splendid and invaluable 'Poster to Poster' collection. As usual, I am indebted to the team of dedicated checkers and correctors of my text, led by the redoubtable Charles Allenby, faced this time with the additional demands of map checking.

Finally, I must express my gratitude, first to those anonymous cartographers who one hundred years ago drew by hand the original artwork for the attractive and informative maps that were the inspiration for this book, and second to Dr Beeching, whose report, published fifty years ago, ensured that there were plenty of lost branch lines for me to explore.

PICTURE CREDITS

Photographs used in this book have come from many sources. Some have been supplied by photographers or picture libraries, while others have been bought on the open market. In the latter case, photographers or libraries have been acknowledged whenever possible. However, many such images inevitably remain anonymous, despite attempts at tracing or identifying their origin. If photographs or images have been used without due credit or acknowledgement, through no fault of our own, apologies are offered. If you believe this is the case, please let us know because we would like to give full credit in any future edition.

Unless otherwise specified, all archive photographs and postcards are from the author's collection.
l = left; r = right; t = top; b = bottom; m = middle

Photographs by Paul Atterbury

Paul Atterbury 3, 8 all, 9 all, 16tr, 18br, 19 bl & cr, 20cl, 21b, 22tr, 30br, 31br, 32tr, 33br, 37, 41br, 42br, 43br, 45b, 48–9 all, 52tr, 53bl & br, 55bl, 56tr, 57cl & cr, 68b, 69tr, 70cl & b, 71b, 78br, 79br, 80c, 81cr & bl, 83, 89tr & br, 90tr & bl, 94, 100, 101b, 102br, 108cr, 109br, 110bl, 113, 118b, 119br, 120br, 121cl & cr, 123, 128cr & br, 129tr & br, 130cl & cr, 131br, 132br, 138bl, 139tr, 140br & br (inset), 141, 142–3 all, 151, 158cr & br, 161, 166bl, 167cl & cr, 168b, 169cr, 170tr & cr, 180cr & br, 186cr & br, 187tr & cr, 196c, 197bl & br, 198bl, 199c & br, 200cr, 202, 206b, 207cl, 208tr & b, 220c, 221cr, 222bl, 223b, 224c, 231tr & bl, 236b, 237tr & cl, 238cl, 248bl, 249br, 250br, 251b

Other images

JW Armstrong 162–3bc, 186cl, 189t
JH Aston 120cr, 242tr
Hugh Ballantyne 58t, 96bl
RW Beaton 131bl
RK Blencowe 62cl
SV Blencowe 19tr, 38cl, 70t, 120tl, 152tl, 200br, 216tl, 221cl
Peter F Bowles 18c, 23br, 244b
J Brackenbury 59b
J Britton 251t
IS Carr 169br, 188bl
HC Casserley 44bl, 125tl, 136, 245br, 250cl
Peter Colins 177br
ColourRail 17br, 45cl, 211tr, 214c, 220cl, 238bl, 249cr
Philip Conolly 21cl
S Creer 96–7br, 131cl
Hugh Davies 104–5tl
L Elsey 245bl

Mike Esau 245cl
D Fereday Glenn 84bl
Kenneth Field 173tr, 176tl
C Gammell 1, 7cr, 22b, 24cr, 41c, 56cr, 64bl, 96tl, 105bl, 109cr, 111bl, 126, 153br, 166cr, 177tr, 192tl & bl, 194, 197tr, 201bl & br, 204, 206cr, 220br, 222cr, 224bl, 225t, 226b, 227tr, bl & br, 228tr, 238br, 239b, 240t, 245tr, 246, FR Geater 39b
JG Glover 176–7b
Sue Gordon 44br
John Goss 105tr, 125cr, 242bl
Peter W Gray 125br
Gregory 39tl, 64–5br, 109cl
L Hanson 111tr
Tony Harden 39tr, 43cl & bl, 52bl, 69b, 73, 78cl & cr, 79cr, 82r, 90br, 91cr, 92br, 101c, 105cr & br, 108cl & br, 110cr, 118c, 129bl, 132cr, 134b, 138cr, 139br, 140cr & br, 147 all, 148c & b, 149c, 158tr, 159c,

162tl, tr, cl & bl, 163tl, tr & br, 170br, 171br, 172tl and bl, 173br, 174tr, 176tr & bl, 181br, 189b, 196br, 198c, 199bl, 201cr, 207br, 209tl, 216tr & b, 217tl, tr & br, 223cr, 233tr, 236c, 239t, 241t & b, 248cr, 249cl, 250bl
JC Haydon 6tl, 55cr
Tom Heavyside 211bl
RN Joanes 22c, 102cr
LB Lapper 34tr
MJ Lee 242cr
A Moyes 209bl
James Murdoch 31cr, 33tr, 35b, 47l, 84tl, 100b, 148t, 170bl, 180cl, 190–1ct, 192–3br, 211cl, 212
RB Parr 16b
RC Riley 17bl, 81br, 104bl
RF Roberts 168tl & tr
P Rutherford 54br
JF Sedgwick 200bl

WS Sellar 222br, 242br
EE Smith 149bl, 181tr
JJ Smith 190tl
NE Stead 178, 244tl
Douglas Thompson 35tr, 36b, 44cl, 119bl, 130br, 132bl
RE Toop 24tr
CHA Townley 225b
WL Underhay 12tl
M Walers 171tl
AG Well 84br
HF Wheeller 46tr
CFD Whetmath 23tr
AJ Wickens 154–5br
Stephen Wilkins 177tl
E Wilmshurst 138br
www.disused-stations.org.uk/
Nick Catford 146bl; Paul Wright 91bl & br
MH Yardley 6br